Brave New
Families

Brave New Families

Biblical Ethics and Reproductive Technologies

Scott B. Rae

Baker Books

A Division of Baker Book House Co
Grand Rapids, Michigan 49516

© 1996 by Baker Book House Company

Published by Baker Books
a division of Baker Book House Company
P.O. Box 6287
Grand Rapids, Michigan 49516-6287

Printed in the United States of America

Library of Congress Cataloging-in-Publication Data

Rae, Scott B.
 Brave new families : biblical ethics and reproductive technologies / Scott B. Rae.
  p. cm.
 Includes bibliographical references and index.
 ISBN 0-8010-2077-8 (paper)
  1. Family—Biblical teaching. 2. Human reproduction—Biblical teaching. 3. Human reproduction—Religious aspects—Christianity. 4. Human reproduction—Moral and ethical aspects. I. Title.
 BS680.F3R34   1996
 241′.66—dc20   96-14443

In chapter 1, "Potential Objections and Responses: For the Sake of Virtue" is excerpted and revised from its original publication in *Ethics and Medicine* 10, 1 (spring 1994): 11–21.

In chapter 4, "Substance Versus Property-Things" and "The Human Being as a Substance" are excerpted and revised treatments of material co-published with John A. Mitchell in *The Silent Subject: Reflections on the Unborn in Society*, edited by Brad Stetson (Westport, Conn.: Praeger, 1996).

For information about academic books, resources for Christian leaders, and all new releases available from Baker Book House, visit our web site:
http://www.bakerbooks.com/

Contents

"[Rae] describes in a reader-friendly manner the incredible complexities of the advancing reproductive technologies. He strikingly and effectively analyzes the ethical issues inherent and places them in the contrasting context of biblical theology, natural law, and the Western legal tradition of procreative liberty. Out of these varying and contrasting moral contexts he carefully delineates his line of reasoning and its application to pastoral counseling of infertile couples. His erudite and compelling arguments are invaluable in guiding the Christian counselor and ethicist committed to credible scientific rigor and ethical decision-making."—**Reed Bell, Sr.**, Pediatrician and former Medical Issues Advisor to Focus on the Family

"I can recommend Rae as a careful thinker. He seems to consider all sides of an argument and is balanced in his evaluations of the works of others. He is also sufficiently bold to suggest new ideas where these seem warranted by the facts."—**Robert Rakestraw**, Professor, Bethel Theological Seminary

Acknowledgments

I am grateful to a number of friends and colleagues who have helped to make this book a reality. My colleagues at Talbot School of Theology and Biola University, particularly Walt Russell, J. P. Moreland, Klaus Issler, Doug Geivett, Paul Cox, and Kenman Wong, have given me an invaluable resource: their belief in me and their encouragement to publish my work because they believe it has value. I am blessed to have such colleagues with whom I share the task of advancing the kingdom of God.

Two other friends and colleagues made significant contributions to the book by stimulating my thinking and helping get it into print. John H. Coe, Rosemead School of Psychology, Biola University, contributed the section in chapter 1 on virtues in forming moral decision making. We published this material together, and I have revised it from its original form. I am grateful for his contribution. John A. Mitchell provided helpful material on the moral status of fetuses and embryos. This material too was jointly published, and I have revised excerpts from the original publication. I am grateful to Mr. Mitchell for his substantial contributions in this area.

My family bore most of the costs of my writing this book. My wife, Sally, and my sons Taylor, Cameron, and Austin (who was in utero during most of the process) are my treasures. I appreciate their patience as I finished the book. I am also grateful to Sally for her expertise on the emotional and spiritual aspects of infertility.

The conclusion in particular and the texture of the book overall bear the imprint of her experience. I gratefully dedicate the book to my family; I hope that this work will be useful to those desiring children and making the hard choices about assisted reproductive technology.

Introduction

John and Mary have been trying to have a baby for the past three years. They have been married for about five years and are in their early thirties, and their desire for a child has increased as more of their friends have begun to have children. When they first began to try to conceive a child, they were told that pregnancy frequently doesn't happen on the first or second attempt. But nobody told them that after three years of faithfully trying to get pregnant, they still would be childless. Each friend who has a baby is a reminder of their inability to achieve one of their fondest dreams.

After the first few months of unsuccessful attempts at conception, they began to ask themselves if there might be some sort of biological problem with one or both of them. They saw their doctor, who told them that there was really nothing to worry about at such an early stage. In fact, he told them that a couple is not technically infertile until they have been actively trying to get pregnant for a minimum of twelve months. So they kept trying. They employed all the "home remedies" for infertility that their well-meaning friends suggested. Mary took her temperature daily, since an increase in the woman's body temperature is a fairly good indicator that she is ovulating. They went a step further and bought the best ovulation-predictor kits on the market to assess more accurately the time at which she might be ovulating. They even tried to reduce the stress in their lives by arranging some romantic getaway vacations around ovulation times, when they could relax and be free of the normal pressures of life.

As the struggle to have a child progressed into the second year and they were now considered technically infertile, they tried to see if there was something medically wrong with either of their reproductive systems. John went to a clinic to have his sperm tested for count and motility. John's sperm count was a little bit low, but still within normal range. Mary went to her doctor again to make sure that she was ovulating and that her fallopian tubes were not blocked. Mary's fallopian tubes were not blocked, and it was reasonably certain that she was ovulating each month. Every test came back within normal range, so they concluded that all their reproductive systems were working as they should be. There appeared to be no logical explanation for why Mary was not yet pregnant.

By this time, it was painful to be around couples with small children. Being around the newborns of their friends was especially difficult. It seemed that these new parents could talk about nothing else except their children. Subjects like labor and delivery, breast feeding, lack of sleep, diapers, teething, and strollers dominated their conversations and reminded Mary and John how much they wanted to share the experience of their friends. Their friends tried to be sensitive to them but found it difficult to contain their enthusiasm for their new little bundles of joy. John and Mary began slowly to distance themselves from these friends because it was too difficult to be around them. They even stopped going to church on Mother's Day and Father's Day. It seemed that their church didn't acknowledge that some members desperately wanted children but so far could not have them. Other family-oriented holidays such as Thanksgiving and Christmas were harder to celebrate too, particularly when it meant being around their extended family, since all of their brothers and sisters are married and have children.

Before they were married, John and Mary looked forward to a pleasurable and gratifying sex life. They never imagined that sex would become a chore and would remind them of past failures to conceive a child. As they experienced continuing difficulty conceiving a child, Mary would grow more depressed and cried often on that one day each month when she got a painful biological reminder that she was not pregnant. They wondered out loud if having a child was worth going through all of their trouble. They even contemplated a life without children. They started looking into adoption as an alternative, but they were still not quite ready to give up trying to have a child.

One thing that made their infertility so difficult was the way it affected each of their self-images. For Mary, being a fulfilled woman included the experience of being a mother. She had a deep longing to conceive and experience childbirth and the bonding with her newborn that her friends talked about with such intimacy. She felt like less of a woman because she was failing to achieve one of her most significant callings in life. John felt that his manhood and virility were threatened, and he too felt like less of a man because of his failure to impregnate his wife. They certainly did not expect that infertility would have such a powerful impact on the way they saw themselves.

After roughly two years of trying and reaching what they thought was their breaking point, they remembered that one of their friends had seen an infertility specialist who had helped them become pregnant. They recalled seeing some television programs and reading in newspapers and magazines about new reproductive techniques that were doing miracles with infertile couples. But they had also heard about the risks, potential complications, and high costs involved. They had never given any of these techniques much serious thought, believing that such extreme measures would not be necessary. They decided it was time to check into reproductive technology for themselves.

The infertility specialist they saw was empathetic with their situation. They did not know if he was a Christian, but he expressed more care for them than many of their well-meaning Christian friends whose advice to them was to trust God or to accept childlessness as his calling for them. The specialist explained to them that there were a variety of reproductive technologies available to them, and that the expense could be the only constraint they would face. He told them about a dizzying array of techniques, each with its own set of abbreviations. There was AIH, AID, GIFT, ZIFT, and IVF. Some were very expensive, and caused them to wonder how they would pay for them. Others involved less money, and they were encouraged about that. One aspect caught them off guard, however. The doctor explained that some of these techniques would involve only their genetic materials. But other techniques necessitated a third person contributing either genetic material, that is, the egg or the sperm, or the womb in which the child would be gestated. In some cases, a woman, called a surrogate mother, might provide both egg and womb. They left the meeting with the doctor somewhat encouraged that their situation was far from hopeless, but also confused about which treatment or treatments to try.

In church they had heard their pastor occasionally make a passing reference in his sermons to these techniques. He seemed concerned that infertile couples were not trusting God to give them a child, but John and Mary were confident that they had trusted God through the process so far, and they had prayed consistently as they tried to get pregnant. He also seemed concerned that so many of these techniques were so unnatural, and that bothered John and Mary too. He had also expressed hesitations about a couple using another person to help them conceive and bear a child. John and Mary knew that some of these techniques involved third-party contributors, and they didn't know quite what to think about that. Thinking about these reproductive technologies gave them hope, but some unsettling questions were raised too.

If you were a pastor, how would you counsel John and Mary? How would you help them discover what light the Bible offers concerning the moral and spiritual implications of the various reproductive technologies? What kind of advice would you give to them? Or if you were in John and Mary's place, what would you do? Which avenue, if any, would you pursue? Or would you forego all artificial reproduction and either adopt, accept childlessness, or continue to try naturally to conceive?

If you and your spouse are struggling with infertility, this book is for you. My wife, a marriage and family therapist specializing in infertility, tells me that the average couple she counsels has not thought much about the ethics of reproductive technology. This book will help you evaluate the various technologies and the moral and legal considerations of each choice. I have tried to analyze these technologies from the perspective of evangelical theology to help you draw some conclusions about which technologies are morally permissible and consistent with biblical ethics.

If you are a professional or layperson who is involved with infertile couples and has, at some time, found yourself wondering, as a Christian, what to say to a couple contemplating some of these technologies, this book is for you too. Many people who try to help infertile couples find themselves with nothing substantive to say to them, and as a result, their advice is often trite, superficial, and though well-intentioned, sometimes harmful. This book will enable you be more helpful to those infertile couples you know.

If you are teaching a class in a church, college, or graduate school on social issues, medical ethics, or reproductive ethics, then this book is for you and your students. I have tried to make a very complicated subject understandable to people who may be thinking seriously about reproductive technology for the first time, and to professionals, who may have underestimated the complexity of the moral and legal issues infertile couples face.

Overview of the New Reproductive Technologies

In the last twenty years, medical science has made some remarkable accomplishments in the field of reproductive technology. When used successfully, these technologies are the miracle of life for couples who have often spent years trying to have a child and have exhausted all other avenues for conceiving a child on their own. But many of these techniques raise major moral questions and can create thorny legal dilemmas that must be resolved in court.

The term *reproductive technologies* refers to a wide spectrum of treatments for infertility. These include the following:

Artificial insemination by husband (AIH) is the mechanical insertion of the husband's own sperm into his wife's body. Usually the sperm, obtained by masturbation, is treated in the lab and then injected into the wife's body using a syringe without the needle attached.

Artificial insemination by donor (AID) is used when the husband is unable to produce suitable sperm for fertilization of his wife's eggs. Usually, the sperm of two or three anonymous donors is mixed together to insure anonymity and then inserted into the woman's body. Normally, the donors sign a waiver of parental rights, indicating that they give up any parental claims to the child produced with their sperm and that they will not attempt to establish any contact with a child born through use of their sperm. Thus the husband of the woman who actually bears the child is assumed to be the child's legal father.

Egg donation is the female equivalent of AID, in which a woman, sometimes anonymous and sometimes not, contributes one or more eggs to an infertile couple. Usually the eggs are fertilized with the sperm of the husband in the infertile couple in the lab, and the fertilized eggs, or embryos, are inserted in the uterus of the wife of the infertile couple, where it will gestate until its birth.

Gamete intrafallopian transfer (GIFT) is a process by which the wife's eggs are removed surgically and reinserted with sperm in the fallopian tubes where fertilization can occur naturally. This is usually preceded by using hormone treatments to stimulate production of a number of eggs during the woman's cycle.

In vitro fertilization (IVF), the first well-publicized reproductive technology, is a process in which fertilization takes place "in vitro" or in glass, outside the body. Here too the woman's body is stimulated hormonally to produce a number of eggs that are surgically removed, fertilized in a petri dish, and then surgically reinserted in the woman's uterus. This is the procedure that produces test-tube babies.

Embryo transfer is a more delicate procedure in which a woman donates her eggs to an infertile couple. But instead of being removed, the egg is fertilized inside her body. She is artificially inseminated by the husband of the infertile couple, and when conception occurs, the embryo is "flushed" out and transferred to the uterus of the infertile wife, who will carry and give birth to the child.

Zygote intrafallopian transfer (ZIFT) is a process much like IVF. The only difference is that the embryos are reinserted into the woman's fallopian tubes, where they have a better chance of implanting. This technique is also more expensive than IVF.

Surrogate motherhood is probably the most controversial of all the reproductive advances made recently. The ones that have not gone according to plan have been the material for some dramatic television miniseries (see the case of Baby M, for example). To call surrogacy a new reproductive technology is a bit misleading since it is neither new nor does it normally involve much technology. It dates back to Old Testament times (Gen. 16, 30) and normally involves only artificial insemination. Some distinctions in the kinds of surrogate motherhood (also called surrogacy for short) are helpful. *Genetic surrogacy* is where the surrogate mother contributes the egg and uterus, that is, she is artificially inseminated by the husband of the infertile couple and actually gives birth to the child, turning him or her over to the couple shortly after birth, similar to adoption. *Gestational surrogacy* is where the surrogate contributes only the uterus, (commonly called a "rent-a-womb" scheme) with the egg coming from the wife of the infertile couple. The wife's eggs are fertilized by her husband's sperm by means of in vitro fertilization, then implanted in the surrogate mother, who will carry the child during pregnancy and give birth. This is usually done when the wife of the infertile couple can produce eggs but for some reason cannot carry a child to term. Both of these types of surrogacy can be done for a fee, called *commercial surrogacy*, or by a family member or close friend, out of the goodness of her heart. This is called *altruistic surrogacy*. In most cases, the surrogate is a genetic surrogate who expects to be paid. In commercial surrogacy, the couple who contracts the surrogate usually employs a surrogacy broker, who recruits and screens the surrogate, drafts the contract, and monitors the process until the child is turned over to the contracting couple, the point at which the surrogate's work is complete.

Cloning of embryos has recently been done with human embryos. This procedure has been used with animals for some time, but in 1993 was done for the first time with human embryos by infertility researchers who were trying to help infertile couples keep the cost of IVF down. Instead of removing a number of the woman's eggs and fertilizing them in the lab, they removed one or two, fertilized them, and essentially copied them, creating more embryos that could later be implanted in the woman's body should they be necessary. For the most part, scientists duplicated in the lab what the body does when identical twins are produced. This technology is very new and very controversial, but promises to be helpful to infertile couples in the future.

Prenatal genetic testing is also on the leading edge of new reproductive technology. This procedure can help an infertile couple know the genetic makeup of the child that the woman is carrying. Scientists can even do some genetic testing of embryos prior to implantation. This technology makes available the future possibility of sex and trait selection for a child.

Micromanipulation is one of the newest reproductive technologies. Here a surgical (by laser) opening is made in the woman's egg, enabling the sperm to more easily penetrate and fertilize it. Sometimes the sperm is directly injected into the egg.

One group of these techniques involves primarily medical intervention into natural reproductive processes (fertility drugs, AIH, GIFT, ZIFT, IVF, and micromanipulation). A second group of these technologies goes further and requires contribution from another person in order to achieve conception and/or birth (AID, egg donation, embryo transfer, and surrogate motherhood).[1] In some cases, the genetic material of the third party is required, and in others, such as gestational surrogacy, it is not.

These new technologies make a wide variety of reproductive arrangements possible for couples and single persons today.

1. To be exact, GIFT, ZIFT, and IVF normally involve the genetic materials of husband and wife only, though they can be used with donor genetic materials also. For egg donation to work, one of the above techniques must also be employed.

Some of them are routine treatments for infertility, but others are more novel ways of having a child. Here is a sample of the ways procreation can occur through these new medical technologies (see if you can pick out the different technique(s) that are required to make each procreative arrangement happen):

1. A man who cannot produce sperm and his wife want to have a child. She is artificially inseminated with the sperm from an anonymous donor, or a mixture of donors, conceives, and bears a child.
2. A woman who cannot produce eggs and her husband want to have a child. They hire a woman to be inseminated with the husband's sperm and to bear the child for them.
3. A woman is able to produce eggs but is unable to carry a child to term. She and her husband "rent the womb" of another woman to gestate the embryo that will be formed by laboratory fertilization of the husband's sperm and his wife's egg.
4. A married couple desires to have a child, but the woman wants to avoid any interruption in her career for pregnancy, so her sister offers to carry the child for her. She accepts and the child is born successfully.
5. A lesbian couple want to have a child. One of the women provides the egg, and after it is fertilized by donor sperm, the embryo is implanted in the uterus of her partner.
6. A couple desiring to have children cannot produce any of the sperm or eggs necessary for conception. So the woman's sister will donate the egg, and the man's brother will donate the sperm. Fertilization will occur in vitro, that is, outside the womb, and the embryo will be transferred to the wife of the couple, who will carry the child.
7. Two homosexual males want to rear a child. To do so, one man's female friend donates the egg and the other man donates the sperm (or it could be a mixture of both of their sperm). Another woman is hired to carry the child.
8. A postmenopausal woman in her early sixties with grown children wants to have another child. She is given a donated egg, has it fertilized by donor sperm, and the embryo

is implanted in her body for her to carry and give birth to the child.

From a theological perspective, both groups of reproductive technologies (the ones that do not involve third-party contributors and those that do) raise ethical issues. These issues are viewed within the context of one's understanding of the theology of the family and reproduction that is outlined in Scripture and Christian tradition. For example, Roman Catholic tradition, based on natural law, has taught that most interventions in the reproductive process are immoral because they interfere with the natural order of creation (and procreation) that God has ordained.[2] Other Christian traditions allow for technological intervention but do not allow any third parties into the process. We will evaluate both groups of reproductive technologies from the perspective of the biblical teaching on the family.

The Current Increase in the Incidence of Infertility

In the past few years, we have seen a great deal more attention paid to infertility than at any time in recent history. Certainly some of that is due to the remarkable technological advances in reproductive medicine. In the major media outlets, there is a steady stream of information about infertility and reproductive technologies. As I watch the newsmagazine programs and read the print media, rarely does a month go by without media focus on some aspect of procreation. Are society and the media simply talking about infertility more frequently, or is there actually a greater incidence of infertility than in previous decades? Studies suggest that infertility has increased and is occurring more frequently than in previous generations. That raises the question, What is causing this higher rate of infertility today?

A couple is considered infertile if they have been unsuccessfully trying to conceive a child for twelve consecutive months.

2. See chapter 2 for a more extended discussion of the Roman Catholic contribution to reproductive ethics.

Unless there are evident problems, many infertility specialists will not consult with a couple until they have been trying to conceive for at least a year. Since the mid-1960s, the incidence of infertility has increased at an astronomical rate, over 300 percent, affecting an average of 10 to 15 percent of married couples in the United States.[3] That comes to roughly 2.3 million couples in the United States for whom these advanced technologies are their only hope to have a child of their own.[4] Figures in Great Britain are roughly similar, with an average of 10 percent of married couples facing infertility.[5] It is estimated that approximately one-third of the cases of infertility are due to a problem with the husband's reproductive system, such as a low or zero sperm count, or the inability of his sperm to reach and penetrate the egg in order to fertilize it. A woman's infertility is often more complicated. It can be due to factors such as irregular ovulation, problems in the uterus that prevent an embryo from implanting there, blockage in the fallopian tubes that prevents the egg from reaching a place where it can be fertilized, or hormonal imbalance. The biological causes of infertility can be very complex, and many couples may never know exactly why they are having trouble conceiving a child. Even with the ability of technology to "work miracles" with infertile couples, one gets the sense that the womb is still the "secret place" that the psalmist describes, to which only God ultimately has access (Ps. 139:15).

Perhaps the most frequently mentioned cause of the higher incidence of infertility today is that many couples are waiting longer to have children than in previous generations. It is not uncommon for couples to wait until their careers are established and they are well into their thirties or early forties to begin a family.

3. See Claudia Wallis, "The Saddest Epidemic," and "The New Origins of Life," *Time*, September 10, 1984, 46–50.
4. Nancy Wartik, "Making Babies," *Los Angeles Times Magazine*, March 6, 1994, 20.
5. For the figures in the United Kingdom, see Athena Liu, *Artificial Reproduction and Reproductive Rights* (Aldershot, England: Dartmouth, 1990), 1–2. She is citing the well-known Warnock Report, the report of the British government's commission on artificial reproduction. The full title is *The Report of the Committee of Inquiry into Human Fertilisation and Embryology* (London: HMSO, Cmnd. 9314, 1984).

As the eggs and sperm age, they are less likely to successfully combine and produce conception. In addition, the older couple faces a greater risk of some type of genetic problem that would produce a miscarriage. This is the reason that women over thirty-five are normally encouraged to have prenatal genetic testing, to see if there is some genetic deformity in their child.[6]

A second generally accepted cause of the current increase in infertility is the epidemic rise in sexually transmitted diseases. The sexual revolution in the 1960s and 1970s that liberalized sexual attitudes and practices brought with it a dramatic increase in venereal diseases. In many cases, damage to the uterus and fallopian tubes can be traced to these infections, and such damage makes it more difficult to conceive and carry a child. Damage to the uterus can also be caused by use of certain birth-control devices such as some intrauterine devices (IUD) and abortion. Women who have had abortions, especially women who have had multiple abortions, frequently find it difficult to conceive a child when they desire to do so.

Stress and the pace of life today also may contribute to infertility. It is difficult to establish a direct causal link between stress and infertility, but some studies have indicated that there is a connection between infertility and the increase in two-career marriages.[7] There is little doubt that both husband and wife working full time has increased the amount of stress in the home. Whether that is a direct cause of infertility is not clear, but it is a factor that should not be ignored.

The Infertility Industry

In the United States, approximately 350 centers offer reproductive technologies to alleviate infertility. There are infertility clinics in almost every major metropolitan area in the United States, and in Great Britain and Australia. In fact, much of the initial re-

---

6. For more on the ethics of prenatal genetic testing, see chapter 9.
7. Robert R. Bell, *Marriage and Family Interaction*, cited in Stanley Grenz, *Sexual Ethics: A Biblical Perspective* (Dallas: Word, 1990), 143, 246.

search in this area was conducted in England and Australia. The American Fertility Society and the Society for Assisted Reproductive Technology publish data on most of these clinics in the United States annually. There are numerous medical and scientific journals that publish the latest studies on various reproductive technologies.

Though these clinics exist explicitly to help infertile couples achieve their dream of having a baby, we should not forget that infertility is also big business. For example, in 1991, more than 33,000 assisted reproductive-technology procedures were attempted, making it a $2 billion per year industry.[8] Many health insurance companies now cover part if not the majority of the expenses involved. Some of the treatments are relatively inexpensive. But for the more sophisticated technologies, the cost can easily run into thousands of dollars. For couples who are fortunate and do have a child, the money is often immaterial to the joy of realizing their dreams. But the failures far outnumber the successes,[9] and many couples will spend thousands of dollars and be no closer to achieving their goal of having a child than when they started. Though the reproductive industry has been generally well received by society, it has not been immune from criticism. Its critics claim that the practitioners are exploiting desperate infertile couples and misleading them by not clearly presenting the rates of success and failure.

Overview of the Book

In assessing the morality of each of these reproductive technologies, we must first lay some foundational groundwork. That will be the focus of chapters 1 through 4. We will examine a theology of the family relative to reproduction that will set some of the main parameters for the Christian couple (chap. 1). We will use

8. Wartik, "Making Babies," 20.
9. The success rate for live births coming out of these more advanced technologies such as IVF, GIFT, ZIFT, and micromanipulation is approximately 15 percent. Ibid., 21. It is a bit higher for GIFT.

this to evaluate the Roman Catholic prohibition of most reproductive technologies based on the notion of natural law (chap. 2) and the Western legal tradition of procreative liberty based on the Constitution (chap. 3). The crucial issue that will form a bridge into the remaining chapters is the question of the personhood of the fetus and embryo (chap. 4). If embryos and fetuses are persons from the moment of conception, that belief affects one's moral understanding of some of these reproductive technologies.

In chapters 5 through 10, we will look at the specific reproductive technologies that are being used today. We will discuss artificial insemination and egg donation in chapter 5. IVF, GIFT, ZIFT, embryo transfer, and micromanipulation sperm injection are discussed in chapter 6, since they have a number of features in common. Surrogate motherhood is more controversial both in Christian and secular circles, and we will explore its debated issues in chapter 7. The rest of the book will take up some of the more novel reproductive techniques. Human embryo cloning, recently done for the first time in the United States, will be discussed in chapter 8; prenatal genetic testing, both of fetuses in utero (a more developed technique) and embryos, a very recent development, in chapter 9; and fetal therapy, with its corresponding issue of forced cesarean sections for imperiled fetuses, in chapter 10. The book will close with some encouragement to infertile couples and guidelines for friends and professionals who deal with infertile couples.

Though I have tried to make the book accessible to someone with little background in this area, the issues that we will address together are complex, and I would do you the reader and the subject a disservice to deal with them simplistically. I have tried to make the medical technology involved understandable to a layperson. The moral discussion of these technologies presumes no formal background in ethics, but my intent is to do justice to the moral complexity of these issues. This approach is most likely to benefit both the professional and the layman.

1

Reproductive Technologies and a Theology of the Family

Introduction

Some time ago, a woman in our church approached me excitedly to tell me about an unusual occurrence that was taking place in her family. Motivated by altruism, her daughter had agreed to be a surrogate mother for the daughter-in-law. The egg of the daughter-in-law and the sperm of her husband had been fertilized in vitro and successfully implanted in the uterus of their daughter, who was, at that time, two months pregnant. The fact that it was a case of gestational surrogacy, in which the surrogate has no direct genetic relation to the child she is carrying, made it morally permissible in the eyes of the woman who told me about the situation. In addition, the fact that it was done out of purely altruistic motives added to its moral acceptability. The idea that someone could think that such an act would be morally objectionable was preposterous to her. This was an example of Christlike unconditional love at its best. Yet the response she received from others in the church was not so enthusiastic. There were significant questions raised about another person beside husband and wife contributing to reproduction, even though there was no new genetic material being introduced and even though the surrogate was an extended family member. Many people in the community of God's people are skeptical of any reproductive interventions,

23

not to mention those that involve another person in collaborative reproduction.

In this chapter and the one that follows, the biblical and theological parameters for procreation will be explored. This involves addressing two primary questions. First, does the biblical teaching on the family and reproduction allow for the interventions of reproductive technologies that interrupt the natural processes that God has set up? In other words, does the Roman Catholic natural-law doctrine as applied to reproduction reflect the biblical teaching? This will be the focus of the next chapter. Second, does the biblical teaching on the structure of the family allow for participation of third parties in collaborative reproduction? This is the focus of this chapter. Of course, if the answer to the first question is negative, then the second question becomes moot. I will argue that the Scripture does allow for some reproductive interventions, thus taking issue with Roman Catholic natural-law doctrine. I will also argue that the doctrine of the family establishes that the use of third parties in collaborative reproduction goes against God's intended creation model. I suggest that Scripture is skeptical about such arrangements, but even though some use of some reproductive technologies may violate the model of creation, it does not follow in every case that they are morally prohibited. Even if they are morally permissible, I argue that issues about virtue and character must be considered in determining whether such arrangements ultimately are satisfactory.

Theology of the Family Related to Reproduction

The more difficult of the two primary questions concerns those technologies that require a third party in collaborative reproduction. Does the biblical teaching on the structure of the family preclude any third-party involvement? Or is the structure of the family a cultural construct that can change as social conditions change?

Though a great deal has been written on the structure of the family, it is rare that the subject of reproduction is addressed in these works. Gender issues have driven most of the discussion of the structure of the family, and as a result, the bearing of family structure on reproduction has been neglected.[1] Perhaps one of the principal reasons for this neglect is the lack of a developed concept of the family in the Scripture. The Bible assumes a great deal about the family's structure without much of a systematic defense of it. However, I will argue that the family structure presented in Scripture is normative and is based on the creation account.

The extended family or clan was a major component of social life in biblical times, and its structure has been remarkably consistent throughout biblical history up to the present day. With new ways of reproduction that do not require sexual intercourse society has been challenged to think of the family structure in different ways. This nuclear structure, consisting of a heterosexual couple producing children within the context of marriage, has been the consistent pattern for the family throughout most of the history of civilization. But is it the divinely instituted norm, in such a way that any third-party involvement in reproduction is precluded?

Perhaps a second reason for the paucity of biblical material on the family structure is because it was made so clear at the creation mandate in Genesis 1–2. That is, the family structure was assumed in Scripture because it was grounded in creation. There is a normative family structure established by the creative word of God that expresses itself in the order of creation.[2] The natural order of the family is established by the God of nature, who embedded a specific structure of the family into his creation.

In Genesis 1–2, there is a critical link between the man and woman in the context of marriage and the procreation of children. Though the family is not the direct result of the command in Genesis 1:27 to "be fruitful and multiply," the institution of the family is clearly related to it.

---

1. There are a handful of exceptions to this trend. They include Helmut Thielicke, *The Ethics of Sex* (New York: Harper and Row, 1964), Ray S. Anderson and Dennis B. Guernsey, *On Being Family* (Grand Rapids: Eerdmans, 1985), and Oscar E. Feucht, *Family Relationships and the Church* (St. Louis: Concordia, 1970). In general, Protestant works on the ethics of reproductive technologies have been scarce, and the field has been dominated by Roman Catholic moral theologians.
2. Anderson and Guernsey, *On Being Family*, 17.

Though there are two creation accounts in Genesis 1–2, they are complementary and not contradictory. Genesis 1 provides the broad panorama overview of creation. Genesis 2 views the most important aspects of creation—the creation of man and woman and their relationship to each other and to God—in more detail. Thus the account of the creation of man and woman that is described in Genesis 2:18–25 actually fits into the broader overview of Genesis 1. To be specific, it occurs after the divine initiative in 1:26 to create mankind and prior to the command to the newly formed couple in 1:27 to begin procreating and populating the earth. Thus, the creation of mankind is described generally in 1:26 and specifically in the male and female of the species in 2:18–25. The first command that is recorded by Scripture is the command to reproduce (1:27).

The key phrase in 2:24 is considered by most evangelicals to be the place where marriage is instituted. There are numerous reasons for this notion. First, the way that this text is quoted in other places in the New Testament makes it clear that it was originally intended for married couples (Matt. 19:5; Eph. 5:32).[3] Second, the term *leave* is used to suggest that, against common ancient Near Eastern cultural practice in which the bride moved in with the groom and his family, a man and woman who will be intimately related (as the term *cleave* suggests) are to separate from their families of origin and begin a new family unit of their own. Third, the concept of one flesh clearly involves a sexual unity (though not limited to that), and throughout the Scripture, it is evident that sexual relations are restricted to the setting of marriage. Thus it would appear that 2:24 is the place where marriage as a divine institution is begun.

Placing the more specific account of the creation of male and female and the subsequent institution of marriage back into the broader context of the creation in Genesis 1:26, the command to

3. The exception to this is in 1 Corinthians 6:12–20, where Paul argues against sexual promiscuity on the basis of Genesis 2:24. He is not speaking to married couples here, but his point is limited to the one-flesh relationship that is associated with sexual intercourse, thus making promiscuity wholly inappropriate for the believer. This is magnified by the indwelling Christ in the believer, so that Christ is actually joined to the person with whom one has had an affair.

procreate is thus given to Adam and Eve in the context of their leaving, cleaving, and becoming one flesh, that is, in the context of marriage. Though it is true that Adam and Eve are representative in a broader sense of the first male and female of the species, it is also true that this sets the precedent for heterosexual marriage and procreation within that setting. Though it clearly does not suggest that every male and female must be joined in marriage, it does indicate that marriage is to be between male and female, and only in marriage is procreation to occur. In other words, God has set up procreation to be restricted to heterosexual couples in marriage. There is continuity between God's creation of the family in Genesis 1–2 and the command to procreate within that context.[4] This structure of the family seems to be basic to God's creative design, however extended the family became due to cultural and economic factors.

The specific terms *bone (etsem)* and *flesh (basar)* in Genesis 2:23–24 are often used figuratively to indicate family relationships. When the two terms are used in combination (Gen. 29:14; Judg. 9:2; 2 Sam. 5:1) or in parallel (1 Chron. 11:1; 2 Sam. 19:12–13), or when flesh *(basar)* is used alone (Gen. 37:27; Lev. 18:6; 25:49; Neh. 5:5; Isa. 58:7), the notion of a blood family is normally present. It would appear, then, that the use of these terms in Genesis 2:23, when Adam declares that Eve is his bone and flesh, suggests that the normative family is in view in the creation account.

There is then a continuity between the relationship between a couple in marriage and procreation (as well as parenthood, since Scripture assumes a similar continuity between the biological and social roles of parenthood). It could be argued from the creation account that not only marriage but sexual unity in marriage is the only arena in which procreation may occur. Most conservative Roman Catholics argue for a complete continuity between sexual

4. This is not to say that single-parent families are any less genuine families in the sight of God, only that procreation cannot occur in that setting. Single-parent families often began as two-parent families, and procreation occurred in the proper context. Divorce, however tragic, does not prevent the resulting single parent and children from being a legitimate family.

relations in marriage and procreation. That notion is normally grounded in natural law, which is rooted in the order of creation.

However, the creation account does not mandate such close continuity between sexual intercourse and procreation. One could argue that certainly Scripture did not anticipate or address the complex methods of reproduction that are in use today. In addition, the perspective of the creation account on sexual relations must be balanced by other parts of Scripture that extend the purpose of sexual relations beyond procreation alone. Certainly sex is reserved for marriage, but simply because the creation account links marriage and procreation, it does not follow that procreation must always follow from marital sexual relations. The notion of one flesh, though it certainly involves physical intimacy, goes well beyond the physical alone to include all aspects of emotional and spiritual unity. Marriage is to be characterized by oneness between the partners, of which the physical is a part. The teaching of the creation account is that procreation is to take place within the oneness of a total marriage relationship, not necessarily a specific instance of sexual intercourse.

There were examples in the Old Testament law that were designed to safeguard this creation ideal of the family. For example, the prohibitions against illicit sexual relations functioned to preserve the family from breakdown and assumed the creation structure of the family as normative. In the sexual code in Leviticus 18, every sexual relationship except that between a heterosexual couple in marriage is prohibited. Incest, homosexuality, adultery (and specifically cultic prostitution), premarital sex, and even bestiality are forbidden. Though there is no specific reason given for these prohibitions, it is clear that these actions violate the normative structure of the family that is rooted in creation. Keeping the creation ideal of the family intact and free from influences that would undermine it was considered central to the preservation of Israel as a society set apart as God's holy nation (Exod. 19:6).

Even though the creation account does present a normative structure of the family that would appear to preclude third parties from being involved in collaborative reproduction, one should recognize that some novel reproductive arrangements are used in the Old Testament. For example, levirate marriage (Deut. 25:5–10;

Ruth 3–4) was employed to continue the lineage of a woman's deceased husband should she be left childless at his death. Norman L. Geisler suggests this practice provides a biblical precedent for third-party involvement in a form such as artificial insemination by donor.[5]

However, levirate marriage is not analogous to other third-party collaborative reproductive techniques for two reasons. First, no third party was technically introduced into the reproductive matrix since the childless woman in view was a widow. Not only was the husband being replaced for purposes of reproduction, but his death made the levirate arrangement necessary. Second, this is not a case of simply inseminating the woman so that she could give birth, with the sperm donor taking no parenting responsibility. The near kinsman actually married the widow and took full responsibility for supporting her and the child who would be born out of their marriage. If anything, levirate marriage supports the creation model by keeping reproduction within the context of marriage.[6]

A second novel reproductive arrangement found in the Old Testament is surrogate motherhood. This appears to have been a widely accepted cultural practice in the ancient Near East and was employed by both Abraham and Jacob in the patriarchal narratives (Gen. 16; 30). There does not appear to be any condemnation attached to the use of surrogates to alleviate female infertility, except in the case of Abraham and Hagar. However, in the Abraham and Hagar narrative, the issue at hand is not the use of a surrogate, but Abraham's and Sarah's lack of trust in God to keep his covenant promise to make their descendants numerous and to make him a great nation. Thus it is not clear that with such a unique case as Abraham's in his role as covenant mediator that any normative biblical teaching on third-party collaborative reproduction can be deduced.

Though Jacob, too, is a patriarch who carries on the covenant, in his case there is no other issue of faith as was the case with Abra-

---

5. Norman L. Geisler, *Christian Ethics* (Grand Rapids: Baker, 1990), 187.
6. Levirate marriage does introduce the issue of polygamy, but that is a separate issue from third-party collaborative reproduction.

ham. In Genesis 30, Rachel is childless, and Leah has had a number of children. Rachel is so grieved that she instructs her maid to have sexual relations with Jacob. She considers the child who results from this union completely her own. The maid, acting as a surrogate, has no parental rights to the child she has borne. This would seem to be a case in which surrogacy is accepted as a normal practice, with good results for all the parties involved.

However, one cannot assume that an accepted cultural practice is necessarily a moral norm that transcends culture. Scripture is replete with cultural practices that are not considered normative for today. For example, polygamy appears to have been an accepted practice in the ancient world, yet it is not considered normative, particularly when viewed against the backdrop of the creation ideal of monogamy. Slavery was accepted in both Testaments, yet no one can imagine a society today in which people own slaves. Simply because surrogacy existed as a practice in biblical times is no justification to accept its use as a reproductive alternative today. For reasons that are not clear, God tolerated many practices that were not in accordance with his original design. Some of these were tolerated even though they were not consistent with his creation design for marriage and the family. The Mosaic legislation on divorce (Deut. 24:1–4; Matt. 19:3–9) is a clear example of this, and the pattern for marriage in Matthew 19 is clear that it was "from the beginning," a plain reference to the creation account. Just because surrogacy was tolerated in the patriarchal era, it does not follow that its use today is legitimate, especially given the connection in the creation account between the context of heterosexual marriage and procreation.

On the other hand, it is significant that the Old Testament allowed some deviations from God's creation model. Surrogacy is a clear exception to the general rule that procreation was to take place between husband and wife in marriage. Polygamy was allowed, again clearly an exception to the model of monogamy set up at creation. Divorce was permitted, even though it too violated the creation model of permanent monogamy (Deut. 24:1–5). It is true that just because these practices were tolerated, that does not establish them as normative. But simply because they violated the model set up at creation, it does not follow that in every case they are not morally permitted. They may not be the best option, but they may not be prohibited either. Few people view alternative reproductive arrangements made necessary by infertility as the best option. But simply because it is not the best option, fully consistent with the model of creation, it does not follow that it is morally prohibited. Thus, appeal to creation model, without further argument, may not be sufficient to settle the debate concerning the moral acceptability of third-party contributors to the procreative process.

However, when the New Testament appeals to the model of creation to mediate a controversy, that appeal usually settles the issue. For example, Paul appeals to creation in Romans 1:18–32 to inform his judgment on homosexuality. Homosexuality goes against God's design for human beings set up at creation. That is considered the principal argument employed, though he does refer to the negative consequences of deviating from the model for sexuality set up at creation. Similarly, when dealing with the roles of women in the church and the home (1 Cor. 11:8–9; 1 Tim. 2:11–15), he appeals to the model of creation and little else to settle the issue.

The biblical data is thus not as clear as we would wish. The Old Testament permitted some deviations from the creation model without them being sin. But when the New Testament uses the creation model to support its case, there is not much further argument needed or given. That is why it is difficult to say that the Scripture absolutely prohibits all third-party contributors to procreation because they violate God's model set up at creation. They are not the best alternatives, but they may be morally allowed nonetheless. But the model of creation and the New Testament's appeal to its authority tilts the biblical balance against third-party contributors. Thus it seems best to say that Scripture is ambiguous about third-party contributors to reproduction, without saying that Scripture teaches a prohibition of such arrangements. I would recommend that Christian couples not pursue third-party contributors, but on the basis of Scripture, I am not prepared to call every use of them sinful.

One could also object to the connection between marriage and procreation by citing the widely accepted practice of adoption as a violation of it. Adoption is clearly a separation of the biological and social roles of a parent, and is not consistent with the link between marriage and procreation/parenting.[7] However, adoption is widely recognized as an exception to the general rule, or an emergency solution to the tragic situation of an unwanted pregnancy. Just because a discontinuity between procreation and parenthood is occasionally permitted in cases of adoption, it does not follow that any such intentional separation of the biological and social roles of parenthood is allowed. Emergency solutions such as adoption usually make for poor operating norms, and just because the exceptional case is allowed, that does not justify it as the norm.

In general, reproductive technologies that do not introduce third parties into the reproductive matrix can be considered consistent with the biblical theology of the family.[8] Those that enable an infertile couple to conceive using medical technology without third-party collaborators can, for the most part, be embraced by evangelicals as morally responsible. Scripture is skeptical about those that do involve a third-party contributor.

Potential Objections and Responses: For the Sake of Virtue[9]

Thus far a reasonable argument has been made for a theology of the family in which two-party reproductive technologies alone are consistent with the biblical and creation norms. However, someone might object that I have merely assumed without argument that what is normative from creation is also morally obligatory and that to act contrary to a norm is to do what is morally prohib-

---

7. It would be more accurate to say that adoption breaks the link between procreation and parenting, though most children that are put up for adoption are born to unwed mothers. Thus the link between marriage and procreation has been violated as well.

8. See the discussion of in vitro fertilization in chapter 6. On the surface, this practice would be consistent with the biblical notion of the family, but it has other moral concerns that are addressed.

9. I am indebted to my friend and colleague Dr. John H. Coe for his contribution to the original draft of this section.

ited. That is, I can imagine an objection that insists that an act may be contrary to what is morally normative and at the same time be morally permissible. The examples of Abraham and Jacob are arguably illustrations of third-party reproductive arrangements which, though not normative, are nevertheless morally permissible. In fact, there may be a number of actions or situations that are not biblically normative but are arguably morally permissible (whether explicitly condoned in Scripture or not), for example, masturbation, adoption, one-parent families, divorce, lying, birth control, and numerous third-party reproductive technologies discussed above.

For the sake of the argument, let us assume that though third-party reproductive matrixes are against the biblical/creation norm, they are nevertheless morally permissible. In that case, how are individuals to decide what is best for their situation? What moral or other factors are relevant to the discussion for an infertile couple looking for wisdom? It will become evident in our discussion that determining some act to be morally permissible is only the beginning of moral deliberation. Many further issues concerning the implications of an action on one's character and overall happiness must be considered. That is, just because something is morally permissible does not mean that it is morally beneficial for one's character, situation, and overall aim at a happy life. Of course, this raises the whole question of virtue and the excellent life which has been purposefully ignored until now.

Though questions about moral obligation, prohibition, and permissibility are not irrelevant to discussions of virtue, they are secondary to questions about what the wise person of good character would do, how certain choices affect one's character, and what kinds of choices lead to a skillful and happy life. Certainly fortunate circumstances are important for the good life. But wisdom and experience teach us that the manner in which we experience life, as a result of our character, is perhaps most central to living well. For without a good character, in which virtue is central, even the best of circumstances may not be enjoyed as they could. Let us apply the general discussion of virtue to a couple, Ted and Mary, who inquire into the moral legitimacy of third-party reproductive technologies. It has been determined that they cannot have their own children on account of Ted's infertility. Furthermore, they believe that the AID technology is morally permissible though not the biblical/creation norm. Still, they feel sufficiently uneasy about this so that they come to you for theological and moral counsel. It should be readily apparent that the Christian virtues and their corresponding emotions are primary candidates for moral investigation, for the couple is faced with a bad or difficult situation (male infertility) in light of their desire to get something good (a child). In other words, there is more to moral decision making than whether something is or is not permitted.

In general, it should be kept in mind that the biblical/creation norm involves a two-party reproductive matrix. As the norm, it represents what God had in mind for healthy and well-functioning relationships and families. Going against this norm, as in the case of third-party reproductive technologies, may be morally permissible, especially in a fallen world, but not typically without some cost (cf. the relational price that Abraham and Jacob paid, the jealousies which raged etc.).

Furthermore, the couple must come to terms with their own character, God's goal in developing their ability to deal with bad and troubling situations in light of living well with him and others (James 2:2ff.). The couple needs to consider whether their emotional commitment to having a child has obscured their view of important biblical virtues such as trust in God's sovereignty, patience, perseverance, and faith in God's plan for them. Perhaps too much hope has been placed in having a natural child or too much emphasis has been given to the role a natural child plays in happiness. The virtuous person also grows to hope in the Lord, in the fact that someday all hurts will be healed, all injustices made right, and all natural evils transformed to pure joy. Perhaps the couple needs to entertain the virtue of despairing over what is normative, despairing over having a natural child, despairing even over the use of these morally permissible reproductive technologies. The purpose of such despair and the reflection that accompanies it engenders manifold possibilities: what good there might be in not having a natural child; what character development might occur as a result of hoping in God alone; what one might learn of the virtue of charity in adopting a child (as exemplified in God's love toward the Gentiles); what it is to participate in the sufferings of Christ, who despaired of avoiding the cross. Some couples, conversely, may hope in God to the unwise exclusion of entertaining any hope in or even considering any human means of having a natural child. Perhaps these couples despair too quickly of receiving any natural good. This may be a defense against experiencing any unrequited hopes, something with which they may be too familiar. Again, many issues should be introduced for reflection and experience.

As a way of getting at some of the issues of virtue, the couple should be encouraged to come to terms with their fears, both real and illusory. Perhaps some have hoped to excess as a way to defend against their fears that perhaps the best for them would be to despair of having a natural child. Some may find it too painful even to consider that it might be best for their character and their particular situation to accept the situation (the bad) as it is and find God's good in it. Perhaps the couple in question has been unwilling to face this fear. However, some couples may be overly fearful, feeling and believing that God always wants them to embrace the hardest way. Perhaps these type of couples find themselves overwhelmed with such irrational fears. A good moral counselor will help couples understand and process their fears in view of the goals for a healthy emotional life.

In general, the moral counselor assists couples in reflecting upon what kind of persons they are, what kind of person it takes to make certain kinds of decisions, what kind of person will result from making certain kinds of decisions, and how certain kinds of characters experience various consequences. Notice that the focus is less upon following certain rules and more upon what God intends for human life and character. Thus, by introducing the concept of virtue, our original moral quandary of whether to engage in third-party reproductive technologies has taken on many dimensions. This line of moral deliberation not only provides rich resources for reflecting upon the good life but also accounts for many of the truly human dimensions that common sense brings into any complex decision.

Conclusion

The biblical teaching on the family is consistent with some technological interventions in reproduction, but those that introduce a third party into the process raise questions. In general, artificial insemination by husband, GIFT, and in vitro fertilization can be used, assuming that the other moral difficulties involved with in vitro fertilization (embryo storage and selective termination) are addressed. But artificial insemination by donor, egg donation, and surrogate motherhood cannot be used without violating the divinely ordained continuity between the context of marriage and procreation.

However, for argument's sake, it was suggested that third-party reproductive technologies may be morally permissible even though they are a violation of what is normative in creation. Nevertheless, moral deliberation concerning the employment of these reproductive technologies should not be limited to determining what is morally permissible or prohibited (sinful). Good moral reasoning should also consider virtue and human character, complex matters that are relevant to obtaining the good life.

2

Roman Catholic Natural Law and Reproductive Technologies

Introduction

Roman Catholic theologians have provided the vast majority of religiously based discussions of reproductive technologies.[1] Both historically and recently, Roman Catholic theology has had a great interest in bioethics and values related to procreation. Much of the Catholic church's interest in procreation relates to its stand on contraception. This longstanding tradition prepared Roman Catholicism to respond to the reproductive technological developments that have occurred in the past few years. The church's application of Catholic tradition to the development of numerous artificial methods of birth control, including abortion, made for a ready transition to the discussion on reproductive interventions. As a result, the Catholic church has been in the forefront of other religious traditions in addressing the reproductive revolution. This chapter will examine the official Catholic doctrine on procreation as expressed in two primary documents. As

1. For example, when my students ask me for theologically oriented resources that deal with reproductive technologies, I am able to recommend sources almost exclusively by Roman Catholic authors. It would not be surprising if my experience is the norm for evangelicals interested in bioethics. Those few evangelical sources that did exist tended to treat the subject simplistically.

one might expect, response to Vatican doctrine in this area has generated a great deal of dissent, as not everyone agrees with the Catholic church. The main lines of criticism, both from within and without the Catholic church, will be discussed.

Catholic theologians since the Middle Ages have traditionally held that God has revealed moral values outside of the Bible, and that by reason, observation, and experience, all human beings can, to some degree, understand what God requires of them. In fact, natural law dominated Catholic moral theology until very recently, and many of the official Catholic documents on moral matters have reasoned from natural law at the expense of using Scripture to support their positions. The appeal of natural law was that it created common ground for discussion with unbelievers who could not reasonably be expected to appreciate the authority of Scripture. Natural law includes the broad generally accepted moral principles deduced from reason and experience as well as specific moral prescriptions that are grounded in nature, or creation.[2] For a church intent on embracing the world and making its influence felt in a society increasingly hostile to religion, the use of natural law made good sense, because it enabled the church to have meaningful dialogue with the world and also gave the church a chance at persuading the world without dependence on Scripture, a source of authority that the world does not accept. That methodology is certainly appropriate today as Christians attempt to persuade an increasingly secular society of the reasonableness of Christian morality on the issues of the day.

The use of natural law understandably created tension with the Reformers who insisted on *sola Scriptura* or Scripture alone as the source of moral authority for believers. Many evangelicals today are critical of natural-law reasoning for much the same reason. Historically Protestants have been skeptical of natural law, due to their emphasis on the way sin has affected the mind's ca-

2. Catholic moral theologians refer to these as the "order of reason," which means that moral principles are deduced from reason and experience, and the "order of nature," which is tied to the order of creation. Most evangelicals think of this order of nature when they hear the term *natural law*, yet it is not the dominant strand of natural-law doctrine.

pacity to discern God's revelation outside Scripture. However, just because there are limits on how much a person can know from natural law, it does not follow that natural law does not exist. Protestants acknowledge general revelation, the belief that God has revealed himself outside of Scripture, but they are less optimistic than Roman Catholic theologians about the degree to which a person can discern God's ways outside of Scripture.

In Roman Catholic thought, the tradition of natural law has emphasized the strict continuity between procreation and parenthood. According to the natural law of procreation, sexual relations result in conception and childbirth. In the same way that God designed an acorn to grow into an oak tree, he likewise designed sexual relations to come to fruition in the birth of a child. Thus there is a God-ordained, natural continuity between sex in marriage and parenthood. Every sexual encounter has the potential for conception, and every conception has the potential for childbirth and parenthood. This is why sex is reserved for marriage, and why Catholic tradition makes little room for any reproductive technology that would interfere with a natural process that is the result of creation. It also rules out any third-party involvement that would replace one of the partners in the marital relationship. Only with husband and wife in the bond of a heterosexual marriage is it morally legitimate to procreate children. Further, there is a natural and fundamental unity between sexual relations and procreation. Procreation cannot occur apart from marital sexual intercourse, and every conjugal act in marriage must be open to procreation as the natural result of God's creation design.[3]

Catholic tradition related to procreation has its roots in the moral theology of its most dominant figure, Saint Thomas Aquinas, who lived in the thirteenth century and systematized Catholic ethics, providing the basis for discussion up to the present day. It would be difficult to overstate his importance to

<hr/>

3. For further information on Catholic teaching in this area see Edward Collins Vacek, S.J., "Catholic Natural Law and Reproductive Ethics," *Journal of Medicine and Philosophy* 17 (1992): 329–46. His work will be referred to later in this chapter.

Roman Catholic ethics.[4] He held that in evaluating some acts, the critical factor is the structure of the act, not the intentions of the person performing the act or the consequences produced. A structural break in an action—something that prevents an act from achieving its divinely ordained final end—is prohibited. With respect to Catholic doctrine, since the intended end of intercourse is the procreation of children, any action that prevents this end is prohibited. That is, any action that does not allow sex to achieve its God-ordained end violates the intrinsic integrity of the act. Every sexual act has an inherent procreative meaning that is an integral part of the act itself. Thus in every sexual act, husband and wife must be open to procreation and cannot do anything that would break the structural unity of that act of sexual intercourse. That is why neither intentions nor circumstances can supersede the essential nature of the act. The structural unity of certain actions, including procreation, cannot be broken. This is considered a universal truth since it is rooted in the unchangeable nature of a human being, and for this reason Catholic tradition puts contraception on the same moral level with abortion. Both have broken the procreative meaning essential to the act of intercourse. Thus contraception and abortion are immoral since they prevent the essential procreative purpose of sex from being accomplished. In addition, most reproductive technologies that attempt to assist the procreative purpose are considered immoral, because the inherent continuity between intercourse and procreation has been broken. In contraception and abortion, sex is divorced from its procreative purpose. In assisted reproduction, procreation is separated from its essential roots in sexual intercourse.

Humanae Vitae

Contemporary Catholic teaching on procreation is revealed in two official Vatican documents. The first of these is called *Hu-*

4. For further reading of the *Summa Theologica*, the primary ethical and theological work of Aquinas, and commentary on it, see Peter Kreeft, *The Summa of the Summa* (San Francisco: Ignatius, 1990). For an evangelical and largely favorable assessment of the theology of Thomas Aquinas, see Norman L. Geisler, *Thomas Aquinas: An Evangelical Appraisal* (Grand Rapids: Baker, 1991).

manae Vitae: On the Regulation of Birth. It was issued by Pope Paul VI on July 25, 1968. (On the tenth anniversary of this encyclical, the first test-tube baby, Louise Brown, was born in England.) The pope was taking aim at the rise of contraception, and this encyclical is considered the foundational modern philosophical and theological contribution to Catholic reproductive ethics. The general tenor of the encyclical is that "marriage and conjugal love are *by their nature* [emphasis added] ordained toward the begetting and educating of children. Children are really the supreme gift of marriage and contribute very substantially to the welfare of the parents."[5] That is, God ordained marriage for the procreation of children to the benefit of the parents. This is in addition to long-standing Catholic tradition dating back to Aquinas that procreation is largely for the benefit of the species, not the individuals involved.

The crux of the pope's argument is his restatement of the Thomistic doctrine of the essential unity of sexual relations in marriage. Every individual "marriage act," that is, sexual encounter in marriage, must be open to the possibility of creating new life. The reason for this is that when God designed sexual relations, he invested the action with two inseparable meanings, the unitive and the procreative. These are both parts of the essential structure of the action, neither of which can be separated from the other. Thus, contraception is judged a moral evil because it keeps the procreative side of the act from being fulfilled. The pope put it this way:

> That teaching [that every sexual act must be open to procreation], is founded upon the inseparable connection, willed by God and unable to be broken by man on his own initiative, between the two meanings of the conjugal act: the unitive meaning and the procreative meaning. Indeed, by its intimate structure, the conjugal act, while most closely uniting husband and wife, capacitates them for the generation of new lives, according to laws inscribed in the very being of man and of woman. By safeguarding both these essential

5. Paul VI, Encyc. *Humanae Vitae*, July 28, 1968, par. 9. The encyclical was published in English in A.A.S. IX (September 30, 1969) 9: 481–518. This citation is taken from p. 486.

aspects, the unitive and the procreative, the conjugal act preserves in its fullness the sense of true mutual love and its ordination towards man's most high calling to parenthood.[6]

The structure of the sex act is clearly bound up with God's creative purposes for man and woman in marriage. The intimate and unbreakable connection between the unitive and procreative purposes of sex was willed by God, is inherent to each sex act, and is necessary to give each sex act its fullness that God originally designed for it. This statement is foundational to official Catholic teaching on reproduction and it lays out the primary tenet that married individuals must not intentionally separate by any means the two divinely ordained and essential structural elements of sex in marriage: the *unitive,* which enables husband and wife to experience the oneness of marriage, and the *procreative,* which enables them to transmit life to the next generation, reflecting the creative hand of God. These two elements are rooted in the nature of human beings, and ultimately in the will of God who created that nature in them. The pope states, "To use this divine gift [of sex in marriage] destroying, if only partially, its meaning and purpose [by separating the unitive and procreative] is to contradict the nature of both man and woman and of their most intimate relationship, and therefore it is to contradict the plan of God and His will."[7] Thus the encyclical is based on natural law because the teaching is grounded in that which is natural for human beings and the natural process, both of which are natural because they are ordained by God. Contraception, sterilization, and elective abortion are all prohibited by the teaching of this encyclical.

Of course, whenever sex does not result in pregnancy, that is not necessarily a violation of the intrinsic structure of the act if the couple is open to creating life and takes no measures to actively prevent it. In those cases, God prevented pregnancy naturally. That is why natural family planning according to what is called a rhythm method of birth control is acceptable in Catholic teaching. The difference between using a rhythm method and artificial

6. Ibid., par. 12, p. 488.
7. Ibid., par. 13, p. 489.

birth control is that the former makes use of a legitimate natural process, the times of the month when the woman is not ovulating and cannot become pregnant. In the latter, the couple is interrupting a natural process with artificial methods.

Donum Vitae

A second influential Vatican document was issued on February 22, 1987. It is called the "Instruction of Respect for Human Life in Its Origin and on the Dignity of Procreation."[8] It is often referred to as *Donum Vitae*. It was written by Cardinal Joseph Ratzinger, the Prefect of the Congregation for the Doctrine of the Faith, the Vatican office that serves as the theological overseer for the Catholic church, insuring its adherence to Catholic tradition. This document addresses assisted reproductive technology and attempts to apply Catholic teaching on procreation to the various new reproductive technologies. It cites the earlier *Humanae Vitae* in several important places, and it is apparent that the instruction is a further application of the spirit of *Humanae Vitae* to a set of new questions. The document lays out the key moral principles governing the discussion and then replies to specific questions related to different reproductive technologies.

The instruction acknowledges that science and technology are significant expressions of the dominion that God originally entrusted to mankind at creation, of which medicine in general is a major part. But that does not mean that technology can be exempt from moral assessment. That is, moral principles from natural law serve to limit technology appropriately.[9] The fundamental values that limit the application of reproductive technology are twofold: "the life of the human being called into existence and the special nature of the transmission of human life in marriage."[10] The first of these values has to do with the moral status of the embryo (and fetus, by extension) and the concern to protect embryos

---

8. This document is published in *Origins* 16, 40 (March 19, 1987): 698–710.
9. Ibid., 699–700.
10. Ibid., 700.

from the moment of conception. The instruction goes into great depth in discussing the embryonic right to life from conception until death and also deals with questions about prenatal diagnosis, research and experimentation on embryos, and the use of embryos in reproductive technologies such as in vitro fertilization.[11] In general, reproductive methods that involve intentional destruction of embryonic life are not morally allowed.[12]

The second fundamental value related to assisted reproduction is "the special nature of the transmission of human life in marriage." Here the instruction reaffirms the essential teaching of *Humanae Vitae*, that all human procreation must take place in marriage and be connected to a specific sex act. The instruction states that "from the moral point of view a truly responsible procreation vis-a-vis the unborn child must be the fruit of marriage. . . . The fidelity of the spouses in the unity of marriage involves reciprocal respect of their right to become a father and a mother only through each other. . . . In marriage and in its indissoluble unity [is] the only setting worthy of truly responsible procreation."[13] Therefore, any reproductive interventions that involve third-party genetic or gestational contributors would not be allowed.[14] The instruction insists that these interventions violate the reciprocal commitment between the spouses in marriage, violates the right of the child, can hinder developing personal identity, and potentially damages the stability of the family for society.[15] The only reproductive technologies that are possible for faithful Catholic couples are those that use the genetic material of husband and wife. Artificial insemination by donor (AID), egg donation, and surrogate motherhood are not consistent with Catholic teaching.

11. For further discussion of in vitro fertilization and other methods of assisted reproduction, see especially chapter 6.

12. Based on the discussion of the moral status of fetuses and embryos in chapter 4, there is not much debate between evangelical pro-life Christians and the teaching of this instruction.

13. "Instruction," 704–5.

14. The instruction uses the term *heterologous artificial fertilization* to describe these. For technologies that use the genetic material of husband and wife, the instruction uses *homologous artificial fertilization*.

15. Ibid., 705.

In keeping with *Humanae Vitae*, the instruction goes further and evaluates reproductive technologies that do not involve third-party contributors. In answer to the question, "What connection is required from the moral point of view between procreation and the conjugal act?" the instruction quotes the central point of *Humanae Vitae*, which inseparably links the unitive and procreative meanings of sex in marriage.[16] Furthermore, it states that "the same doctrine concerning the link between the meanings of the conjugal act and between the goods of marriage throws light on the moral problem of homologous artificial fertilization (AIH), since it is never permitted to separate these different aspects to such a degree as positively to exclude either the procreative intention or the conjugal act."[17] Thus the only morally legitimate way for fertilization to occur is between husband and wife in marriage and as a result of a specific act of intercourse. The intrinsic nature of the act of sex is rendered incomplete by separating sexual relations from procreation. The instruction puts it this way:

> From the moral point of view, procreation is deprived of its proper perfection when it is not desires as the fruit of the conjugal act, that is to say, of the specific act of the spouses' union. . . . The moral relevance of the link between the meaning of the conjugal act and the goods of marriage as well as the unity of the human being and the dignity of his origin, demand that the procreation of a human person be brought about as the fruit of the conjugal act specific to the love between spouses.[18]

Thus, morally legitimate procreation must occur as the result of a specific sexual union in marriage. Any separation of the intent to procreate from its roots in married sex is not legitimate. For Catholic teaching, there is no significant moral difference between birth control, which isolates the unitive aspect of sex in marriage, and reproductive technologies, which isolate the procreative aspect of sex and remove it from normal sexual intercourse. The individual reproductive interventions are judged as actions in and of

16. Ibid.
17. Ibid., 706.
18. Ibid.

themselves and cannot be justified by appeal to the overall sexual relationship of the couple, the other good consequences that may result if a child is born to the couple, or even from the sex that may immediately precede or follow the specific reproductive intervention. The problem is that the inherent nature of the sex act is violated. With in vitro fertilization, for example, the instruction states that "the generation of the human person is objectively deprived of its proper perfection: namely that of being the result and fruit of a conjugal act in which the spouses can become cooperators with God for giving life to a new person. The act of conjugal love is considered in the teaching of the Church as the only setting worthy of human procreation."[19] Therefore, in vitro fertilization, zygote intrafallopian transfer, embryo transfer, and artificial insemination are all judged to be morally problematic.

The instruction does make an important distinction between a technology that *assists* normal intercourse and one that *replaces* it in the process of trying to conceive a child. Anything that assists intercourse is considered a part of God's wisdom that can be utilized in reproduction. The important aspect is that the unity of sex and procreation is maintained. What this means more specifically is that conception must occur according to its intended design. The movement of genetic materials may be assisted, but use of technology may not replace normal intercourse. For example, fertilization must always occur inside the body, and masturbation may not be used as a substitute for sex in order to collect sperm outside the body to be reinserted into the woman. The instruction puts it this way: "Thus moral conscience does not necessarily proscribe the use of certain artificial means destined solely either to the facilitating of the natural act or to ensuring that the natural act normally performed achieves its proper end. If the technical means facilitates the conjugal act or helps it to reach its natural objectives, it can be morally acceptable. If, on the other hand, the procedure were to replace the conjugal act, it is morally illicit."[20]

An example of a reproductive technology that assists intercourse without replacing it is what is called low tubal ovum trans-

19. Ibid., 707.
20. Ibid.

fer (LTOT). This procedure extracts and relocates the egg to a place where fertilization can occur. This is performed in cases in which the woman is infertile due to a blockage in her fallopian tubes. The physician who performs LTOT is able to bypass the blockage and place the egg lower in the fallopian tubes or even in the uterus, where conception can now occur by natural intercourse. The sperm still follows its natural course and fertilization occurs in the body.

However, LTOT has some medical problems involved. Most clinicians believe that conception occurs in the higher regions of the woman's fallopian tubes and that the path of the embryo from the upper regions of the fallopian tubes to the uterus is an important part of the embryo's development that enables it to attach itself successfully to the wall of the uterus. Should fertilization take place in the lower regions of the fallopian tubes or in the uterus, it may increase the chances of a miscarriage.

To correct this, a related procedure called tubal ovum transfer (TOT) has been developed. The egg is removed and relocated at a higher part of the fallopian tubes, giving implantation of the embryo, assuming the egg is successfully fertilized, a better chance to occur. This procedure would not be helpful to some women with blocked fallopian tubes, since the embryo would still need to travel the length of the tubes to reach the uterus. However, the procedure would be helpful for couples who have trouble conceiving for other reasons. Both LTOT and TOT have been declared consistent with Catholic teaching because they assist rather than replace intercourse and because fertilization occurs naturally within the body. In both procedures the sperm is inserted through normal intercourse, although in TOT, the sperm must be treated and then reinserted in the woman's fallopian tubes. This is done by use of a silicon sheaf, much like a condom, that seals itself after the initial expulsion of sperm in intercourse. The sperm that is left over after this initial expulsion is then treated and reintroduced into the woman's body to enable fertilization to occur and thus to enable intercourse to achieve its intended goal. Some Catholic ethicists insist that this is within Catholic teaching since masturbation is avoided as a means of collecting the sperm. Others, however, conclude that because the sperm does not travel its normal route, but is taken outside the body and reinserted into the woman after being treated, it has partially replaced intercourse instead of simply assisting it. This has caused some conservative Catholic moral theologians to question the moral legitimacy of TOT, though it is not specifically prohibited by either *Humanae Vitae* or *Donum Vitae*. The debate over this procedure shows the fine distinctions that are sometimes necessary in assessing the morality of some new reproductive technologies.[21]

A further example of a widely used reproductive technology that the Vatican instruction seems to allow is GIFT.[22] In this procedure the woman's eggs are removed and joined with the sperm in a catheter that keeps them separate. Both sperm and egg are re-inserted into the fallopian tubes so that fertilization can occur in the body. As long as the sperm is not collected by masturbation, but through normal intercourse with something like a sheaf to collect the sperm, many Catholic moral theologians agree that GIFT assists and does not replace normal intercourse. However, the steps that GIFT and TOT normally use vary somewhat from Catholic teaching. Most infertility clinics that offer GIFT, for example, assume that sperm will be collected by means of masturbation. The same is true for artificial insemination, though it may be possible to collect sperm for artificial insemination by use of the sheaf as well. But sperm collection by means of normal intercourse strikes many people as awkward, and does not normally enable the couple to obtain the best sperm sample since the majority of the sperm are ejaculated during the initial expulsion in intercourse.

Catholic Dissent from Official Church Teaching

As one might expect, not everyone in Catholic circles agrees with the Vatican position. The instruction was the subject of a great deal of comment, much of it critical. Some of the criticism came

21. For more discussion on the technicalities of ovum transfer and its moral assessment by Catholic theologians, see Donald DeMarco, *Biotechnology and the Assault on Parenthood* (San Francisco: Ignatius, 1991), 205–38.
22. For further discussion on this technique, see chapter 6.

from outside the Catholic church,[23] but a good deal of the critique of the Vatican's position has arisen from Catholic scholars. Non-Catholic commentators have echoed most of the criticism that has come from Catholic moral theologians.

Too Narrow a View of Sex and Procreation

The primary criticism of the Vatican's position prohibiting most reproductive technologies is that it takes a much too narrow view of sex and procreation. There is more to the question of which reproductive technologies are morally allowable than whether or not they replace or assist normal intercourse. The view that every child must come from a specific act of sexual intercourse between husband and wife is said by critics to limit moral decision-making about reproduction unnecessarily, and that whether to use a specific reproductive intervention requires broader criteria and a more holistic view of marriage and procreation.

The instruction asserts that when a child is conceived through reproductive technologies, it is not the fruit of the spouses' love.[24] But this does not follow, unless one assumes that sexual intercourse is the only way love in marriage can be expressed.[25] Sexual love is only one of many expressions of love in marriage, and love between the couple can be expressed in their efforts to conceive a child apart from their sexual relationship. Other expressions of love include the shared longing for a child, cooperation and support for each other in the process (often required to a greater degree when the couple is infertile), and affirmation of each other's respective masculinity and femininity, which infertility undermines.[26] For example, a husband's emotional sup-

23. See, for example, the statement by the Ethics Committee of the American Fertility Society, entitled "Ethical Considerations of the New Reproductive Technologies In Light of 'Instruction on the Respect for Human Life in Its Origin and the Dignity of Procreation,' *Fertility and Sterility* supplement 1, 49, 2 (February 1988).

24. Instruction, 708.

25. Richard A. McCormick, "The Vatican Instruction on Bioethics: Two Responses," *America* 156 (1987): 247–48.

26. Edward C. Vacek, S.J., "The Vatican Instruction on Reproductive Technology," *Theological Studies* 49, 1 (1988): 110–31, at 115.

port for his wife during the arduous process of in vitro fertilization and the mutual support needed when the process has not yet accomplished conception, are clear expressions of marital love in the process of procreation. The child who is conceived to a loving couple who care deeply for each other, who provide a loving, nurturing home, and who use a reproductive intervention is just as much the fruit of the couple's love as is the child who is conceived naturally. In fact, the process of artificial reproduction may even require expressions of love, support, and Christlike self-sacrifice that are not necessary when conception happens naturally and easily.

This criticism maintains that the structure of the sexual act is given too much weight in evaluating the morality of different reproductive interventions. Other criteria must be employed to render a moral judgment on different types of reproductive technologies. The instruction insists that the only relevant criterion is whether the integrity of the conjugal act is maintained, that is, that the procreative and unitive purposes be maintained in each and every sexual act. Any reproductive intervention that separates the two nonnegotiable aspects of the sexual act cannot be morally legitimate.

Catholic critics, most of whom are natural-law adherents in some form or another, suggest other criteria are necessary for making a sound moral evaluation of the use of these technologies. Many Catholic moral theologians who make this point insist that these broader criteria actually have their roots in the thought of Thomas Aquinas, to whom the Vatican also appeals for support of the traditional view. The primary objection to the Vatican position is that the part (the specific sexual act) should be evaluated in terms of the greater whole (the life of the family).[27] That is, the specific act of sex should not be viewed in isolation from the couple's marital and family life together. When reproductive technologies can be used to overcome infertility and help fulfill the couple's deeply held desire for children, the entire family benefits. The benefit of the family, Vatican critics allege, should be

27. Edward Collins Vacek, S.J., "Catholic Natural Law and Reproductive Ethics," *Journal of Medicine and Philosophy* 17 (1992): 329–46, at 341.

viewed with the same if not more emphasis as the inherent structure of the sexual act. Maintaining the integrity of sex in marriage is important and thus there would be a problem with some technologies that would encourage irresponsible use of a person's genetic materials, as could be the case with sperm and egg donation.[28] But other values such as nonsexual love between husband and wife, the natural inclination to procreate children, especially those genetically related to the parents, and the fulfillment of the family in having children are also important. The traditional view that depends on the centrality of the sexual act itself may be causing other important values for family life to be compromised, thereby hindering the natural fulfillment of families.

Catholic moral theology has long depended on what is called "the principle of totality," that is, that the whole has greater moral worth than any individual part. This principle works in medicine in general to suggest that treatment of any part of a person shall not be to the detriment to the person as a whole, and that it is justifiable to destroy a piece of the whole for the sake of the whole. This principle is used to justify amputation and can be applied socially to justify capital punishment. That is, the state can kill a person guilty of a capital offense for the good of the whole community. Organ donation was considered justifiable on the same principle. There is a well-developed line of reasoning in Catholic thought that gives greater weight to the whole than to any one of the parts. Critics of the Vatican position use the principle of totality to justify some reproductive interventions. They insist that the whole includes the couple and the family, and that the part (the sexual act, specifically, the insistence that its inherent integrity be maintained) cannot override the fulfillment and flourishing of the family that is tied (at least for infertile couples) to having children. Reproductive interventions can be acceptable because they provide for other critical values that are key to human flourishing and to accomplishing what God ordained for individuals and families that the entrance of sin prevents without the help of human technological creativity. Thus, the couple's

---

28. For more on this aspect of procreative responsibility, see Sidney Callahan, "Lovemaking and Babymaking," *Commonweal* 114 (1987): 233–39, at 234.

family values, not the isolated sexual act, should be primary in assessing reproductive technologies. Ironically, the Vatican claims that use of these technologies will bring harm to the husband and wife, to their love and marriage, and to the child that is conceived from these technologies. Empirical questions can be raised about each of the claimed harms, and it may be that not allowing couples to access some reproductive technologies on moral grounds may actually cause some of these same harms that the Vatican wishes to prevent.[29]

Unitive and Procreative Aspects of Sex Can Be Separated

A second criticism from Catholic moral theologians is that the unitive and procreative aspects of sex need not go together every time a couple has sexual relations. The Vatican instruction teaches that every act of sexual relations must be open to procreation, thus ruling out contraception and sterilization. Similarly, procreation cannot occur apart from sex in marriage. The critics suggest that the Vatican documents are too rigid on this point, even to the point of absurdity in some cases. Rather, the general connection between marriage and procreation must be maintained. On the whole, the link between the unitive and procreative aspects of sex must be maintained, but not every sexual encounter between husband and wife must encompass both aspects. Catholic moral theologian Richard A. McCormick accepts the general link between the two aspects of sex, but denies that both must be present every time a couple has sexual relations. He states, "It is sufficient that the *spheres* be held together, so that there is no procreation apart from marriage, and no full sexual intimacy apart from a context of responsibility for procreation."[30]

Catholic teaching does make some allowance for natural birth control. The Catholic church does not teach that couples must

29. Vacek, "Catholic Natural Law and Reproductive Ethics," 341.
30. Richard A. McCormick, S.J., "Therapy or Tampering?: The Ethics of Reproductive Technology," *America* 154 (December 7, 1985), cited in Arthur L. Greil, "The Religious Response to Reproductive Technology," *The Christian Century* (January 4–11, 1989): 11–14, at 12.

engage in sex during fertile periods, nor does it fault couples for abstaining during fertile periods in order to space births. If a couple used a rhythm method and never intended to have a child, such a lifestyle could be morally acceptable if there were sound reasons for not having children.[31] If it were, then one would have to ask what the difference is between a couple who abstains during fertile periods temporarily in order to space their children and a couple who abstains during fertile periods for the long term in order to avoid having children. It would appear that the latter couple is using a morally acceptable method of birth control to avoid having children altogether. Acknowledging other informing values would appear to be contrary to the strong emphasis on the inherent structure of the sexual act for determining the morality of reproductive decisions. It might open the door for the Vatican's critics to assert that values other than the structure of the sex act need to be considered in assessing reproductive technologies. At the least, a couple could be using an approved birth-control method—one that the Vatican teaches does not violate the inseparability of the unitive and procreative aspects of sex—to separate the unitive and procreative aspects of sex permanently. The need for this connection between the two aspects of sex reaches an extreme according to some Catholic moral theologians. The Vatican instruction affirms that sex does not lose its value, presumably in both its aspects, even when the couple is permanently infertile.[32] But it seems forced to assert that the sex act has procreative as well as unitive meaning even when the couple has no biological prospect of conceiving a child.[33]

Scripture affirms the essential goodness of both the unitive and procreative aspects of sex, but there does not appear to be any biblical demand that the two aspects always be linked. The creation account establishes that the spheres of marriage and procreation be connected, but it does not require that every time a couple has sexual relations, they be open to procreation. It is true that

---

31. Vacek, "Catholic Natural Law and Reproductive Ethics," 337.
32. Instruction, 708.
33. Vacek, "Catholic Natural Law and Reproductive Ethics," 338.

in the teaching of Thomas Aquinas, concern for the species of the human race was weighted more heavily than concern for the individual family. But it should be clear that human beings have more than fulfilled their obligation to "be fruitful and multiply and fill the earth." In fact, concern for the species, especially in parts of the third world, would appear to mandate separating the unitive and procreative aspects of sex by responsible use of birth control. The Catholic church has been widely criticized for contributing to overpopulation by its prohibition of birth control, based on the church's doctrine that requires keeping the unitive and procreative aspects of sex together.

Scripture affirms that sex has a variety of purposes, all of which are ordained only within the confines of marriage. For example, it clearly teaches that sex is one of the means by which a couple experiences the physical oneness and spiritual unity that is a part of the mystery of marriage (Gen. 2:24; Eph. 5:29–33). Second, sex was established as the means for procreation. Third, it is designed for pleasure and is one of the ways a couple enjoys each other. Scripture views sex as good within marriage if it is an expression of a couple's love for each other. Within this context, any of the purposes for sex are good in and of themselves. In fact, sexual pleasure between married persons is good even if pleasure is the only objective for any particular sexual act.

The Song of Solomon bears eloquent testimony to the high place Scripture gives to sexual pleasure. The royal couple in the Song revel in each other's love, exhibiting a depth of passion that most couples would like to reproduce in their own marriage. The imagery of sex as a meal of choice foods (Song of Sol. 4:13–5:1) indicates that pleasure was the objective of the couple on their wedding night. The way in which they describe each other's bodies in exquisite figures of speech (Song of Sol. 4:1–7; 6:4–9; 7:1–8) makes it clear that pleasure is the purpose for the sex recorded in the book. Interestingly, in the entire book, there is not one mention of children or procreation. If the unitive and procreative purposes of sex must always go together, this is a most unusual omission. It seems to point to pleasure as an inherent and self-sufficient purpose of sex. That is, sex can be for pleasure alone, apart from any procreative intention.

Similarly in 1 Corinthians 7, Paul speaks of sex as a source of physical release and enjoyment, since it is better to marry than to burn with passion (1 Cor. 7:9). Paul commands that husbands and wives come together for sex regularly so that they will not be tempted to look elsewhere for the pleasure of sex (1 Cor. 7:2, 5; this seems to be the meaning of the phrase in verse 2, "because there is so much immorality."). They are commanded not to deprive each other, presumably of the pleasure of sex (and perhaps also the source of physical release), except by mutual consent for temporary periods of prayer and contemplation (1 Cor. 7:5). Husbands and wives are enjoined to fulfill their conjugal duties to each other (1 Cor. 7:3–4), and nowhere in this passage does the apostle mention children. Rather, in this passage the purpose of giving pleasure to one's spouse appears to be the sole and sufficient reason for sexual relations.

Scripture does not appear to teach that unitive and procreative purposes of sex must always be linked. If that is the case, then both birth control (separating out procreation) and some reproductive interventions (separating out the oneness and pleasure purposes) would seem to be morally legitimate. If Scripture allows sex for pleasure alone as a self-sufficient purpose, then it would seem that other purposes for sex are legitimate and self-sufficient as well. Thus, it is biblically allowed to separate the purposes for sex. If it is permissible to separate the pleasure aspect from the procreative by using birth control, then it must be legitimate to separate procreation from sex by using some reproductive technologies.

Prohibiting Reproductive Technology Is Arbitrary

A third criticism is that the prohibition of medical technology to alleviate infertility is arbitrary and overly restrictive, particularly in light of the Vatican's endorsement of technology in general. Critics claim that the use of new medical technology to help couples conceive a child is generally appropriate, parallel to using medical technology to cure other medical conditions. The instruction sanctions scientific research and technology as an expression of human beings' God-ordained dominion over the earth (Gen. 1:28). However, science and technology cannot proceed apart from conscience and morality. There are considerations other than technological efficiency and progress that may place limits on the uses of such innovations. In view of this general support for technology as a legitimate exercise of human beings' dominion over creation, Catholic critics have found it odd and arbitrary that virtually no technology is allowed in the area of procreation. Since human beings are not only allowed but also entrusted with extensive dominion over most other areas of life, it seems inconsistent to deny human beings the same dominion over sex and procreation. This is particularly the case since reproductive technologies are medical technologies. Catholic teaching routinely allows for medical technology to intervene to restore malfunctioning organs and systems to their proper natural function. Many Catholic thinkers have difficulty understanding how reproductive technologies can be consistently excluded from legitimate medical treatment. Not only does medicine intervene, but at times it substitutes for a failing bodily function. For example, dialysis substitutes for diseased kidneys, ventilators substitute for diseased lungs, and pacemakers substitute for critical heart functions, in the same way that some reproductive technologies substitute for diseased reproductive functions.[34] Some would take this even further and argue that the technological developments that enable human beings to more effectively exercise dominion over the creation reflect a part of our creative makeup that comes from our Creator. Professor Sidney Callahan suggests that "the mastery of nature through technological problem solving is also completely natural to our rational species; indeed it is the glory of *homo sapiens*."[35]

From a Protestant perspective, this criticism is stated in terms of the notion of general revelation. As is true with new technology that serves the good of mankind, reproductive technologies are a part of God's general revelation that is universally available. As a part of creation and the mandate given to mankind to exercise dominion over the earth (Gen. 1:26), God gave mankind the ability

34. Ibid.
35. Callahan, "Lovemaking and Babymaking," 234.

to discover and apply all kinds of technological innovations. It does not follow, of course, that mankind has the responsibility to use every bit of technology that has been discovered. For example, many people suggest that certain types of genetic engineering, especially what is called germ-line therapy (a type of genetic surgery in which the gene that is corrected is also passed on to succeeding generations), should *not* be used. Others suggest that nuclear-weapons technology is another innovation that should not have been developed, or at least not used, given its awesome destructive capacity. But for the most part, technological innovations that clearly improve the lot of mankind are considered a part of God's common grace, or his general blessings on creation, as opposed to his blessings that are restricted to those who know Christ personally. This is even more so the case when the technology in question is being used to reverse an effect of the fall. The use of medicine to alleviate infertility, a clear effect of the fall, is parallel to the use of medicine to alleviate other physical effects of the fall, namely, disease. It would appear that many of the reproductive technologies in question would fit under the heading of general revelation, and whether they should be used depends on whether such a use violates a biblical principle or text.

Use of Reproductive Technologies Does Not Separate the Goods of Marriage

A fourth criticism is that use of reproductive technologies does not necessarily separate the goods of marriage. It is not clear that separating the unitive and procreative aspects of sex necessarily involves separating the goods of marriage. The instruction states that, "The same doctrine concerning the link between the meanings of the conjugal act and between the goods of marriage throws light on the moral problem of homologous [involving the genetic materials of husband and wife] artificial insemination. . . ."[36] In other words, there seems to be a critical connection between the essential aspects of sex in marriage and the goods of marriage in general. But critics have pointed out that this does not follow, since the goods of marriage involve the entire relationship be-

---

36. Instruction, 706.

tween the couple (and future children) as opposed to the individual act of sexual intimacy.[37] This reflects a narrow view of the relationship between sex and the rest of the goods that are produced in a marriage. The approach of the Vatican seems to place the objective value of sexual relations in the child produced and the resulting benefit to the species, rather than in the couple or in their family relationship.[38] The danger in this approach is that it hints at the notion that nature uses human beings for its own ends, thereby depreciating the individuals in the marriage as well as the relational aspect of sex.[39]

Desire for a Genetically Related Child Is Part of the Procreative Constitution

Many commentators have pointed out that the strong desire of couples to have a child to whom the parents are genetically related is a widespread inclination that borders on being universal. Though there may be some cultures in which this is not the case, for the majority of the human species there is a strong tendency to procreate and to pass on one's genetic material to the next generation. This is why adoption is considered a last resort for most couples. The overwhelming urge is to have a child to whom they are genetically connected, and normally, only when that is not possible do couples consider adoption. This is often why infertile couples are opposed to a third-party genetic contributor should that be necessary. Given the emphasis in Catholic teaching on the natural process of procreation, critics have wondered why the natural tendency to have a genetically related child has been omitted from consideration. It would seem to be an integral part of the human procreative constitution, and reproductive technologies that can enable that longing to be fulfilled should be considered morally appropriate. Of course, this does not legitimate all measures to have a child, but when medical technology can help fulfill this legitimate desire, it is curious that the Vatican,

37. "Ethical Considerations of the New Reproductive Technologies," 1S.
38. K. Wojtyla, *Love and Responsibility* (New York: Farrar, Straus, and Giroux, 1981), 57–59. The author is better known today as Pope John Paul II. This was written prior to his becoming pope.
39. Vacek, "Catholic Natural Law and Reproductive Ethics," 338.

working from a natural-law framework, has not included what seems to be a significant part of the human makeup. The Vatican might respond that the procreative intention is a significant part of human nature but that there are limits on how human beings can fulfill their normal human inclinations. For example, it would not be right to steal to fulfill the natural inclination to eat. In the same way, it is not morally legitimate to violate the inherent structure of sex in marriage to achieve a normal human longing. But surely this is what medical technology is designed to do, to fulfill our innate human inclination for individual self-preservation by combating disease, one of the effects of the entrance of sin into the world. And if it is true that the Vatican position reflects an overly narrow view of the relationship between sex and procreation and an arbitrary exclusion of infertility techniques from the realm of human technological dominion over the creation, then it would appear legitimate to use reproductive technologies to help fulfill the innate procreative constitution of human beings. Reproductive technologies would be an extension of sex in marriage, providing, by medical technology, that which the body can no longer do for itself, and thereby restoring a natural function to fulfill a natural inclination for which infertility is a treatable obstacle.

Conclusion

Official Catholic teaching has prohibited most reproductive technologies. The instruction did not specifically comment on some new technologies such as GIFT and ovum transfer, and there is likely to be considerable debate in the future over the moral acceptability of these recent techniques. But the reasoning behind the Vatican's rejection of most reproductive interventions is not likely to change. The insistence that the unitive and procreative aspects of sex must be inseparably linked is still the foundation for contemporary official Catholic teaching. Thus any technology that replaces normal sex is not morally legitimate. Technologies that assist normal intercourse are morally acceptable within this framework. As a result, artificial insemination, in vitro fertilization, embryo transfer, and surrogate motherhood have all been rejected. Critics, from both inside and outside the Catholic church, have argued that the official church teaching in this area takes too narrow a view of sex and procreation, that the unitive and procreative aspects of sex in marriage can be legitimately separated, that the church arbitrarily prohibits the use of reproductive technology given its acceptance of medical technology in general, that reproductive technologies do not necessarily separate the goods of marriage (in fact, they may even promote some of them), and that the church is underemphasizing the natural human inclination for a genetically related child.

There seems to be no compelling reason to prohibit infertile couples from using reproductive technologies in general. They are a part of God's general revelation to human beings, part of his equipment for human creativity, graciously given to the human race to enable us to exercise appropriate dominion over the creation. More specifically, since dominion in general clearly includes dominion over the human body, medical technology is one of God's greatest gifts to the human race, enabling human beings to overcome one of the principal effects of the entrance of sin into the world, disease. Infertility is undoubtedly an effect of the fall of mankind into sin, and medical technology to reverse it is generally morally appropriate. Within proper biblical parameters, reproductive technologies that use the genetic materials of husband and wife are morally appropriate. These include artificial insemination by the husband, in vitro fertilization, GIFT, and ZIFT.[40] To be sure, Scripture looks skeptically at third-party contributors. The Christian couple trying to conceive a child and be faithful to Scripture at the same time should be careful about employing third-party genetic or gestational contributors. Thus artificial insemination by donor (AID), egg donation, and surrogate motherhood are options about which the couple should be very careful. As chapter 7 will point out, most types of surrogate motherhood are immoral and should be illegal. Most of the de-

40. For discussion of the parameters on the direct use of these techniques, see chapters 5 (for artificial insemination) and 6 (for in vitro fertilization, GIFT, and ZIFT).

bate over third-party contributors occurs with AID and egg donation, and couples should be very careful and hesitant about using these techniques. But there is no compelling reason to assess reproductive technologies as negatively as does official Roman Catholic church teaching.

3

The Western Legal Tradition of Procreative Liberty

Introduction

In looking at the moral acceptability of various reproductive technologies, the Roman Catholic tradition stands at one end of the spectrum, being the most restrictive. At the other end of the spectrum is the law's treatment of most reproductive technologies. The legal tradition of procreative liberty has tended to grant broad freedom to couples to use a wide variety of reproductive technologies and arrangements in order to achieve their goal of conceiving a child. The tradition of biblical ethics, discussed in chapter 1, stands squarely in the middle between the more restrictive Catholic teaching and the more permissive legal consensus. With the exception of commercial surrogate motherhood, which has gained neither widespread legislative nor judicial support, the tradition of procreative liberty gives couples the legal right to use virtually any reproductive technique to have a child. Though the United States Supreme Court has not specifically addressed any specific reproductive technology, including surrogate motherhood,[1] states in

1. A number of state Supreme Courts have addressed surrogacy, including California (*Johnson v Calvert*, 114 S Ct 206 [1993]) and New Jersey in the well-publicized Baby M case (*In re Baby M*, 537 A2d 1227, NJ [1988]). To date, fourteen states have passed laws prohibiting commercial surrogacy and making the contracts void. For a detailed discussion of these state laws and the state of the law internationally, see Scott B. Rae, *The Ethics of Commercial Surrogate Motherhood* (Westport, Conn.: Praeger, 1994), 146–58.

general have refused to write laws that would interfere with a couple's or a single person's liberty to have a child.

Procreative liberty as a legal right is a strongly held tradition, tied closely to the right to privacy. This tradition has strongly affected the way society views most reproductive technologies. Since there are few legal limits on the use of reproductive technology, public policy has imposed only minor restrictions to regulate the infertility industry, with the exception of surrogate motherhood. Couples expect that procreative decisions will be theirs and theirs alone. These attitudes make it difficult for any religious tradition to suggest moral limits on the use of reproductive interventions, particularly if it desires to see its moral stand on these technologies become the law.[2] Because the discussion of reproductive technologies is set against the backdrop of a long-standing legal tradition of procreative liberty in the United States, any public policy on reproductive technologies that does not take this tradition into account will face significant obstacles in the process of being enacted into law and of withstanding Constitutional challenge once enacted.

This chapter outlines the legal right to use a variety of reproductive technologies and arrangements. This is a different issue from the moral right to utilize these techniques. The moral aspects are the primary focus of the other sections of this book. The chapter will discuss the following issues:

1. *The legal precedent.* The key Supreme Court cases that have formed the fabric of procreative legal freedom will be discussed, with attention given to the moral arguments that supported the legal verdicts. These cases had great significance in developing a moral consensus supporting the legal right of couples to procreate children.

2. *Analysis of procreative liberty.* The conclusion that the legal tradition allows for third-party participation in the repro-

2. The Vatican *Instruction on Respect for Human Life in Its Origin and on the Dignity of Procreation* makes it clear that the ideal is that Roman Catholic moral teaching in this area become the law. See part 3, "Moral and Civil Law: The Values and Moral Obligations that Civil Legislation Must Respect and Sanction In This Matter," *Origins* 16, 40 (March 19, 1987): 699–710, at 708–10.

ductive process will be explored and defended. This section will defend the notion that procreative liberty applied to methods of reproduction can be extended to noncoital methods. However, it must be emphasized that simply because the law allows for broad procreative liberty by extension of the existing legal precedent, that does not mean that it is moral for couples to exercise that liberty.

3. *Limits on procreative liberty.* Various cautions are urged in the exercise of third-party procreative liberty. These cautions are from the perspective of the law, not necessarily biblical ethics. The limits on procreative liberty from biblical ethics were addressed in chapters 1 and 2, and further limits will be discussed throughout the book.

The point of this chapter is not to make a moral argument for the right to reproduce in general. Rather, this chapter examines the legal and moral background to the notion of procreative liberty. When you think about these various technologies, it is important to consider what public policy should be in this area, that is, what might be enacted into the law as well as what your own individual moral decisions about these technologies should be. Any proposed law that would regulate or restrict the availability of reproductive technologies must be consistent with the legal and moral traditions of procreative liberty if it is to have much chance of becoming law and being upheld as Constitutional.

The Legal Precedent

As the legal precedent for procreative liberty developed, the focus of the cases shifted from general concerns about family life to a more narrow concentration on contraception. The cases that dealt with contraception were based on the reasoning that came out of the earlier, more general cases. Though the earlier cases may not appear at first glance to apply to reproductive technologies, they are important in that they lay the foundation upon which the edifice of procreative liberty is built.

Given the centrality of abortion to the discussion of procreative liberty in general, the absence of the key abortion cases from this discussion may appear curious.[3] As important as these cases are to the general debate over procreative liberty, they are not essential to the debate over reproductive technologies. A significant part of the discussion about different reproductive techniques relates to the freedom of a couple to conceive a child using noncoital methods and third parties in the conception/gestation process, putting the method of reproduction outside the parameters set by the traditional family. The issues in reproductive technologies and procreative liberty center on conception, not abortion. Procreative liberty issues are at stake prior to any point at which abortion would be contemplated. One place where abortion might be relevant to the various reproductive methods is in surrogate motherhood, that is, whether the contracting couple in surrogacy have the right to limit the legal abortion right of the surrogate. Most agree that once the child is conceived, a surrogacy contract cannot limit the abortion rights of the surrogate. Thus the key abortion cases are not discussed because they are not directly relevant to the procreative liberty issues that are specific to the use of various reproductive technologies.

Meyer v Nebraska[4]

In the first of the cases in which the United States Supreme Court established the tradition of procreative liberty, the Court continued to broaden the scope of the liberties protected by the Fourteenth Amendment. Though the Constitution does not specifically recognize the right to privacy, the Court has continually expanded the notion of liberty to include various zones of privacy inherent in the due-process clause.

In *Meyer v Nebraska*, the Court affirmed that the protected Constitutional liberties include the freedom for an individual "to

3. These cases include *Roe v Wade*, 410 US 113 (1973), *Doe v Bolton,* 410 US 179 (1973), *Planned Parenthood of Central Missouri v Danforth*, 428 US 52 (1976), *Webster v Reproductive Health Services*, 109 S Ct 3040 (1989), and *Planned Parenthood v Casey*, 112 S Ct 2791 (1992).
   4. 262 US 390 (1923).

marry, establish a home and bring up children."[5] The state cannot interfere with one's decision to establish a family. Though noncoital means of reproduction were not in view in this case, some have argued that the freedom for coital reproduction extends by implication to methods that use some of the new reproductive technologies, such as IVF and AID.[6] However, this decision clearly confined procreative liberty to married couples, and the Court appeared to assume that children (conceived by normal means) are to be brought up in a home occupied by a heterosexual married couple.

Pierce v Society of Sisters[7]

Though this case did not deal with conception, the decision affirmed the liberty of parents to rear their children in the manner in which they see fit. (The state of Oregon in this case was prevented from mandating that parents send their children to public schools until the age of sixteen.) It clearly limited the power of the state to interfere in the realm of family matters. This is a foundational decision that was later applied more specifically to privacy as it relates to contraception and abortion. Though the case does not address procreative liberty per se, this decision was instrumental in beginning to define the zones of privacy that were later specified to include procreation as chief among them. Here the Court made the phrase in the *Meyer* decision more precise, that an individual has the freedom to "bring up children." Assuming that the way in which that is done does not harm the child in a way that the state could readily prevent, the state does not have the authority to mandate how parents

---

5. Ibid., 399.

6. See, for instance, John Robertson's statement about this and other Supreme Court decisions. He states, "In dicta, however, the Supreme Court on numerous occasions has recognized a married couple's right to procreate in language broad enough to encompass coital and most non-coital forms of reproduction." He then cites the *Meyer* case as one example. "Embryos, Families and Procreative Liberty: The Legal Structure of the New Reproduction," *Southern California Law Review* 59, 5 (July 1986): 958.

7. 268 US 510 (1925).

should rear their children. "It is an unreasonable interference with the liberty of parents and guardians to direct the upbringing of the children, and in that respect violates the Fourteenth Amendment."[8]

Skinner v Oklahoma[9]

The Court in this case struck down a mandatory sterilization law for habitual criminals, particularly those guilty of "felonies involving moral turpitude." The defendant was convicted of robbery on three different occasions, and facing sterilization, he sued, charging that the statute violated the equal protection clause of the Fourteenth Amendment. The Court ruled that the law was discriminatory, "laying an unequal hand on those who have committed intrinsically the same quality of offense and sterilizes one and not the other [the law mandated sterilization for robbery but not for embezzlement], it has made as invidious a discrimination as if it had selected a particular race or nationality for oppressive treatment."[10]

In addition, the Court ruled that the law denied an essential civil liberty, and the language suggested that the right to procreate is so basic as to be inalienable. "We are dealing here with legislation which involves one of the basic civil rights of man. Marriage and procreation are fundamental to the very existence and survival of the race. [When sterilized] He is forever deprived of a basic liberty."[11] Thus, the right to marry and start a family established in *Meyer* cannot be forfeited by any criminal behavior.

Griswold v Connecticut[12]

In this landmark case, the Court struck down a Connecticut law forbidding the use of contraceptives, and in doing so, affirmed the right of marital privacy. Though the Constitution does

8. Ibid., 534.
9. 316 US 535 (1942).
10. Ibid., 541.
11. Ibid.
12. 381 US 479 (1965).

not specifically mention many of the rights that are now clearly recognized as consistent with it, the Court recognized that the right of privacy in marriage is within the penumbra of specific guarantees made by the Bill of Rights.

The Court here established the notion of peripheral rights.[13] Among these are the right to privacy.[14] "This case, then, concerns a relationship lying within the zone of privacy created by several fundamental constitutional guarantees. We deal with a right of privacy older than the Bill of Rights."[15] Here the Court affirmed the notion of substantive due process, that within the structure of the Fourteenth Amendment certain liberties exist irrespective of their specific mention in the Constitution. These unwritten liberties were identified by the Court in keeping with the spirit of those liberties protected by the Bill of Rights.[16] Clearly the Court placed the decision not to procreate within the zones of privacy, consistent with earlier decisions that affirmed the freedom to procreate.

Eisenstadt v Baird[17]

This case broadened the right to use contraception, recognized by *Griswold*, to include unmarried individuals as well as married couples. The Massachusetts law in question made it a felony for anyone except a licensed physician or pharmacist, at a physician's direction, to distribute contraceptives. The law provided that contraceptives be distributed only to married couples, and was struck down by the appeals court as a violation of the equal protection clause of the Fourteenth Amendment. That decision was affirmed by the Supreme Court.

---

13. Citing *NAACP v Alabama*, 357 US 449, the Court ruled that the First Amendment protects freedom of assembly and privacy in one's associations. "While not expressly included in the First Amendment, its existence is necessary in making the express guarantees fully meaningful." Ibid., 483.

14. Ibid., 484.

15. Ibid., 486.

16. In his concurring opinion, Justice Goldberg stated, "I do agree that the concept of liberty protects those personal rights that are fundamental, and is not confined to the specific terms of the Bill of Rights." Ibid., 486.

17. 405 US 438 (1972).

The Court rejected the state's claim that the law was grounded in a concern for public health, concluding that it was only a mask for its real purpose of preventing premarital sexual activity.[18] In doing so, the Court affirmed the direction set in *Griswold* that keeps the government from intruding into the private realm of the bedroom.[19]

In the majority opinion, Justice Brennan clarified the right to procreative privacy.

> If under *Griswold* the distribution of contraceptives to married persons cannot be prohibited, a ban on distribution to unmarried persons would be equally impermissible. It is true that in *Griswold* the right to privacy in question inhered in the marital relationship. Yet the marital couple is not an independent entity with a mind and heart of its own, but an association of two individuals each with a separate intellectual and emotional makeup. If the right of privacy means anything, it is the right of the individual, married or single, to be free from unwarranted governmental intrusion into matters so fundamentally affecting a person as the decision whether to bear or beget a child.[20]

The Court affirmed a fundamental privacy right in decisions to prevent conception. These decisions are so fundamental to an individual's goals, aims, and happiness in life that decisions in this area are to be left to the individual, assuming that no harm comes to the parties to the decision or others affected by it. This case thus marked an important shift in the way procreative privacy; rights are recognized. The *Griswold* decision assumed that a marriage constituted a separate entity that should not be subject to intervention by the state. It protected only married couples from such intervention. *Eisenstadt*, however, affirmed the individuality of the people within the marriage relationship. Thus the

18. Ibid., 452.
19. Justice Douglas used a graphic illustration in *Griswold* to make this point. "Would we allow the police to search the sacred precincts of marital bedrooms for telltale signs of the use of contraception? The very idea is repulsive to the notions of privacy surrounding the marriage relationship." *Griswold v Connecticut*, 381 US, at 485–86.
20. Ibid., 453.

right of privacy was extended beyond the marital couple as a unit to the individuals that make it up. In this way, *Griswold* now can apply to individuals irrespective of their marital status.[21]

Stanley v Illinois[22]

In a case that has important implications not only for procreative liberty but also for parental rights, the Court reversed a decision by the Illinois Supreme Court that denied Stanley a hearing to determine his fitness as a parent prior to the state placing his children for adoption. The Illinois law in question held that upon the death of a single mother, the children were to be declared wards of the state and placed in guardianship, irrespective of the unwed father's claim to parental rights. Stanley was thus denied a hearing to determine his parental fitness. He charged that he was being denied his rights under the due process clause of the Fourteenth Amendment. The Court recognized a fundamental right of parents to associate with and rear their children:

> The private interest here, that of a man in the children he has sired and raised, undeniably warrants deference and, absent a powerful countervailing interest, protection. It is plain that the interest of a parent in the companionship, care and custody of his children comes to this Court with a momentum for respect lacking when appeal is made to liberties which derive merely from shifting economic arrangements.[23]

21. M. Louise Graham, "Surrogate Gestation and the Protection of Choice," *Santa Clara Law Review* 22 (1982): 310–11. She states, "*Eisenstadt* recognized that the marital relationship was not a unity, but rather an association of two emotionally and intellectually distinct individuals. Thus the right of personal privacy belonged to individuals, rather than to the marital unit, and it extended to all adults regardless of their marital status." Because privacy was extended from the family to the individuals that constitute the family, procreative liberty was extended also from the family unit to the individual. Thus, it can be said that the right to privacy goes beyond individuals within a marital unit, to individuals outside the family unit as well. Once privacy was seen as applying to individuals instead of family units, the door was open to the exercise of procreative liberty outside the normally defined family unit.
22. 405 US 645 (1972).
23. Ibid., 651.

However, the Court went further and made broad statements about the significance of the family and the fundamental rights that derive from recognition of it. "The Court has frequently emphasized the importance of the family. The rights to conceive and to raise one's own children have been deemed 'essential,' 'basic civil rights of man,' and 'rights far more precious than property rights.' The integrity of the family unit has found protection in the Due Process Clause and the Equal Protection Clause of the Fourteenth Amendment."[24] Though this case addresses not procreative liberty but parental rights, clearly both sets of rights are consistent with the broad notion of liberty recognized by the Court. Decisions concerning both begetting and rearing children are to be left to parents unless there is a compelling state interest that justifies intervention.

Moore v City of East Cleveland[25]

This case reversed an appeals court decision that upheld a city housing ordinance that limited occupancy of single-family homes to nuclear families. In this case, that definition excluded a family in which a grandmother chose to live with her son and two grandsons. The law was struck down as an arbitrary limit on the due process clause.

Two important points were made in the concurring opinion of Justice Marshall. First, the city cannot define a family in the way it did, restricting it to the nuclear family. This definition effectively excluded the notion of the extended family living together under the same roof, which the Court recognized has a long history and plays an important role when the nuclear family faces economic hardship or loss of one of the parents. Second, classifying families in this way "unconstitutionally abridges the 'freedom of personal choice in matters of family life [that] is one of the liberties protected by the Due Process Clause of the Fourteenth Amendment.'"[26] The family and family-related decisions, such

24. Ibid., 651.
25. 431 US 494 (1977).
26. Justice Marshall was citing *Cleveland Board of Education v LaFleur*, 414 US 632, 639–40 (1974).

as marriage, having children, and the manner in which they are reared, are within a zone of privacy protected by the penumbra of rights guaranteed by the Constitution. This is an example of the Court's tendency to defend a narrow privacy right with broad language about the overriding right to privacy. Though the Court has yet to hear a case dealing with a specific reproductive technology, one could argue that the reasoning in this case surely supports procreative decisions that involve different definitions of family and noncoital means of reproduction that involve third party participants.

Carey v Population Services International[27]

The Court affirmed a lower court decision that struck down a New York law that restricted the sale of contraceptives to minors, allowed contraceptives to be purchased only from a licensed pharmacist, and prohibited anyone from advertising contraceptives. The Court ruled that the restrictions were not sufficiently narrowly drawn and thus unnecessarily burdened procreative liberty.[28] In addition, the Court held that minors have procreative liberty as well as adults and thus the law discriminated against them. Here the Court held that procreative freedom takes precedence over the state's concern to deter increasing sexual activity by minors. Finally, the prohibition against advertising violated the freedom of expression clause of the First Amendment. The language of the decision goes beyond the narrow issue of contraception and the right to prevent conception. If that were the only aspect of procreative liberty being protected, then one could possibly argue that the decision protects only the right not to become pregnant, and the application to reproductive technologies in general would have to be made by implication or analogy. But the decision explicitly protects the

27. 431 US 678 (1977).
28. This reasoning is similar to that used in *Doe v Bolton*, 410 US 179 (1973), that restricting abortions to licensed hospitals unnecessarily limited a woman's access to an otherwise protected right. Cited in *Carey*, 431 US, at 688. However, the Court did acknowledge that "even a burdensome regulation may be validated by a sufficiently compelling state interest." Ibid., 686.

right to achieve pregnancy. After the Court cited the long precedent for privacy in family matters,[29] it applied the *Griswold* decision to this case. "The decision to bear or beget a child is at the very heart of this cluster of constitutionally protected choices. That decision holds a particularly important place in the history of the right to privacy. Decisions *whether to accomplish or prevent conception* are among the most private and sensitive."[30] The Court's summarized by stating, "Read in light of its progeny, the teaching of *Griswold* is that the Constitution protects individual decisions in matters of *childbearing* from unjustified intrusion by the State."[31] Thus, the Court specified that procreative liberty concerns not only decisions to use contraceptives, but also not to use them. Whether the language is broad enough to include reproductive technologies is open to debate, but it appears that the full range of procreative decisions is in view, even though the Court had not contemplated any of the future reproductive technologies at that time.

Analysis of Procreative Liberty

Apart from the *Skinner* sterilization case, which affirmed that not even habitual criminal activity is a sufficiently compelling state interest to strip someone of the right to reproduce,[32] the procreative liberty cases fall into two principal categories. The first set of cases protects the liberty not to procreate, that is, the right not to conceive, or the freedom not to complete a preg-

29. "It is clear that among the decisions that an individual may make without unjustified government interference are personal decisions relating to *marriage* (*Loving v Virginia*, 388 US 1,12, 1967), *procreation* (*Skinner v Oklahoma*, 316 US 535, 541–542, 1942), *contraception* (*Eisenstadt v Baird*, 405 US 453–454, 460, 463–465), *family relationships* (*Prince v Massachusetts*, 321 US 158, 166, 1944), and *child rearing and education* (*Pierce v Society of Sisters*, 268 US 510, 535, 1925; *Meyer v Nebraska*, 262 US 390, 399, 1923)." Ibid., 685.

30. Ibid., 685.

31. Ibid., 687.

32. In fact, in light of *Skinner*, it is difficult to imagine circumstances that could justify forced sterilization, if habitual criminal activity is not considered a valid basis for so doing.

nancy.[33] This set includes the abortion and contraception cases. The second set of cases encompasses the right of parents to rear a child already brought into the world and protects families from state intervention that would dictate by whom and how those children are to be reared.[34] This set of cases includes the family-rights cases, such as *Meyer, Pierce,* and *Moore.* The Court in these cases assumes coital means of reproduction within the context of the traditional family setting. Clearly none of these cases directly addresses questions raised by surrogacy or by reproductive technologies such as IVF and embryo transfer. Though the second set of cases provides the broad language of freedom in family-related matters, the first is more directly relevant to procreative liberty, since these cases deal with the specific decision about whether to bear children.

The cases affirm the legal right to engage in sexual relations without a reproductive intent and to take the necessary precautions to insure that conception and birth do not occur. However, the critical question for the discussion of reproductive technologies is whether that freedom can be extended to protect the freedom to engage in reproduction without sexual relations. In other words, does procreative liberty include the freedom to separate aspects of procreation and recombine them, even in collaboration with others?[35] Though the Court has not specifically recognized these rights, are they logical extensions of liberties that have already been recognized? In addition, what, if any, are the limits on the use of these freedoms?

One helpful distinction that will limit the discussion in this area is that between the freedom *to* procreate and freedom *in* procreation.[36] The former deals with the decision to conceive, gestate, and/or rear a child. With the exception of adoption decisions

33. The limit on the freedom not to carry a pregnancy to term is limited by the viability of the fetus. After viability, the legal right to terminate the pregnancy becomes the right not to carry or rear a child to whom one could give birth.

34. The limit on this is parental unfitness or neglect/abuse of the child.

35. This is essentially the definition of procreative liberty put forth by John A. Robertson in "Procreative Liberty and the Control of Conception, Pregnancy and Childbirth," *Virginia Law Review* 69 (April 1983): 410.

36. This distinction is made by Robertson, ibid., 410.

that are made during the pregnancy or after birth of the child, these are decisions that are made prior to conception. Thus, in some cases the decision about rearing the child is not made prior to conception, though in most planned pregnancies, the decisions to conceive, gestate, and rear a child are all made before the woman involved becomes pregnant. Freedom in procreation concerns pregnancy management decisions, that is, the freedom to control the various aspects of pregnancy. The freedom to procreate includes the freedom to decide when, with whom, and by what means one will procreate. The decision to involve a third party comes under this heading.

Given the Court's tendency to use the broad language of procreative freedom in addressing more limited issues such as contraception and abortion, the precedent for recognizing other reproductive freedoms seems well within the Court's intent. For instance, in *Carey*, the Court appeared to justify not only decisions about contraception, but also decisions about whether to bear or beget a child. *Carey* specified the principle that was inherent in both the *Griswold* and *Eisenstadt* decisions, that the individual, married or unmarried, is to be free from state intervention in the general area of procreative decisions,[37] not only to prevent but also to achieve conception. Thus, the language of these key decisions provides a basis for extending the narrow range of specific constitutionally recognized procreative liberties. One can argue that coital procreative liberties, clearly assumed in these decisions, should be extended to include noncoital means of reproduction as consistent with the established legal precedent.

Actually, noncoital means to deal with male infertility such as AID (which involve a third party) are already legally recognized, and the law has been formulated to protect children born out of these arrangements from illegitimacy and to provide for their

37. As stated in the *Eisenstadt* decision, "If the right of privacy means anything, it is the right of the individual, whether married or single, to be free from unwarranted governmental intrusion into matters so fundamentally affecting a person as the decision to bear or beget a child" (405 US at 453). Clearly, the contraception decision is couched in broader terms that validate the freedom to make procreative decisions.

support. Though the Supreme Court has not ruled on a case involving such third-party arrangements, it would appear to be a consistent extension from arrangements to relieve male infertility to those that relieve female infertility. This would involve the use of a surrogate mother[38] to replace the infertile female, as opposed to the use of a sperm donor to replace the infertile male in AID situations. To deny protection to surrogacy while allowing it for AID would discriminate against infertile women and would likely be found in violation of the equal protection clause of the Fourteenth Amendment.

Clearly there is a significant difference between the one-time contribution of a sperm donor and the nine-month involvement of a surrogate mother. The closer analogy to sperm donation is not surrogacy, but egg donation. However, the fact that surrogacy and sperm donation are not precisely analogous does not undermine the need for consistency in treating male and female infertility. Just because there are two aspects to female infertility (egg production and gestation) as opposed to one for males (sperm production) does not mean that remedies for female infertility should not be as equally protected as remedies for male infertility. The point of the comparison between male and female infertility is not the inequality of contribution in sperm donation and surrogacy; it is that both are valid medical ways to alleviate infertility.

If the issue is framed as the extension of reproductive liberties for fertile couples to infertile couples,[39] again there does not seem to be a significant leap. Rather, this application involves a consistent extension of liberties already recognized. The basis for valuing procreation exists for both fertile and infertile couples, and noncoital collaborative reproduction should be legally protected since there may be no other way for the infertile couple to repro-

___

38. The term *surrogate mother* is misleading since, in most cases, she is the actual mother of the child, having contributed genetic material to the child. In reality she is the surrogate wife in that she replaces the father's wife in the childbearing function. The father's wife is the real surrogate parent, in that she replaces the woman who bore the child in the social and relational parenting role.

39. This way of framing the issue is taken from Robertson, "Procreative Liberty, and the Control of Conception, Pregnancy and Childbirth," 428.

duce.[40] The couple's interests in reproducing (such as passing on one's genetic heritage, values, and family line) are the same, whether infertile or not. The values that are inherent in having a child (such as a feeling of family completion and the powerful longing to love and care for one's offspring) are the same, whether the couple is infertile or not. The biological effect, that of uniting sperm and egg, is the same, whether the couple is infertile or not. Thus, the interests in having a child and the biological effects involved in normal coital reproduction between a fertile husband and wife are the same as those that employ noncoital or collaborative means. In fact, the desire for a child is likely to be even stronger for infertile couples who have experienced the trauma associated with infertility. They are likely to consider the child more of a "miracle" and will appreciate the "gift" of a child more than those who have not had difficulty in reproducing. These similar interests and values are the basis for extending this freedom to include third-party collaborators in the process of reproduction. The third-party contributor provides the missing factor that the couple lacks due to the natural allotment of reproductive capacities. The couple is otherwise qualified to be parents and if fertile would clearly be free to reproduce. Since married and fertile couples have the freedom to beget children, married and infertile couples must also have this freedom. To deny them this liberty would be to discriminate against them based on biological disadvantages that they did not choose and for which they are not responsible.

The *Eisenstadt* decision extended procreative liberty[41] to unmarried persons, and the extension of positive procreative liberties to unmarried persons is again logically based on liberties already recognized.[42] Single persons have the same desires and

40. The rights of unmarried persons to procreate outside of marriage will be considered in the next section.

41. Even though *Eisenstadt* dealt specifically with contraception, the decision made it clear that the right to privacy included not only contraception but the right to be free from government intrusion (apart from compelling state interests) in matters of bearing or begetting a child. Thus, the reasoning behind the legitimacy of contraception also includes the positive side of reproduction, that of producing a child rather than preventing such a process.

42. See Robertson, "Procreative Liberty," 418–19. Further see Robertson, "Embryos, Families and Procreative Liberty," 962–63.

needs for children as married persons and the same competency to parent. Moreover, they attribute the same personal significance to reproduction as do married persons. Procreation can be as central to the life of an unmarried person as it is to a married couple, and the freedom of single persons to bear and rear the children they have already conceived is well established. One cannot imagine an unmarried woman being forced by the state to abort or give up for adoption the child she is carrying. Thus, the shift to the freedom to conceive a child in the first place is a minor, not a major, shift. There seems to be no compelling reason to legally limit procreative freedom solely to married couples, though the demands placed on a single parent warrant significant caution before one encourages unmarried persons to exercise this freedom.

Limits on Procreative Liberty

In general, from a legal perspective, procreative freedom may be limited by law on the same basis as other freedoms may be limited: the prevention of harm to the parties involved. Of course, use of these liberties may also be limited by moral or spiritual considerations, though it is unusual for the state to limit them by law based solely on a moral or religious tradition. The freedom to reproduce in general, whether using noncoital collaborative means or the traditional method, may be limited, if harm to the child may result.[43] For instance, the likelihood that a severe genetic disease will be transmitted to the child may establish a moral obligation not to reproduce, depending on factors such as the disease involved, its social costs, and the risks involved. However, the risk of physical harm to the child from noncoital or collaborative means appears to be minimal, and the use of these means to prevent such transmission of disease would almost certainly be justified. In addition, if the couple, specifically the mother, were unwilling to provide proper prenatal care for the

43. Hull, Richard T., "Introduction: Claims about the Right to Assisted Reproduction," in *Ethical Issues in the New Reproductive Technologies*, ed. Richard T. Hull (Belmont, Calif.: Wadsworth, 1990), 16–17.

developing child, this should place moral limits on the right to reproduce. A mother's alcoholism, exposure to toxic chemicals or sexually transmitted disease during pregnancy, or drug use all place the child at great risk of being born with significant defects, and in some cases lead to premature fetal death. Unless the couple is willing to provide adequate care to a child in the womb, there is a moral obligation not to conceive. A further limit that comes out of a concern not to harm the child would be the inability of the couple to perform the functions of parenthood. These range from mental retardation to inadequate financial means to support a child.

In collaborative reproduction, protection of the collaborators from harm would also justify restrictions on procreative liberty, though the state has no responsibility to protect mature adults from the folly of their choices.[44] Such harm to the collaborators is most evident in the regret, at times severe,[45] that surrogate mothers may experience when they give up the child they have borne to the contracting couple. Yet the state is usually not justified in restricting people's freedom to undertake risky behavior that many would consider foolish, such as skydiving or employment as a stuntman. However, if there were evidence of clear harm to the parties involved in the collaborative process, restrictions on it could be justified. For instance, performing the procedures involved could justifiably be limited to licensed medical facilities and practitioners.[46]

Collaborative reproduction also raises the issue of psychosocial harm to the child. Since the child is cut off from at least half of his biological lineage, and perhaps deceived by not being told about it, there is the prospect that the child will suffer from identity confusion about his or her genealogy. This confusion is compounded if the social parents make no attempt to tell the child about his or her birth circumstances (or perhaps attempt to cover them up and deceive the child), and the child does discover them, which usu-

44. Robertson, "Procreative Liberty," 433–34.
45. See, for instance, the anguish and extreme depression experienced by Mary Beth Whitehead following her release of Baby M to the Sterns (chap. 7).
46. Robertson, "Procreative Liberty," 434.

ally occurs. Collaborative reproduction thus has the ability to separate the different aspects of parenthood, and this separation could contribute negatively to a child's sense of self-esteem. Yet this separation between gestation and rearing occurs regularly in adoption, and though there are examples of children who adjust poorly to adoption and other blended family arrangements, many children thrive with adoptive parents. Though the desire to connect with one's biological lineage is undeniable and often overpowering, there is little evidence that this separation of aspects of parenthood has produced tangible harm to the adopted children. In fact, one could argue that surrogacy arrangements would be less disruptive than adoption, since in surrogacy there is usually some genetic link to the parents who are rearing the child.[47] Further, it is clear that this genetic confusion, should it occur, is not comparable to the child never having been born at all.

Yet the adoption parallel is hardly exact. Though it is undeniable that adopted children do cope and even thrive, there is a significant difference between after-the-fact crisis management and preplanning to duplicate the same conditions.[48] Adoption is clearly a rescue operation that delivers the child from an emergency situation in which the birth mother is unable or unwilling to take on rearing responsibilities. Rescue solutions normally make for poor operating standards, and the fact that children do cope in adoption settings hardly justifies intentionally creating similar situations. However, the difference between the rescue situation of adoption and the preplanned setting of surrogacy does not by itself serve as a bar to surrogacy arrangements. It does, though, raise questions about the appropriateness of the adoption analogy as a justification for surrogacy.

One might also appeal to the adoption parallel to justify the attempt of couples to connect biologically to their future offspring through the genetic link that surrogacy provides. Just as adopted children often have a strong desire to connect with their natural parents, so do prospective parents have a desire to connect to

---

47. Robertson, "Embryos, Families and Procreative Liberty," 1000.

48. Sidney Callahan, "Lovemaking and Babymaking: Ethics and the New Reproductive Technology," *Commonweal* (April 24, 1987): 235.

their future children. But the courts have not as yet accorded any fundamental rights to adoptees to connect to their biological lineage, even though the desire may be very strong. As Professor Joan Hollinger states, "Is it reasonable, then, to expect that an adult's claim for constitutional protection for an interest in connecting to future generations through the use of noncoital means of reproduction would be taken more seriously than the adoptee's desire to be linked back in time to his or her genetic heritage?"[49] No fundamental right to connect genetically to one's parents has been established, though the intense desire to do so is understandable. Should there, then, be a right to have a genetic connection to future generations? When assessing the potential harm to children born of collaborative reproductive arrangements, past legal precedent has placed the burden of proof on those who would limit the freedom to show evidence of tangible harm. Yet it is not possible to prove harm before the fact, since there has not been adequate time since the first surrogate birth to assess any kind of harm to the children. Even with children born from AID, there has not been enough long-term study to reach any conclusions about harm. As a result, the approach of those who strongly favor surrogacy is to proceed with minimal restrictions, working only from the adoption parallel. Given the current uncertainty about harm to the child, it may be more prudent to err on the side of caution than freedom. This is already the case with adoption, as the state regularly intervenes when the well-being of children is at stake. There is great care taken to insure that adoptions protect the child's best interests, illustrated by careful adoption proceedings, custody decisions, and the voluminous laws that regulate adoption. As Professor Sidney Callahan states, "Should not medical professionals be similarly responsible in carrying out the interventions which will, in essence, give a couple a baby to rear?"[50]

A further cause for caution in the broadening of procreative liberty is revealed in the way that some have extended procreative

49. Joan Heifetz Hollinger, "From Coitus to Commerce: Legal and Social Consequences of Non-coital Reproduction," *University of Michigan Journal of Law Reform* 18 (summer 1985): 879–80.
50. Callahan, "Lovemaking and Babymaking," 236.

liberty beyond the use of noncoital means or collaborators simply to alleviate infertility. University of Texas law professor John A. Robertson, for instance, argues that these reproductive means may be used ethically irrespective of the purpose.[51] These purposes include gender or genetic trait selection and transfer of the burden of carrying and delivering a child to another who is more willing. It is irrelevant to Robertson whether the woman who will be the social parent has health reasons for wanting someone else to gestate and bear her child. It would appear that reasons of comfort and convenience would be sufficient to exercise this aspect of one's procreative freedom. This freedom would also include the right to abort fetuses based on desired gender and trait features. The only limit on this right appears to be the responsibility not to harm the child that is developing in the womb.[52]

Two principal arguments are used to support this extension of procreative liberty. The first is based on the factors that make reproduction significant for people. Robertson states, "Reproduction occupies a central position in the lives of many people who consider reproduction meaningful *only if the child has certain characteristics such as good health* . . . , people are free to not to add a child to the family *if the characteristics and traits that make having a child meaningful are missing* [emphases added]."[53] As a result, couples and individuals are free to take whatever steps they desire to insure the characteristics that make reproduction meaningful, within the limits prescribed by the obligation not to harm the child.

51. He states, "The right of married persons to use noncoital and collaborative means of conception to overcome infertility must extend to any purpose, including selecting gender or genetic characteristics of the child or transferring the burden of gestation to another." See Robertson, "Procreative Liberty, and the Control of Conception, Pregnancy, and Childbirth," 430–32.

52. Without entering the details of the abortion debate, it would seem that Robertson has difficulties justifying abortion for sex selection while at the same time restricting use of reproductive technology out of a desire not to harm the child. Even if one grants that the fetus does not have personhood until some point during the pregnancy, or even until birth, it does not follow that it cannot be harmed. It seems illogical to be so concerned about the potential child's health that one restricts procreative liberty to safeguard it, while at the same time allowing the destruction of the fetus for reasons such as gender preference.

53. Ibid., 430.

However, the traits that make reproduction meaningful could include more than simply good health. Robertson also includes gender and trait selection, though he admits that many of the most desirable traits such as beauty and intelligence are affected by so many complicated genetic combinations that engineering them is very difficult.[54] But there does not appear to be anything in principle that would prevent parents from doing this if it were technologically possible. One can certainly understand and justify the desire of parents to do practically anything to prevent severe genetic diseases or other serious deformities that would drastically alter their experience of parenthood. But to place gender and trait selection in the same category as severe genetic diseases seems unwarranted and makes the significance of parenthood dependent on characteristics that are subjective and frequently irrelevant. It is difficult to see how specific traits such as eye color or hair color would dramatically alter the significance of having a child. Though there is nothing wrong with a desire for certain physical traits, using collaborators and noncoital means to insure them seems extreme. Basing the meaningfulness of having a child on such traits is far too subjective, and hardly justifies the lengths that Robertson would permit people to go in order to maximize desirable traits. Given the difficulty involved in enforcing a restriction on the use of reproductive technology in this way, it would not be desirable to make it illegal, but it could be useful to discourage use of scarce medical resources for this purpose, particularly when the basic health-care needs of millions are not being met.

A more significant problem occurs with the allowance to use reproductive technologies to select for gender, not to mention the right to abort for sex selection. Given the strong male bias in most cultures when it comes to offspring, the likelihood of disrupting the gender balance among the population seems fairly high.[55]

54. Ibid., 431–32.
55. Consider the experience in China, where it has been common for parents who are allowed to have only one child to abort female fetuses or to allow them to die (or even actively work to end their lives) following birth. However, in a scenario such as this, there may be a compelling state interest at stake for which Robertson would limit the use of collaborative techniques.

Furthermore, the bias against female offspring is itself troubling, for the same reasons that a bias against adult women is inherently troubling, especially if this bias is considered a factor that makes reproduction meaningful. It is difficult to justify use of collaborative reproduction for any purpose other than preventing severe genetic diseases.

A second argument for a broad use of noncoital and collaborative means is the parallel between the freedom to choose a mate and the freedom to choose the characteristics of one's child. Robertson states, "Just as people are now free to pick mates (based on certain desirable traits), they would have to be free to pick egg, sperm and gestational donors to maximize health or desirable physical features."[56] Just as one has the right to choose a mate based on features and traits that one finds attractive, he argues, so couples have the right to choose the traits that they find attractive in their children. Though there is nothing harmful in having certain desired traits for one's children, the right to trait selection for one's children does not follow from the right to select a mate of one's choice. There is a significant difference between choosing among people who have already established traits and attempting to create those traits through collaborative/noncoital means of reproduction. The more appropriate parallel to mate selection would be the right of parents to select from various children to adopt based on genetic and trait preferences.

An additional cause for concern and limit on how reproductive technologies might be used involves respect for embryos as persons with the potential to develop into adults. The philosophical defense of this notion will be taken up in detail in the next chapter. If it is true that personhood begins at the moment of conception, then there is no moral difference between embryos, fetuses, and persons outside of the womb. The concern for protecting the right to life of the fetus in the uterus would extend to embryos in infertility clinics. The only difference between fetuses and embryos would be stage of development and location, and to be con-

---

56. Ibid., 431. This even extends to the freedom to use genetic manipulation, should the technology become available to do so, to provide a child with a genetic makeup of the parents' choice.

sistent with a biblical stand on abortion, protection would have to be granted to embryos as well. This would mean that the widespread practice of discarding or experimenting on unimplanted embryos is a problem, as is the intentional creation of embryos for research purposes. Since the law does not recognize the personhood of the fetus, at least until viability, it is unlikely that embryos will receive protection that personhood merits.

Some people, however, are recognizing a distinction between using leftover embryos for research and intentionally creating embryos to experiment on them, experiments that usually destroy the embryos. For example, President Bill Clinton rejected part of the recommendation of the National Institutes of Health Embryo Research Panel and banned federal funding to centers that create embryos specifically and only for research purposes.[57] But he did accept the panel's recommendation that would allow research conducted with leftover embryos created during infertility treatments. It may be that pressing for a law that would prohibit infertility clinics from discarding unused embryos, though philosophically consistent with a pro-life stand on abortion, would be viewed by society as an extreme that might undermine the effort to protect all unborn children.[58] If so, it may be that the more prudent course for supporters of the unborn would be to avoid making a legal issue of embryo protection. The other alternative is to press for legal restrictions to protect embryos, however unlikely such restrictions are to be enacted into law.

A final limit on procreative freedom comes from the obligation to recognize the procreative liberties of all parties involved, for example, the surrogate mother in surrogacy arrangements. Both the natural father and the surrogate mother have procreative liberties

57. Marlene Cimons, "Clinton Bans Funding for Embryo Creation," *Los Angeles Times,* December 3, 1994, A32–33.
58. See, for example, Laurence Tribe, *Abortion: The Clash of Absolutes* (New York: Norton, 1990), where he suggests that the pro-life's insistence on personhood beginning at conception would produce the "absurd" conclusion that embryos used in infertility could not be discarded without violating their right to life. He points to that as an extreme case in an effort to discredit the pro-life movement as a whole.

that deserve protection. In a contract-law approach to surrogacy, in which the contract is fully enforceable, the interests of the infertile couple in forming a family are the only ones considered. For example, in the *Baby M* case, the lower court in New Jersey upheld the contract, based on the freedom of the contracting couple to use noncoital means to establish a family; the interests of a third party were held not to stand in the way of this fundamental liberty.[59] As Boston University law professor George Annas responded, "The right to procreate is determinative in this only if we assume it is exclusively a male right and not one that Mary Beth Whitehead retains."[60] There is no inherent reason to favor one person's procreative liberties over another's, and one of the limits on procreative freedom that should be imposed on surrogacy arrangements is that the right of a contracting couple to use collaborative means to form a family cannot be done at the expense of the surrogate's procreative liberty. She is, after all, procreating too, even as a surrogate, and even if she initially agreed to waive parental rights. As Justice Wilentz stated in reversing the lower court ruling, "To assert that Mr. Stern's right of procreation gives him the right to the custody of Baby M would be to assert that Mrs. Whitehead's right to procreation does not give her the right to the custody of Baby M."[61]

Thus when a surrogacy contract is enforced against the will of the surrogate, the parties are in the unusual position in which one person can exercise his procreative liberties only on the condition that the other's are forfeited.[62] The constitutional freedom to procreate does not include the right to deny someone else's sim-

---

59. *In re Baby M,* 525 A2d 1128, 1164 (1987).

60. George Annas, "Baby M: Babies (and Justice) for Sale," *Hastings Center Report* 17 (June 1987): 13–14.

61. *In re Baby M,* 537 A2d, 1254 (1988).

62. In commenting on the *Baby M* case, in which, initially, the contract was enforced over the desire of the surrogate to keep the child, Paul Armstrong, vice chairman of the New Jersey Bioethics Commission, and Patrick Hill suggest that the term *surrogate mother* is an oxymoron. "Surrogate motherhood is a contradiction in terms," they state. If the surrogate can perform that function only by giving up her procreative rights, it is difficult to see how she can be called a mother. Paul W. Armstrong and T. Patrick Hill, "Baby M: New Beginnings and Ancient Mileposts," *Seton Hall Law Review* 18 (1988): 854.

ilar right to parent.[63] The liberty of one person to procreate does not include the right to deny another's freedom to rear and associate with the child to which that other has made a genetic and/or gestational contribution. As stated by the New Jersey Supreme Court in the *Baby M* case, "There is nothing in our culture or society that even begins to suggest a fundamental right on the part of the father to the custody of the child as part of his right to procreate when opposed by the claim of the mother of the same child."[64] Thus, a conflict of procreative liberties exists in surrogacy that must be resolved if the use of collaborative reproduction is to be constitutionally consistent.

Conclusion

Though the long tradition of procreative liberty opens the door to use of various reproductive technologies, that does not mean that the liberty is absolute. Significant Constitutional limits can be placed on the exercise of this liberty. In addition, recognizing the right does not obligate society to provide access to the necessary means to employ it, and society is not obligated to encourage the practice. Further, there are moral limits on individual couples that may preclude use of technologies that are legal. Primarily, these moral considerations come from religious traditions that normally today are not considered the foundation for law unless they reflect a broad societal consensus or widely shared values. That is to say, though a Christian couple might have the legal right to use virtually any of these reproductive technologies, it does not follow that they are morally correct in using them. Chapters 5 through 10 will outline the moral and biblical restrictions on the use of these individual reproductive techniques.

63. That is not to say that a woman cannot agree to function as a surrogate and then voluntarily waive her parental rights. A surrogate's fundamental rights are denied only when the terms of the contract are enforced against her will, and she is denied her right to associate with the child she has borne.
64. *In re Baby M*, 537 A2d, 1246 (1988).

4

The Moral Status of Fetuses and Embryos

One of the fundamental philosophical issues underlying the discussion of reproductive ethics is the status and corresponding rights of fetuses and embryos. That is, who counts as a person, and, more specifically, when does personhood begin and end? While the implications of this analysis extend to a variety of ethical issues, such as abortion and euthanasia, the application in this chapter will be to the moral status of the unborn. It will be argued that embryos and fetuses (hereafter referred to synonymously) are fully and equally human persons.

How one views the unborn will, of course, greatly influence one's view of abortion. But it will also give parameters for use of some new reproductive technologies. For example, if personhood begins at the point of conception, then embryos fertilized in vitro and kept in storage for further use are human beings. Using them for experimental purposes or discarding them if they are not necessary is morally problematic. In addition, if prenatal genetic testing reveals genetic anomalies in the fetus, then the decision to end the pregnancy on that basis is very problematic, since it is a human being whose life is being taken. Further, if in the process of cloning embryos, some are destroyed or damaged, that is a problem because that which is being cloned is not simply a clump of cells, but a human being. It is critical to properly understand the nature of the fetus/embryo in order to avoid moral difficulties in the use of the various reproductive technologies.

Substances Versus Property-Things

Developing a proper philosophical view of unborn human beings first requires drawing a distinction between substances and property-things.[1] In the tradition of Aristotle and Thomas Aquinas, acorns, dogs, and human beings are examples of substances. Every substance is an individuated essence that has certain properties, such as the arrangement of spots on a dog or the IQ of a human being, and exists as a deeply unified whole that is ontologically prior to its parts; that is, a substance is more than the aggregate sum of its parts and properties. Most importantly, a substance possesses a defining, internal principle within its essence that informs its lawlike change and behavior. Conversely, a property-thing is an ordered aggregate. A car is an example of a property-thing, existing as a loosely unified aggregate of externally related parts. There is no underlying bearer of properties existing ontologically prior to the whole, and no internal, defining essence that diffuses, informs, and unifies its parts and properties. It is merely a collection of parts, standing in external space and time relations that, in turn, gives rise to a bundle of externally related properties that are determined by those parts.

The same is not true with a substance, say, a dog. The properties of a dog are different than the properties of an automobile. The properties of the dog are grounded in, unified by, and emerge from the dog's essence. Thus, a dog is more than the external organization of its parts functioning in a given way. Its properties are deeply unified and related internally as part of its essential nature. Its properties exist only in the context of a coherent, ontological whole. Conversely, a car has no nature beyond its additive properties, bundled together to form a loosely unified whole. Lacking an internal essence or nature, an ordering principle is externally imposed upon a set of parts to form a bundle of properties by human convention. Possessing an internal nature, then, is possible only for substances, all of which belong to a natural kind and exist in a manner essentially unique to a particular

1. I am indebted to my colleague John A. Mitchell for his substantial contribution to the original published version of this section.

class of beings. Their essential nature informs their being and gives them the essential properties peculiar to their natural kind. All members of a given species possess the same essential nature. That nature either is or is not exemplified by some particular.

So, while substances possess an internal nature, property-things do not. There is no internal, ordering principle on which to base a car's unity, govern its change, or guide its movement toward an end or purpose. Instead, there are only modifications caused by external forces. Specifically, human minds designed and built the automobile by configuring its materials into a functional pattern. These materials had no inclination of themselves to be so structured and are externally related in an artificial manner. The shape, location, and function of the materials could have been radically different, and each component could have been used for an entirely different purpose than constructing an automobile.

By contrast, that which moves a puppy to maturity or an acorn to an oak tree is an internal, defining essence or nature. This nature directs the developmental process of the individual substance and establishes limits on the variations each substance may undergo and still exist. The acorn will not grow into a dog and the dog will not become an oak tree. Consequently, a substance functions in light of what it is and maintains its essence regardless of how it changes. For it is the underlying essence of a thing, not its state of development at a given point, that constitutes what it is. We would not, for example, say that an oak sapling is of a different kind than an adult oak tree. As a substance grows, it does not become more of its kind, but rather, it matures according to its kind. The realization of its potential is controlled by the substance's essence. The capacities for the acorn one day to develop a trunk, branches, and leaves are already embedded within the acorn, prior to their realization. This is true whether the acorn actually grows into a tree or not, since such development is dependent on conditions that are independent of the acorn's essential nature. When such conditions are met, however, including the proper soil and environment, the acorn will express these latent capacities in the fullest sense. The absence of such conditions is irrelevant to the essential nature of the acorn.

A further distinction between substances and property-things is that substances maintain their essential identity through change, while property-things do not. An individual substance endures through change because it is more than the sum of its parts. The properties of a substance can change without altering the thing itself. A dog, for example, can lose a tooth or sheds its fur, but it remains the same dog throughout these processes of change because the dog is not an aggregate sum of its parts. Instead, the whole is prior to the parts and these parts exist in virtue of their internal relations to each other, grounded in the essence of the dog. By contrast, a property-thing is a whole that is constituted by its parts. Since property-things are identical to the sum of their bundled properties and ordered parts, a change in any property or part necessarily causes one "entity-stage" to end and another to begin. Thus, property-things have no enduring essences to ground their identity through change.

The Human Being as a Substance

A human being is not a property-thing but a substance. While space does not permit an exhaustive defense of this view beyond what has already been said, it will be helpful to briefly sketch four lines of argument in its favor.[2] First, every human organism is an ontological whole whose parts, properties, and capacities are related internally. The "human" identity of bodily organs and structures of consciousness presuppose their participation in the whole of which they are parts and structures. Second, every human being exhibits species-specific behavior, betraying an essential nature that is common to all members of the human species. All growth and development is governed by and restricted to the lawlike process informed by the essential human nature. Third, absolute personal identity through change suggests a substance view of a human being. Introspective awareness of oneself through change, that is, the ability to reflect on the changes one is encountering, lends support to the claim that persons are sub-

2. I thank J. P. Moreland for his insights regarding this issue.

stances that endure through change. Fourth, the notion of moral responsibility and criminal justice presupposes a substance view of a human being, because we hold the "same" person responsible for crimes committed, even if the accounting for them occurs long after the crimes were committed. For example, suppose that someone did not come to trial and a verdict until seven years after the crime. We still hold that person responsible, regardless of how he or she has changed. If a human being is a property-thing, then the person who is tried would be a different person than the one who committed the crime.

It is true that each of these claims has been disputed. The crucial point is that if this thesis regarding human beings is true, then human beings are substances, not property-things. Before we apply the preceding discussion to the question of the ontological status of the unborn, we need to consider briefly two objections to the view that humans are substances. These criticisms focus primarily on problems with the notion of essential natures.

One objection is that "essence" of a thing is merely a facade. For example, philosopher J. M. Thoday suggests that genetic variations are so significant among members of any given population that, regarding human beings, "there are as many human natures as there are men."[3] The obvious question for Thoday is why he refers to all men as having human natures. What unifies this group of things under the classification "human"? He may respond that each human being has an individually distinct human nature, and thus may be grouped into the set we refer to as "humans": (e.g., {human nature$_1$, human nature$_2$, human nature$_3$ . . . human nature$_n$}). But this clearly does not solve the problem. For now the question is, what unifies the members of this set to warrant calling it the set of individual human natures? We must eventually point to a universal human nature that allows us to refer to the unified group of

3. J. M. Thoday, "Geneticism and Environmentalism," in *Biological Aspects of Social Problems,* ed. J. E. Meade and A. S. Parker (Edinburgh: Oliver Boyd, 1965), 101, as quoted by Daniel Callahan, "The 'Beginning' of Human Life," in *What Is a Person,* ed. Michael F. Goodman (Clifton, N.J.: Humana, 1988), 41.

things we call humans. For ". . . unless there is some tacit, generalizable understanding of what the word 'human' means, some universal signification, then it could not be used to describe more than one organic entity."[4]

A second argument against the substance view suggests that entering a species is a process. Speaking of the human species, philosopher Lawrence Becker asserts,

> Human fetal development is a process analogous to metamorphosis, and just as it makes good sense to speak of butterfly eggs, larvae, and pupae as distinct from the butterflies they become (to say that they are not butterflies) so too it makes sense to say that human eggs, embryos, and fetuses are distinct from the human beings they become—that they are not human beings, only human becomings. When can we say that the fetus is a human being rather than a human becoming? Surely only when its metamorphic-like process is complete—that is, when the relatively undifferentiated mass of the fertilized human ovum has developed into the pattern of differentiated characteristic of the organism it is genetically programmed to become.[5]

Becker's view is riddled with problems. First, he fails to distinguish between the way we describe what we see and what a thing actually is. From the fact that we draw a distinction between "pupae," "larvae," and "butterfly," it does not follow that each is its own species. Becker himself acknowledges that "caterpillars and butterflies are both stages in the same insect."[6] Though the former is modified in its physical form into the latter, the essential nature of the one insect is identical in both cases. Likewise, though we distinguish between human newborns and adults, it does not follow that they are of different species. Nor does it follow that because we distinguish between human fetuses and two-year-old children, they belong to different species.

To illustrate this problem with Becker's view, consider a man

4. Daniel Callahan, "The 'Beginning' of Human Life," in *What Is a Person,* ed. Michael F. Goodman (Clifton, N.J.: Humana, 1988), 41.
5. Lawrence Becker, "Human Being: The Boundaries of the Concept," in *What Is a Person,* ed. Michael F. Goodman (Clifton, N.J.: Humana, 1988), 60.
6. Ibid., 60.

entering a room.[7] One can enter a room gradually, be half way in, three-quarters of the way in, and then fully in the room. During all stages of entrance, the man must exist fully to do the entering. Likewise, to be in the process of entering the human species, I must first be, in toto. I cannot be in the process of coming into being, since I must first exist to enter any process. To be a mere "human becoming" is an incoherent notion.

A second problem with Becker's view is the suggestion that the fetus becomes a human being only after "its metamorphic-like process is complete . . . [when] . . . the relatively undifferentiated mass of the fertilized human ovum has developed into the pattern of differentiated characteristics of the organism." This judgment is highly arbitrary, especially when applied to human beings, since the development process continues for decades after birth. Thus, it is difficult to see when Becker's "metamorphic-like" process is complete. Size and shape, as well as physical and mental capacities, continue unfolding well into the teenage years and beyond. Certainly the eighteen-year-old is no more human than the five-year-old; but since the older person is further along in the growth process, Becker's distinction implies this conclusion. It seems apparent that both the child and the adult are equally human. Moreover, the most obvious explanation for this equality is that they both possess a common human nature that informs and directs the "metamorphic-like" process throughout the stages of human growth and development. Arguably, the same essential nature directs the process before birth.

Personhood and the Unborn

The following argument defends the personhood of the unborn.

1. An adult human being is the end result of the continuous growth of the organism from conception.
2. From conception to adulthood, there is no break in this development, which is relevant to the ontological status of the organism.

7. Roderick Chisholm, *On Metaphysics* (Minneapolis: University of Minnesota Press, 1989), 58.

3. Therefore, one is a human being from the point of conception onward.[8]

Though few would deny premise 1, and premise 3 clearly follows from 1 and 2, the success of this argument rests on the truth of 2. To deny that the fetus is fully human from conception, one must point to an ontologically significant (substantial) modification that occurs between conception and birth. There is no good reason to believe that such a break occurs at any point in the process (as opposed to important but normal developments within the life of one organism). Some disagree with this claim, however, and point to either "criteria for humanness" or "decisive moments" at which the fetus first acquires the status of personhood.

The most common decisive moment, and the one currently endorsed by the United States Supreme Court, is *viability*, that is, the point at which the fetus is able to live on its own outside the womb. Currently, the average fetus is viable at roughly twenty-four to twenty-six weeks of gestation. Once this point is reached, some argue, the fetus acquires the status of personhood by virtue of its ability to live on its own, no longer dependent on a uterine environment though still dependent on medical technology.

"Viability" as a determinant of personhood is unhelpful, if for no other reason than because viability cannot be measured precisely. It varies from fetus to fetus, and medical technology is continually pushing viability back to earlier stages of pregnancy. Moreover, since viability continues to change, this raises questions about its reliability as an indicator of personhood. But proponents of viability argue that while it is possible for medical advances to push back the limit of viability, say at twenty weeks' gestation, there may be a point beyond which there is no reasonable prospect of pushing it back any earlier. Given this scenario, viability will be a more stable concept, and thus a more reliable determinant of personhood.

But what does viability actually measure about a fetus? The concept of viability is a commentary, not on the essence of the fe-

8. Cf. Richard Werner, "Abortion: The Moral Status of the Unborn," *Social Theory and Practice* 4 (spring 1975): 201–22.

tus, but on the ability of medical technology to sustain life outside the womb. Viability relates only to the fetus's location and dependency, not to its essence or personhood. There is no inherent connection between the fetus's ability to survive outside the womb and its essential nature as a human being. Thus, while viability is a helpful measure of the progress in medical technology, it has no bearing on what kind of a thing the fetus is or is not.

Perhaps the next most commonly proposed decisive moment is *brain development*, or the point at which the brain of the fetus begins to function, at roughly forty-five days of pregnancy. The appeal of this decisive moment is the parallel with the definition of death, which is the cessation of all brain activity. Since brain activity is what measures death, or the loss of personhood, some argue, it is reasonable to take the beginning of brain activity as an indication that personhood has begun. This decisive moment, however, is unhelpful as well. The problem with the analogy to brain death is that the dead brain has no capacity to revive itself again. It is in an irreversible condition, but the fetus only temporarily lacks first-order brain function. Its electroencephalogram (EEG) is only temporarily flat, whereas the dead person has a permanently flat EEG. In addition, the embryo from the point of conception has all the necessary capacities to develop full brain activity. Until around forty-five days' gestation those capacities are not yet realized, but are latent in the embryo. However, that a capacity is latent has no bearing on the essence of the fetus, since that capacity is only temporarily latent, not irreversibly lost. Thus, there are significant differences between the fetus who lacks the first-order capacity for brain activity in the first four to five weeks of pregnancy and the dead person who lacks both the potentiality and the actuality for any brain activity whatsoever. Brain activity thus fails as the decisive moment for personhood, then, is a nonstarter.

A third suggested decisive moment is *sentience*, or the point at which the fetus is capable of experiencing sensations, particularly pain. The appeal of this point for the determination of personhood is that if the fetus cannot feel pain, then there is less of a problem with abortion, and it disarms many of the pro-life arguments that abortion is cruel to the fetus. As is the case with the other decisive moments, however, sentience has little inherent connection to the personhood of the fetus, since it confuses the experience of harm with the reality of harm. Simply because the fetus cannot feel pain or otherwise experience harm, it does not follow that it cannot be harmed. If I am paralyzed from the waist down and cannot feel pain in my legs, I am still harmed if someone amputates my leg. In addition, to take sentience as the determinant of personhood, one would also have to admit that the reversibly comatose, the person in a persistent vegetative state (a person who has sustained a very serious head injury leaving only the brain stem functioning), the momentarily unconscious, and even the sleeping person are not persons. One might object that these people once did function with sentience and that the loss of sentience is only temporary. But once that objection is made, the objector is admitting that something else besides sentience is determinant of personhood, and thus sentience as a decisive moment cannot be sustained.

Another suggested decisive moment is *quickening*, or the first time that the mother feels the fetus move inside her womb. Historically, this has been the first evidence of life to be detected clearly, prior to the development of sophisticated medical technology such as ultrasound. Upon close examination, it becomes clear that quickening as a determinant of personhood is unacceptable because the essence of the fetus cannot be dependent on someone's awareness of it. This criterion confuses the nature of the fetus with what one can know about the fetus. In other words, this decisive moment confuses epistemology (knowledge/awareness of the fetus) with ontology (the nature or essence of the fetus). A similar confusion is involved in the use of the *appearance of humanness* of the fetus as a decisive moment for personhood. The appeal of this view is primarily emotional, in that as the fetus comes to resemble a baby, one begins to associate it with the kind of being that one would normally consider a full human being (e.g., a newborn). But what the fetus looks like has no inherent relationship to what it is, and from the point of conception, the fetus has all the capacities necessary to one day exemplify the physical characteristics of a normal human being. The appearance of the fetus, then, is an unhelpful criterion for human personhood.

A few assert that *birth* is the decisive moment at which the fetus acquires personhood. But this assumption is deeply problematic. It seems intuitively obvious that there is no essential difference between the fetus on the day prior to its birth and on the day after its birth. The only difference between the prebirth and postbirth fetus/newborn is her location. But birth says nothing about what kind of thing the fetus is; it merely offers a commentary on her location. But just because I change venues, it does not follow that there is any essential change in my nature as a person. Likewise, just because the unborn human changes its location, this does not change its essential nature as a fully human being.

A final suggested decisive moment is *implantation*, and proponents of this view offer at least three reasons in its defense. First, it is at implantation when the embryo establishes its presence in the womb by the "signals" or the hormones it produces. Second, since anywhere from 20 to 50 percent of the embryos spontaneously miscarry prior to implantation, some suggest that implantation is critical, not only to the development of the embryo, but also to its essence. Proponents also suggest that if we claim that a full person exists before implantation, then we are morally obligated to save all the embryos (something that very few people hold). Third, twinning, or the production of twins, normally occurs prior to implantation, and, according to some, this suggests that individual personhood does not begin until after implantation.

Though placing personhood at implantation would have little effect on the abortion question (since most induced abortions occur well after implantation), the ethical implications of this decisive moment are significant. First, if correct, it would make any birth-control methods that prevent implantation, such as many forms of the birth-control pill and the "abortion pill," RU-486, morally allowable, since an embryo that has yet to implant is not considered a person. Further, leftover embryos that are kept in storage in in vitro fertilization could be discarded or experimented with without any moral problem, since those embryos do not possess personhood.

Several things can be said against the arguments for implantation as a decisive moment. First, just because the embryo establishes its presence by the hormonal signals it produces, it does not follow that personhood is established at this point. The essence of the fetus is independent of another's awareness of its existence, whether that awareness is physical awareness, as in quickening, or chemical awareness, as in the production of specific hormones. Second, just because up to 50 percent of conceived embryos spontaneously miscarry, it does not follow that personhood comes at implantation, since the essential nature of the fetus is not dependent on the number of embryos that do or do not survive to implant. Moreover, even if the preimplantation embryo is a full person, as I contend, we are not morally obligated to save them all since there is no moral obligation to interfere in the embryo's natural death. Not interfering to prevent a spontaneous miscarriage differs from killing an embryo just as removing life support from a terminally ill patient and allowing death to occur differs from actively killing the patient.[9] Third, just because twinning occurs prior to implantation, it does not follow that the original embryo was not a full person before the split. In fact, it is equally possible that two persons existed prior to implantation, and individualized only after that point. At the least there was a minimum of one full person prior to twinning. Thus implantation fails to serve as an ontologically decisive moment for personhood.

Given the inadequacies of the decisive moments, some philosophers suggest that a human person must meet one of these criteria: consciousness . . . and in particular the ability to feel pain; reasoning, the developed capacity; self-motivated activity; the capacity to communicate; the presence of self-concepts.[10] To this list, ethicist Joseph Fletcher adds self-control; sense of the future and the past; the ability to relate to others; and curiosity.[11] The en-

9. There is some debate on the parallel between killing and allowing to die in euthanasia. See, for example, James Rachels, *The End of Life* (New York: Oxford University Press, 1987).

10. Mary Ann Warren, "On the Moral and Legal Status of Abortion," in *Morality in Practice,* ed. James A. Sterba (Hartford: Wadsworth, 1986), 144–45. Quoted by W. F. Cooney, "The Fallacy of All Person-Denying Arguments for Abortion," *Journal of Applied Philosophy* 8, 2 (1991): 163.

11. Joseph Fletcher, "Indicators of Humanhood: A Tentative Profile," *Hastings Center Report* 2 (1972). Cited by Scott B. Rae, "Views of Human Nature at the Edges of Life," in *Christian Perspectives on Being Human: An Integrative Approach,* ed. J. P. Moreland and David Ciocchi (Grand Rapids: Baker, 1993), 239.

tire project of defining personhood in functional terms fails, since a thing is what it is, not what it does. Moreover, the absence of expressed functional capacities does not mean that the individual's ultimate capacities to express those abilities are absent. Instead, if the unborn, defective or otherwise, are for some reason incapable of human skills such as reasoning, communication, willing, desiring, self-reflection, and aspiring, it does not follow that they are not persons.[12] These capacities still exist within the individual human entity as ultimate capacities constituting its essence. Therefore, even if these criteria were among the legitimate indicators of personhood, every human substance, born and unborn, would qualify as a person, since a human being is a substance with all the ultimate capacities for fully expressed personhood.

Simply because someone does not possess the capacity to exercise all the functions that persons normally do, it does not follow that he or she does not possess personhood. An entity losing its function does not mean that the entity itself no longer exists, only that it cannot function or perform all of its functions. If through neurological damage I lose the ability to use my leg, that is one thing. It is quite another to insist that it is the same thing as losing my leg altogether. Even if I never had the use of my leg from birth and will never again have the use of it for the rest of my life, that is not the same thing as having it amputated. Just because some newborns and fetuses, for example, cannot exercise many of the functions of personhood, and through deformity will never be able to exercise them, it does not follow that they do not possess the essence of personhood. Function is grounded in essence, and if function is absent, it is no necessary commentary on the essence of the unborn.

Personhood actually has three important aspects to it: the inherent, the functional, and the social.[13] Inherent personhood re-

---

12. Much of this argument boils down to epistemological, not metaphysical, issues. Our ability to reliably ascertain the functional abilities of the unborn is hardly exhaustive. The budding field of prenatal psychology, experimental as it may be, points to the fact that much of the cognitive/self-awareness capabilities of the unborn remain unexplored.

13. Richard Sparks, *To Treat or Not to Treat: Bioethics and the Handicapped Newborn* (New York: Paulist, 1988), 256–57.

fers to the possession of personhood that comes from membership in the human community by virtue of being a human substance. Functional personhood refers to the ability to perform the functions that characterize a person. Social personhood refers to recognizing one's rights based on an individual's social utility. The functional and social aspects of personhood are grounded in the inherent. The basic definition of personhood is the inherent one, as distinct from one's functions or utility. From the perspective of Scripture, and with centuries of theological precedent, each member of the human species is a creature of incredible intrinsic worth. The faulty logic of attributing personhood based on function is that "to do" or "to function" is made synonymous with "to be." Yet as Roman Catholic ethicist Richard Sparks puts it, "One's value is not wholly or even primarily ability-related. One's basic significance does not depend on the amount of functional abilities one has been endowed with nor on how well one exercises those talents."[14]

The inadequacies of functional definitions of personhood are clearly evident if we try to practice them consistently. Consider the person under general anesthesia. He is clearly not conscious, has no expressed capacity for reason, is incapable of self-motivated activity, cannot possibly communicate, has no concept of himself, and cannot remember the past or aspire for the future. According to the functional criteria, he is not a full person—but this is absurd. In response, it may be argued that the person is only temporarily dysfunctional. But this ad hoc claim is not available without appealing to something outside of functional criteria. Appealing to unexpressed, higher-order capacities as evidence of personhood suggests an essential human nature; that is, defending the personhood of the anesthetized human seems to require pointing to higher-order or even ultimate capacities that are embedded in his human nature. To argue that the person before anesthesia remains a person while under anesthesia, we must point to what that person is, irrespective of his first-order functional capacities. To insist that he remains a person because he had once expressed first-order capacities of consciousness begs

14. Ibid., 260.

the question, since this merely reasserts the functional premise as a defense against this objection.

Finally, if essential personhood is determined by function, it follows that essential personhood is a degreed property. After all, some will realize more of their capacities to reason, feel pain, or self-reflect than others. Moreover, it is undeniable that the first several years of normal life outside the womb include an increasing expression of human capacities. Likewise, the last several years of life may include a decreasing expression of human capacities. Thus, if the functionalist view is correct, the possession of personhood could be expressed by a bell curve, in which a human being moves toward full personhood in the first years of life, reaches full personhood at a given point, and then gradually loses personhood until the end of life. Presumably, the commensurate rights of persons would increase, stabilize, and decrease in the process. Without appealing to something other than function, it is difficult to resist this troubling conclusion. Indeed, intellectual honesty has driven many to embrace this end, and the slope is ever so slippery. Philosophers Helga Kuhse and Peter Singer comment on the ontological status of newborns:

> When we kill a newborn, there is no person whose life has begun. When I think of myself as the person I am now, I realize that I did not come into existence until sometime after my birth. . . . It is the beginning of the life of the person, rather than of the physical organism, that is crucial so far as the right to life is concerned.[15]

While I applaud their intellectual consistency in applying their notion of personhood evenly in ethical issues, their chilling consistency reveals the danger of defining human personhood in functional terms. Not only are the unborn and newborns less

15. Kuhse and Singer, *Should the Baby Live* (New York: Oxford University Press, 1985), 133. It is quickly apparent that Kuhse and Singer equivocate on the question of personal identity. After all, if *I* do not exist until sometime after *my* birth, in what sense is the birth *mine*? The only way for "*my* birth" to be more than a linguistic convention is to admit that "I" existed before I was born, or at least at the time of my birth. But if this is the case, Kuhse's and Singer's attempt to define personhood in terms of function fails.

than persons, apparently all of us are subject to graded person-hood and the correspondingly graded human rights.

To be a person is to possess an essential human nature. The unborn are individual human substances, possessing an essentially human nature; therefore, they are persons. Functional definitions of personhood are arbitrary, metaphysically inadequate, and ethically problematic. Philosophical insight prompts us to remember that a thing is what it is, not what it does. Essence precedes function—to possess an essential human nature is to be a person, regardless of whether one's functional capacities are expressed or not.

Biblical Material on the Personhood of the Unborn

Although the Bible never specifically states that the fetus or embryo is a person, it is misleading to suggest that the Bible has nothing to say on the subject. The general tenor of Scripture is resoundingly pro-life, and though some texts on the surface appear to support a pro-choice position, such support is not borne out by further examination of the texts in context. The Bible does clearly prohibit the taking of innocent life in the fifth commandment, "thou shalt not kill" (Exod. 20:13). The biblical case is made by its equation of the unborn child in the womb with a child or adult out of the womb. It is not sufficient to show that God is deeply involved in fashioning the unborn in the womb and thus cares deeply about the unborn. Given his role as creator of all the universe, the same thing could be said of the animals. God is involved in the creation of animals and cares deeply for them as well. But from that alone, it does not follow that animals have the same rights as persons, since God also gave man dominion over the animal kingdom.[16] To support biblically the person-hood of the fetus, one must show that God attributes the same

16. Such dominion involves the freedom to use creation for mankind's benefit, but man was also given responsibility for creation as God's steward. This responsibility prevents mankind from exploiting the environment under the guise of dominion over it. See Genesis 1:28–29.

characteristics of a person out of the womb to the unborn in the womb. That is, the Bible must use person language in referring to the unborn. The passages cited below are not an exhaustive list of texts that could refer to the unborn, but they represent the clearest passages that attribute the aspects of personhood to the unborn.

In the account of the first birth, when Eve gave birth to her son Cain, this person language is used to describe Cain. In Genesis 4:1, the text states that "Adam lay with his wife Eve and she conceived and give birth to Cain. She said, 'With the help of the LORD I have brought forth a man.'" Here Cain's life is viewed as a continuity, and his history extends back to his conception. Eve speaks of Cain with no sense of discontinuity between his conception, birth, and postnatal life. The person who was conceived was considered the same person who was born. Had Eve not given birth to Cain, she still would likely have said that she conceived Cain, the person.

This continuity between conception and birth is clearer in Job 3:3, "May the day of my birth perish, and the night it was said, 'A boy is conceived.'" This passage is an example of Old Testament poetry called a synonymous parallelism, in which the second line of poetry restates the first one, saying the same thing in different language. The use of this type of parallelism enables one to say that the child who was born and the child who was conceived are considered the same person. In fact, the terms *born* and *conceived* are used interchangeably in the passage, suggesting that a person is in view at both conception and birth. What was there at birth was considered equivalent to what was there at conception. This is strengthened by the use of the term *boy* in the second half of the verse, which speaks of conception. It was not a thing or a piece of tissue that was conceived, but a "boy," a person. This term for "boy" (Hebrew *geber*) is also used in other parts of the Old Testament to refer to a man and a husband. Thus a person, in the same sense that an adult man of marriageable age is a person, was conceived on the night of Job's conception.

Other passages describe God knowing the unborn in the same way he knows a child or an adult. For example, in Jeremiah 1:5, God states, "Before I formed you in the womb, I knew you; before you were born, I set you apart; I appointed you to be a prophet to the nations." Here it seems clear that God had intimate knowledge of and a relationship with Jeremiah in the same way he did when Jeremiah was an adult and engaged in his prophetic ministry. He was called to be a prophet when in the womb. A similar text occurs in Isaiah 49:1, "Before I was born the LORD called me [literally, from the womb the LORD called me]; from my birth he has made mention of my name." Here the person in question was both called and named prior to birth, indicative of a personal interest that parallels the interest God takes in adults. It may be that in Isaiah 49:1, this refers to preexistence before even the womb, since the person in view is the Suffering Servant, Jesus Christ. A further indication that the unborn are objects of God's knowledge occurs in Psalm 139:13–16, in which it is clear that God is intimately involved in forming the unborn child and cultivating an intimate knowledge of that child. One may object to the use of these texts by suggesting that all of these refer only to God's foreknowledge of a person prior to birth. However, in most of these passages, such as Genesis 4:1 and Job 3:3, it is clear that the person who eventually grows into an adult is the person who is in view in the womb.

A second objection that can be raised is that texts such as Psalm 139:13–16 speak only of a person being formed in the womb, not that the person in the womb is indeed a person. However, one must make a distinction between a person who is developing in the womb and a thing that is somehow developing into a person in the womb. Those are not the same things, and these texts seem to indicate that in the womb from conception there is a person with potential for development, not a potential person who is a being that will develop into a person at some point in the gestational process.

Two other passages attribute characteristics of personhood to the unborn. Psalm 51:5 states that "surely I was sinful at birth; sinful from the time my mother conceived me." David here is confessing not only his specific sins of adultery with Bathsheba and arranged murder of her husband, Uriah the Hittite (see 2 Sam. 11–12), but also his innate inclination to sin. This is a characteristic shared by all persons, and David's claim is that he possessed it from the point of conception. Thus, an essential attribute of adult persons, an inclination to sin, is attributed to the unborn. In addition, David is using a synonymous parallelism, and he appears to treat birth and conception as practically interchangeable. Finally, in the New Testament, the term *baby* is applied to a child still in the womb (Luke 1:41–44). The same term (*brephos*) is used to describe the newborn Jesus in Luke 2:16.

The general tenor of Scripture appears to support the idea that the unborn are considered persons by God, described with many of the same characteristics that apply to children and adults. However, a handful of passages seem to indicate that the unborn is less than a full person, and the Bible does not consider the unborn to be the equivalent of an adult in terms of its essential personhood. The primary text that calls this into question is in Exodus 21:22–25, a specific law designed to arbitrate a specific case. The passage states, "If men who are fighting hit a pregnant woman and she has a miscarriage, but there is no serious injury, the offender must be fined whatever the woman's husband demands and the court allows. But if there is serious injury [i.e., to the woman], you are to take life for life, eye for eye, tooth for tooth, hand for hand, burn for burn, wound for wound, bruise for bruise." Pro-choice advocates contend that since the penalty for causing the death of the fetus is only a fine but the penalty for causing the death of the mother is death, the fetus must not be deserving of the same level of protection as an adult. It must have a different status, something less than full personhood that merits life-for-life penalty if taken.

However, there is significant debate over the term translated "has a miscarriage." At best there is no scholarly consensus on the interpretation. The most likely translation is "she gives birth prematurely," implying that the birth is successful, creating serious discomfort to the pregnant woman, but not killing her or her child. The normal Hebrew word for "miscarriage" is the term *shakal,* which is not used here. Rather the term *yasa'* is used. It is normally used in connection with the live birth of one's child. The fact that the normal term for miscarriage is not used here and a term that has connotations to live birth is used suggests that the passage means a woman who gives birth prematurely.[17] This would make more sense of the different penalties accruing to the guilty party. And it may be that the following phrase in verse 23, "if there is serious injury," would apply to either the woman or to the child, so that if the woman did have a miscarriage, that mishap would be punishable under the "life for life" scheme. Even if the correct translation was "she had a miscarriage," it would not necessarily follow that the unborn has less of a claim to personhood, since penalty and personhood are not necessarily related.[18]

Conclusion

Both philosophical reason and the testimony of Scripture suggest that the unborn fetus is a person from the point of conception with all the attendant rights to life. In utilizing the various reproductive technologies, one should be aware that fetuses and embryos are not items that can be discarded if they are no longer wanted or necessary. Couples who plan on using technologies that involve fertilizing and storing embryos in the lab should plan accordingly to insure that human life, even if in embryonic form, not be taken lightly. Further, if prenatal testing is used, couples should be aware that fetuses, even if genetically defective, are nonetheless persons whose right to life deserves protection. Couples should enter into the various reproductive technologies with the awareness that they are creating persons in whatever process they use, for whom they are responsible.

17. For more on this text, see Umberto Cassuto, *Exodus* (Jerusalem: Magnes, 1967), 275, and Gleason L. Archer, *Encyclopedia of Bible Difficulties* (Grand Rapids: Zondervan, 1982), 246–49.
18. Bruce K. Waltke, "Reflections from the Old Testament on Abortion," *Journal of the Evangelical Theological Society* 19 (1976): 3.

5

Artificial Insemination and Egg Donation

Introduction

When we met John and Mary in the introduction to the book, they were struggling with their infertility and asking questions about which assisted reproduction techniques might be an option for them. After appropriate testing was performed to determine where the problem might lie, they were told that their reproductive systems seemed to function well. Their physician could not pinpoint any specific reason why they had not become pregnant. So they ventured off into the brave new world of reproductive medicine to try to conceive the child that they desperately wanted.

In this chapter, you will be introduced to some of the most widely used, least expensive, and least technically complex techniques to assist a couple in having a child. Artificial insemination, either by husband (AIH) or by donor (AID), is usually one of the first techniques employed by a couple seeking medical reproductive assistance. It is used to alleviate male infertility, and because it is relatively risk-free and inexpensive, it is often the first reproductive technology that a couple will try. The female equivalent, egg donation, is much more complicated and expensive. It is often difficult to recruit egg donors because of the difficulty of the procedure. For women who have blockages in the fallopian tubes that prevent the egg from being fertilized, some of the techniques described in the next chapter are more frequently used. But if the woman cannot produce eggs, egg donation is one way that the couple can have a child with at least a genetic connection to the husband. Even though artificial insemination is a relatively simple procedure, it raises complex moral issues that will be addressed in this chapter.

In chapters 1 and 2, which laid out the biblical and theological material related to procreation, it was concluded that the ideal choice for reproduction is a heterosexual married couple. This appears to be the pattern that God set up at creation. Natural-law conclusions that would restrict most reproductive interventions were rejected as inconsistent with the notion of general revelation. Technology that improves the lot of the human race and helps alleviate an effect of the fall of mankind into sin is generally acceptable within specific biblical parameters.[1] Most reproductive technology fits this morally allowable category. It was also concluded that though Scripture is skeptical about reproductive technologies that involve a third-party genetic or gestational contributor, the Bible does not clearly and unequivocally prohibit them. Thus the Christian can cautiously use most reproductive technologies within biblical guidelines, and the Christian couple contemplating techniques that require a third-party contributor should be careful and thoughtful before employing such a technique. Many instances of artificial insemination and all egg donations require this kind of third-party contributor. In fact, artificial insemination and egg donation are the technologies that initially raised the issue of the morality of third-party contributors. For many couples, the major moral impediment to using artificial insemination by donor is that it involves use of donor genetic material. Since that issue was addressed in chapter 2, we will not revisit those arguments. The intent in this chapter is to address other moral and pragmatic concerns raised by use of artificial insemination and egg donation that should be considered by any couple, Christian or otherwise. Though the Scripture is cautious

---

1. See the discussion of GIFT, ZIFT, and IVF for examples of technologies that are generally allowed but with restrictions.

about third-party contributors, there are other causes for concern that cannot be ignored.

Legal and Medical Background

Artificial insemination has been used with animals for some time. The technique was first used with human beings in the mid-nineteenth century. The first AID was performed in the 1890s. Due to widespread religious and social opposition, AID was not widely used until the 1960s. Today, the Congressional Office of Technology Assessment estimates that roughly sixty-five thousand babies are born each year from artificial insemination, approximately half coming from non-husband donor sperm. More than ten thousand physicians provide the service to some 170,000 women annually. Most obstetricians routinely provide the procedure in their offices and infertility clinics offer it as well. Individuals who desire to donate sperm are normally paid fifty dollars per donation, and many donate sperm regularly for some time. Students constitute the group that most frequently donates sperm. It is unusual for women or a couple to spend in excess of one thousand dollars for all fees associated with an insemination.[2]

Egg donation occurs less frequently because of the difficulty in harvesting eggs from a donor woman.[3] But that is not to say that there is no demand or market for donated eggs. With more women waiting longer to start families, it should not be surprising that the need for donor eggs would be increasing. In some cases, the women who are in need of donated eggs are past childbearing age; that is, they are postmenopausal, and a donated egg is the only way for them to have a child. To help meet this need there are roughly sixty-five clinics that offer egg-donation services in the United States today, and in 1990, they reported that they

2. These statistics on sperm donation are taken from U.S. Congress, Office of Technology Assessment, *Artificial Insemination: Practice in the United States Summary of a 1987 Survey-Background Paper*, OTA-BP-BA-48 (Washington, D.C.: U.S. Government Printing Office, 1988).
3. See the discussion of this procedure in chapter 6.

were involved in more than five hundred egg donations.[4] Egg donation is sometimes done in conjunction with IVF egg retrieval. The woman undergoing egg harvesting for IVF can designate some of the eggs to be donated, normally to a specific person. This kind of donation is less common because women undergoing IVF are motivated to harvest and fertilize as many eggs as possible, in order to keep the costs down and the success rate up. Many clinics that offer egg-donation services require that the woman who needs the eggs provide her own donor. There is some anonymous egg donation, but its frequency is not anywhere near the incidence of anonymous sperm donation.

Many donor clinics are willing to help provide the couple with a match for certain traits such as eye and hair color, ethnicity, height and weight, and IQ. One well-known clinic, the Repository for Germinal Choice, in Escondido, California, houses the sperm of "extraordinary" people such as intellectuals and athletes.[5] Some clinics offer couples a higher probability of the gender of their preference, by a technique known as sperm separation.[6] With the Human Genome Project discovering genetic links to a growing number of diseases and predispositions, it should not be surprising to hear of clinics offering such screening in the future. With respect to genetic screening for certain catastrophic diseases, clinics would be responsible if they provided it and couples would be wise to request it.

The law protects the children born from AID and egg donation. The Uniform Parentage Act states that "the donor of sperm for use in artificial insemination of a married woman other than the donor's wife is treated in law as if he were not the natural father of a child conceived thereby."[7] The reason for this presumption, that the legal father of the child is the husband of the woman who gives birth to the child, is twofold: to protect the child from the stigma

4. See Gina Kolata, "Young Women Offer to Sell Their Eggs to Infertile Couples," *New York Times*, November 19, 1991, and Robin Herman, "Egg Donation Centers More Accessible Today," *Washington Post*, July 14, 1992, cited in Andrew Kimbrell, *The Human Body Shop* (New York: HarperCollins, 1993), 83.

5. Kimbrell, *Human Body Shop*, 76–77.

6. Ibid., 77.

7. Uniform Parentage Act, sect. 5 (b).

of illegitimacy and to insure that the child is provided for financially. When a person donates sperm, he usually signs a waiver of parental rights to any child conceived from his sperm. Thus, even if the donor should discover who used his sperm, he would be prohibited from successfully claiming paternal rights to the child. Most states do not greatly regulate artificial insemination and egg donation except to provide for parental rights for the child.

Egg donation has recently come under scrutiny because of allegations of irregularities at the clinic at the University of California, Irvine.[8] Physicians there were accused of taking eggs from some patients and donating them to other patients who were having difficulty in harvesting their own. The charges assert that the physicians neither obtained consent from the donors nor informed the recipients of the egg swapping. This practice will create legal problems as genetic parents pursue court action to claim paretnal rights to children born from their eggs but being reared by other couples who consider the children to be theirs.

Artificial Insemination by Husband

There is general agreement that artificial insemination by husband (AIH) is morally allowed under most circumstances. The exceptions to this are the adherents of Roman Catholic natural law, who hold that any technology that replaces normal sex is not in keeping with the natural reproductive process that God instituted at creation. The official Catholic opposition to AIH is based on the fact that masturbation is needed to collect the sperm from the husband. In this view, that act constitutes replacement of sex, not just assistance. However, some Catholic thinkers suggest that AIH can be used in conjunction with normal sex so that it only assists and does not replace it. They advise a sheath-style condom that seals after the initial expulsion of semen during sex, thereby collecting the sperm. The sperm would then be treated, and the wife would be inseminated with it. This way of collecting sperm

8. Tracy Weber and Julie Marquis, "In Quest for Miracles, Did Fertility Clinic Go Too Far?" *Los Angeles Times,* 4 June 1995, A1, 32.

is not the normal manner in which infertility clinics do AIH, but many are becoming more sensitive to clientele with religiously-based requests for specific variations from normal practice.

A second objection to AIH also comes from parties that object to reproductive technologies in general. Groups and individuals that are concerned with global overpopulation often oppose all solutions to infertility except adoption. They see the procreation of more children as inherently problematic, contributing to what they see as a global environmental threat. Though some Christians suggest that the creation mandate to "be fruitful and multiply" has been amply fulfilled, this is no reason, by itself, to limit a couple to adoption as the only solution to their infertility. There is a good deal of debate over the threat that overpopulation poses, and it may be that having children who become productive people will be a net gain for society. Though adoption advocacy groups do not usually invoke the language of environmentalism to oppose reproductive technologies, groups like RESOLVE have come out publicly against some reproductive arrangements such as surrogate motherhood.[9] It is not hard to understand why these groups oppose the use of many of these technologies, since they reduce the pool of available parents looking to adopt. For the Christian who accepts reproductive technology in general, there is no reason to hesitate to use AIH. It is true that the process does depersonalize procreation to some degree, but for most couples, that is an acceptable price to pay for the technological assistance that helps them conceive a child.

One new way in which AIH is being used is in conjunction with the same drugs that are used in IVF to enable a woman to ovulate more than one egg during a particular cycle. She is given the drug Pergonal to stimulate multiple ovulation, and at the right time during the cycle she is inseminated with her husband's sperm. This increases the chances of achieving a pregnancy, since in most cases, more eggs are released into the fallopian tubes. The risk of this is similar to the risk in IVF, that there might be more than one pregnancy that would result. A couple who intends to

9. RESOLVE is not just an adoption advocacy group, but a more general support and information network for infertile couples.

employ this combination of reproductive assistance should be aware of the risk and should be willing to accept the consequence of becoming pregnant with more children than intended.[10]

Moral Questions about AID and Egg Donation

Moral and pragmatic questions about AID and egg donation must be considered by any couple contemplating use of these procedures. Couples who use AID and egg donation should enter these procedures with an awareness of the potential problems and moral issues involved. It is widely assumed in medical circles that artificial insemination is relatively risk-free, and in most cases there are no complications. Egg donation is more complex, since it involves some minor surgical procedure that carries some risk to the woman. But couples should not be misled by the lack of medical risk in artificial insemination. There are still pragmatic concerns and moral questions that should be considered prior to going forward with AID or egg donation.

Is It Adultery?

One of the most common preliminary questions about AID specifically is whether it constitutes adultery. In the normal practice of AID, the consent of the husband is necessary prior to his wife's insemination. Thus, even though the sperm of a person other than her husband is placed into her uterus, the husband's prior consent makes AID entirely unlike adultery, in which the husband is usually unaware or disapproving of his wife's affair. AID is normally a joint decision. This is an important aspect, since what makes adultery a particularly egregious sin is that it involves such a deep betrayal of trust and a violation of the covenant of marriage.

However, consent of the husband alone does not exempt AID from the charge of adultery. Suppose two couples consent to have

10. In some cases, there might be medical reasons for reducing the number of pregnancies a woman is carrying, but those cases are rare. For further discussion of selective termination, see chapter 6.

an open marriage in which they share sex with each other's spouse. Even though there is technically no betrayal of trust, that still constitutes adultery because the parties engaged in sexual relations with someone outside of the marriage partnership. In this case consent is irrelevant in determining whether or not the people in this open marriage have committed adultery. Though consent is an important part of the normal practice of AID, by itself it is not sufficient to have AID absolved from the charge of adultery. Adultery is defined as a married person having sex with someone other than his or her spouse. AID does not involve sexual intercourse between the donor and the infertile woman. In fact, it would be difficult to imagine a setting that could be so devoid of passion and romance as that clinical setting in which a woman is artificially inseminated. Virtually nothing about the process of AID resembles sexual intercourse except for the artificial introduction of sperm into the woman's uterus. Adultery breaks the one-flesh relationship between husband and wife by introducing another sexual relationship outside of marriage. That, along with the betrayal of trust, is what makes intercourse with someone beside one's spouse adultery. Neither a one-flesh relationship nor a betrayal of trust occurs during normal AID. Thus it is hard to see how consensual AID could be a violation of the seventh commandment that prohibits adultery (Exod. 20:14).

Should Single Women Use AID?

AID makes it possible for single heterosexual women and lesbians to bear children. Many Christian women who strongly desire to have children and would undoubtedly make wonderful mothers cannot fulfill that dream because they have not met a husband. So they turn to AID or adoption as alternatives to have a family. The law is beginning to look more favorably on single women adopting children, and at present the law does not prevent any single woman from pursuing artificial insemination. However, some clinics will not perform the procedure on a woman unless she is married. Others require evidence to show that the child will be cared for adequately by the woman, and it is helpful if she can show that the child will have interaction with a male. Even though the law allows single women to undergo AID, is it moral for them to do so?

For the same reasons Scripture looks skeptically on third-party genetic contributors for a married couple, a single woman should be careful before employing AID to help her start a family. The ideal of children being born into heterosexual marriages is intentional. Both male and female interaction is necessary for healthy child development. This is not to say that single-parent families that result from divorce or the death of a spouse are any less genuine families or that single parents cannot do great jobs as parents. But there is a significant difference between single parenthood that comes about by unintended tragedy and that which comes about by intentional planning. Single parenthood that results from divorce or death is a situation in which everyone attempts to make the best of a difficult situation. It is parallel to the rescue operation that characterizes the adoption of a child who is a result of an unplanned pregnancy. The clear pattern in Scripture is that children are to be procreated into a stable family setting composed of a heterosexual couple. Because single parenthood is acceptable in the emergency scenarios of divorce and death does not mean that it is acceptable when those emergency conditions do not exist. These factors would seem to prohibit lesbians and single heterosexual women from the use of AID to fulfill their dreams of starting a family.

One may object by pointing out that this model of procreation is not black and white, and that even Scripture itself allowed some exceptions to this general rule, thereby perhaps opening the door for third-party contributors. But even in the cases of surrogacy in the Old Testament, the infertile couple was a stable heterosexual couple who took full responsibility for raising and supporting the child. Though the means used to procreate the child deviated from God's original model, the setting into which the child was born did not. So even if Scripture is not clear about the means of procreation, it does seem clear about the setting into which a child is to be born, consistent with what we know to be the best interests of the child.

Other pragmatic considerations that seem to mitigate against single women bearing children by AID are the rigors of raising a child alone. Single parents undoubtedly have one of the most demanding responsibilities of any group in society, and a single woman should think long and hard before voluntarily undertaking such an exhausting responsibility. In addition, evidence is accumulating that shows the need for children to have present, involved fathers in their lives. A growing body of evidence indicates a connection between school dropout rates, delinquency, and crime, and the lack of a father in the home.[11] Given that roughly one-third of children born in the United States currently will be born into single-parent families without a father, society should think carefully before condoning the intentional creation of fatherless families.[12] For example, ethicist Daniel Callahan of the Hastings Center correctly questions the wisdom of intentionally creating families without a father present through use of AID for single women.[13] Though most single mothers can make arrangements to have male influences for their children, they are only periodic at best and are not equivalent to having a two-parent family in which the father is active in the child's life. Clearly, an involved father is best for a child. To be sure, there are situations in which that it not possible due to the father's abandoning his responsibilities. But very few single mothers who are single parents as a result of divorce or death would intentionally plan to undergo the rigors of single parenthood if there were other options. Single women considering this alternative should think about the sacrifices involved and what the child will be missing without a father in the home.

Should Postmenopausal Women Use Donor Eggs?

Some of the most recent controversy about AID and egg donation involves its application to women who have passed the age of natural childbearing. Their bodies can still deliver a child, but once menopause has set in, they lose their egg-producing capac-

11. See David Blankenhorn, *Fatherless America* (New York: Basic, 1994).

12. John Leo, "No-Dad Families," *U.S. News and World Report,* May 15, 1995, 26.

13. Daniel Callahan, "Bioethics and Fatherhood," *Utah Law Review* 3 (1992): 735–46.

ity. Even if they could still produce eggs, once a woman gets close to menopause, her eggs have aged and she runs a greater risk of genetic abnormalities for her child. On the surface, she would seem to be an ideal candidate for egg donation. She has the experience of many years of life to give to a child, and it would seem arbitrary and perhaps even discriminatory to deny procreative liberty to someone because of age.

The most celebrated case of what has been called "granny pregnancies" occurred in 1994 in Italy when, through the use of egg donation, a sixty-two-year-old Italian woman, Rosanna Della Corte, gave birth to a child. Her infertility specialist, Dr. Severino Antinori, had previously enabled a fifty-nine-year-old British woman to have a child. Della Corte wanted the child when her only child, a seventeen-year-old son, was killed in 1991 in a motorcycle accident. She received the eggs of an anonymous donor that were fertilized with her husband's sperm (he's in his sixties also) and she delivered a child by Cesarean section. At age sixty-three she reportedly wants another child. Della Corte presented more of a risk because of her age, but it is well documented that women in their fifties can routinely deliver healthy children successfully. As a result of some of these successes and the ethical concerns they raise, the Italian national medical association issued guidelines that prohibit the use of reproductive technologies by single women, lesbians, and postmenopausal women.[14] Similarly in Britain, no postmenopausal women may have access to assisted reproductive technology. In France, Parliament restricted use of reproductive technologies to infertile, heterosexual couples of child-bearing age.[15]

Though it seems unlikely that many postmenopausal women would want to bear children, those who do present some ethical challenges. Should society place a limit on the age at which a woman can have a child, given the long tradition of procreative liberty in the West and the lack of any age restriction on men? Is it fair to the children being born out of these arrangements to

14. William D. Montalbano, "Physicians Ban Controversial Biogenetics," *Los Angeles Times*, 15 April 1995, A2.
15. Ibid.

have parents who may not live long enough to see their children through childhood and adolescence? Though it may not be enforceable or even wise to prohibit this practice by law, certainly it might be appropriate to use all means available to discourage the practice, since older parents have a greater risk of dying and making orphans of their children. In addition, postmenopausal women will be unable to nurse their children (not a fatal shortcoming), and they will likely have less energy to adequately care for them. It may be that God in his wisdom instituted menopause in order to prevent people from having children past the age when they are generally able to care for and nurture them. To be sure, there are grandparents today who are parenting a second generation of children for a variety of reasons, predominantly due to tragedy that separated the children from their parents. They are providing an essential rescue function. But that is very different from planning a pregnancy that may put the child at risk of being orphaned. At the least, clinics should be responsible and restrict their services to women of child-bearing age. Women should not pursue bearing a child postmenopausally because of the risks to the child. Using assisted reproductive technology to defy nature and overcome menopause is quite different from using it to overcome infertility in couples of childbearing age.

AID and the Impact on the Family

When AID is used with infertile couples of childbearing age, there is often a concern that use of the technology will produce tension and stress in the marriage. The husband is infertile and a substitute is being sought for him. In many cases, there is a feeling of failure and dispensability that is similar to the feelings an infertile woman might have if a surrogate is used. Often anger is directed at the infertile partner, causing further tension in the home. Though these are concerns, they can be addressed through counseling and do not appear to be, by themselves, sufficient to deter a couple from using AID. At the same time, they are not concerns that should be taken lightly.

A second concern is the impact on the child. What does AID do to the child's sense of individual identity? When, if at all, should the parents tell the child of his or her origins? If the parents choose not to tell, does this constitute an unjustifiable form of deception about the child's heritage? These are important questions, particularly since they involve the most important person in the matrix, the child produced by these arrangements. The technology is still so recent that sufficient time has not elapsed to be able to determine the effects of this type of technology on the child. Longitudinal studies are being conducted on children born of surrogacy arrangements, for example, but it is still too early to tell if there are any negative effects on the children. Of course, there are two different approaches to this lack of information. The first is to move ahead until the risks are proven, giving primacy to procreative liberty until harm is established. The second is to move more cautiously, waiting until harm is proven not to occur.

At present, the impact on the child is still an open question. It will likely take at least another decade until enough information is available to draw firm conclusions in this area. It may be that the impact on the children will parallel that of adoption, in which the results are mixed. Some children thrive in adoptive homes while others struggle. But it will be difficult to make any conclusions about the impact on the children until enough data has been amassed.

If and when to tell the child about his or her genetic origins is a more difficult question. It may be appropriate to tell the child when he or she is at an age to be able to handle the information, such as the late teens or early twenties. There does not appear to be any obligation to tell the child of his or her genetic origins during the formative years when it might be harmful or confusing. It would not be deceiving the child to not disclose that information out of a concern for the child's identity and well-being.

The Unknowns Involved in AID

In the early 1980s, a Southern California woman was artificially inseminated with the semen of three anonymous donors mixed together to insure anonymity of the father of the child she hoped would come from the procedure. She did not become pregnant after the insemination and gave up trying to have a child for a time. Roughly twelve years later, the clinic where she was inseminated called her to inform her that one of her donors had recently died of AIDS and that she should be tested immediately. Tragically, she tested HIV-positive, having contracted the virus from this donor. She has since sued the clinic for negligence, and the outcome is still pending as of mid–1995.

Sophisticated screening techniques being used with AID make this scenario unlikely, but the case illustrates the unknowns involved in AID. Though potential donors are screened for diseases and genetic defects, and though prospective parents can choose donors with certain traits they desire, there are still many things about a donor that a couple cannot know, some of which are protected by the donor's right to privacy. Caution should be exercised in the use of AID or egg donation.

Conclusion

Though Scripture does not place a blanket prohibition on the use of donor sperm and eggs, it is skeptical about their use. Couples contemplating AID and egg donation should be careful about employing these techniques given the biblical model for procreation and some of the unknowns about the donor(s) and the impact on the child. Single women should be even more cautious, since raising a child alone is extremely demanding and because Scripture suggests that children be born into a family with an involved father and mother, which is also in the child's best interest. Of all the alternatives for procreation, use of donor gametes should be considered only after all other options such as adoption and other techniques that use the genetic material of the husband and wife have been explored.

6

GIFT, ZIFT, and IVF

Introduction: The Case of James and Jane

James and Jane have been married for the past ten years, the last six of which they have spent trying to conceive a child. After years of frustration at trying to conceive a child naturally, they tried artificial insemination by husband (AIH) a number of times, each attempt ending up in failure. They were uneasy about using donor sperm and decided to try some other options to have a baby by combining her egg and his sperm. On the recommendation of their obstetrician, they contacted the Center for Assisted Reproduction in their area.[1]

After an initial phone conversation, James and Jane made an appointment to meet with one of the nurses in the center. She explained the available options, the procedures involved, the advantages of each, and the costs involved. They were confronted with quite an array of technical terms, and even getting the abbreviations straight at first was a bit intimidating. They recounted briefly their story of infertility, how they had tried unsuccessfully both naturally and artificially, and said they were ready to consider entering the world of technologically assisted reproduction, even though they knew it would turn their lives upside down for

---

1. Centers like this hypothetical one are also called fertility clinics or centers, reproductive centers, or centers for reproductive medicine.

the next few months and take them on an emotional and financial roller-coaster ride.

The nurse explained that the center provided various reproductive services. Usually, the more complicated the procedure and the higher the rate of success, the more expensive it was likely to be. She explained that they were probably candidates for one of the three services in which the center specialized: IVF (in vitro fertilization), GIFT (gamete intrafallopian transfer), or ZIFT (zygote intrafallopian transfer). The nurse indicated that they were all fairly similar procedures, though with some important differences that had to do with the individual couple's specific situation, the rate of success, and the cost involved. She told them that the procedures are medically complicated and that sometimes they involve surgery and ultrasound technology. When James asked about the center's success rate, she brought out a small stack of papers that the center had submitted to the American Fertility Society for publication.[2] She helped interpret the data for them and told them that the center had roughly a 25 percent success rate with these three technologies. While the science of reproductive medicine is still relatively new, their success rates were slightly above the national average.

James and Jane then asked specifically what was involved in each of the three techniques they were considering. The nurse spelled out the process involved with each technology and gave them an estimate of the costs involved. "At the center, the process that we usually suggest first is called GIFT, which stands for gamete intrafallopian transfer. This procedure is appropriate if the husband's sperm is acceptable, that is, if there is enough of it and if it is capable of penetrating the egg. The technical term for this set of circumstances is that there is no 'male factor.' If there is no

2. The American Fertility Society and the Society for Assisted Reproduction compile detailed statistical records on their member clinics annually and publish them in *Fertility and Sterility*, the official journal of the American Fertility Society. Roughly two-thirds of the infertility clinics in the United States are members of the society and submit data to the society for program audits annually. This oversight responsibility is important because of the criticism leveled at the assisted-reproduction industry that it makes false promises and engages in misleading advertising.

male factor and if Jane's fallopian tubes are not damaged, this is the best procedure for you. It is the most successful and most natural of the three procedures you are considering, because fertilization actually takes place where it was designed to occur, in Jane's fallopian tubes. Often, couples who are having trouble having a child and don't have a significant medical reason for their infertility will try GIFT. The first part of the procedure is called egg retrieval. Some clinics call it egg harvesting; others call it oocyte retrieval. By the way, all three of the procedures we're talking about start with egg retrieval. The goal is for Jane to produce as many eggs as possible in one cycle. To do this she would be given a strong medication, either one called Pergonal or an alternative called Metrodin. These are essentially hormones that stimulate her system to produce eggs. Either you [Jane] or your husband must inject it into your system every morning. Sometimes these medications produce side effects, such as occasional headaches, fatigue, and mood swings that are not unusual considering the amount of hormones she will be taking. The amount of medication she will need depends on her system. Some women need more stimulation to produce as many eggs as we want; others need less. Sometimes women need another more expensive drug called Lupron to help the process along even more.

"The next phase of the process must be done in the center. We retrieve the eggs that you have produced during this current cycle. It used to be that egg retrieval required a minor surgical procedure called laproscopy, but that's not necessary any more. Instead the physician, guided by an ultrasound picture of your womb, retrieves the eggs with a needle through the vaginal wall. This can be done with local anesthesia, but sometimes that is not necessary. It sounds painful and complicated, but is not that difficult or painful. Now this is where James comes in. We need a sperm sample from you. I know this can be awkward, but here's how it works. We give you a sterile cup, put you in the men's room, and you give us a sperm sample through masturbation. Now we have all the raw material we need to conceive a baby.

"James's sperm is treated in our lab to make it best prepared to fertilize one of Jane's eggs. The sperm and some of the eggs are put together in a catheter in our lab but kept separate by a divider so that they won't fertilize in the catheter. Then it gets a bit complicated again. The eggs and sperm are then returned to Jane's fallopian tubes, but this time it does take that minor surgical procedure I mentioned earlier called laproscopy. This takes anesthesia, and James will drive you home from the center after it's done. Then we wait for your sperm to hopefully fertilize one of her eggs, and if all goes according to plan, you'll be pregnant. You may end up being pregnant with more than one baby. In fact, if you see a woman with twins or especially triplets, you can bet that she conceived them through GIFT or one of the other procedures you're considering. By the way, all of GIFT is done on the same day.

"There are a couple of other services we offer in addition to GIFT. Since retrieving the eggs is the hardest and most expensive part of the process, it would be a shame to throw the eggs that we don't use away. We suggest that you take the leftover eggs and let us fertilize them in the lab and store them for you if you need them later. Getting pregnant by GIFT is not a sure thing, and if it doesn't happen this time, you will have some embryos in storage that we can implant in Jane if this round of GIFT doesn't produce a pregnancy. The other service we offer is in case you get more than one baby in your pregnancy. If you only want one baby, or could maybe handle two, but you are pregnant with three, we will refer you to physicians in our community who offer what we call selective termination. They have a good track record of reducing the number of pregnancies you are carrying without risking the health of the remaining babies. You may not be interested in that, but some couples are, and I wanted to tell you about it.[3]

"IVF (in vitro fertilization) is different from GIFT in one important way. With IVF, fertilization takes place in the lab instead of inside the body. We use IVF when there is a male factor, that is, when James's sperm count is low or it has what we call low motility. That means that the sperm have difficulty getting to the egg to fertilize it. To put it bluntly, they're not great swimmers! We do all the same things to retrieve Jane's eggs and collect James's sperm, but we put them together in the lab and hope that they will

---

3. Some clinics do not offer selective termination to their clients, but most are willing to refer to a physician who does offer it.

fertilize there. We watch them carefully, and usually within twenty-four hours we'll know how many have fertilized. After forty-eight hours, we put anywhere from one to five fertilized eggs, also called embryos, back into Jane's uterus. We do this by ultrasound, not laproscopy, so surgery is not necessary. We recommend implanting four embryos for the best chance of getting one pregnancy and putting the rest in storage if this first round doesn't produce a pregnancy. Then you save a lot of time, money, and wear and tear on Jane's body if you want to try the process again. All we do is thaw four more embryos and try again to implant them into Jane's uterus. IVF is not as common today, unless there is a male factor and your fallopian tubes are not in good shape for some reason. As with GIFT, you may get multiple pregnancies, and selective termination is an option if you want to consider it.

"If you are not a good candidate for GIFT, we recommend that you think about trying ZIFT. That stands for zygote intrafallopian transfer. We use this procedure when there is a male factor and when Jane's fallopian tubes are in relatively good condition. We retrieve the eggs in the same way, fertilize them in the lab as with IVF, but we transfer the embryos to Jane's fallopian tubes, usually within twenty-four to forty-eight hours of fertilization. We do this because the success rate is higher if the embryos are placed in the tubes. Reinserting the embryos does require minor surgery. The reason for this is that getting the embryos in the tubes requires laproscopy. This means that you will have to stay in the hospital twice, once during egg retrieval and a second time during embryo reinsertion. As with GIFT and IVF, you can store the remaining embryos for later use. That keeps the cost down and reduces the wear and tear on Jane's body that egg retrieval involves.

"Now I'm sure you're interested in the costs of all these procedures. The costs vary depending on how much medication Jane needs to produce the eggs in her cycle. Storing embryos for later use requires an additional expense. Usually the procedures that involve laproscopy are more expensive too. As a general rule, GIFT will cost about twelve thousand dollars. IVF is a bit less expensive since no surgery is required. It costs about ten thousand dollars. ZIFT is the most expensive because it involves fertilizing eggs in the lab and surgery to reinsert the embryos. This procedure costs about fourteen thousand dollars. I don't know what your insurance covers, but I do know that more insurance companies are covering at least part of the cost.[4] We require two deposits, one up front and a second one just prior to your egg retrieval procedure. Any balance left over must be settled at the end of the process."

Moral Evaluation of GIFT, IVF, and ZIFT

In most cases, use of these technologies does not involve a third-party contributor, since the couple involved desires to have a child from their own genetic materials. Thus there would be no concern about violating the creation model for procreation (chap. 1). However, if the woman cannot produce eggs but can carry the child successfully to term, she would be a candidate to receive an egg donation from an outside donor. Egg donation is not an easy process, since the donor must go through the same process as did Jane. A donor woman would take the same medications that Jane took and have the eggs retrieved in the clinic. They would then be fertilized with the husband's sperm. Next the embryos would be implanted in his wife's uterus or fallopian tubes, depending on which procedure had the best chance of success. Most women who consent to be egg donors are close friends or family members of the couple because the process is so involved. In the majority of cases, egg donors are women who are already involved in GIFT, ZIFT, or IVF for themselves. Most infertility clinics offer these procedures if the couple wants to utilize an egg donor. However, the less medically complicated way to do this would be to hire a surrogate mother simply to be artificially inseminated with the husband's sperm and then carry the child to term. That method avoids the costly and arduous process of multiple egg production and retrieval, but it also creates the pros-

4. In some states, such as California, state law requires insurance companies to offer coverage for assisted reproduction. It may be that in those states the premium is so high that it discourages people from buying the coverage, or it may only cover a relatively small percentage of the costs. However, many insurance companies do offer such coverage at a reasonable cost. It is not clear yet whether any health-care reform plan will include coverage for assisted reproduction.

pect of some complex legal problems should the surrogate mother desire to keep the child.[5] If the husband cannot produce sperm, then the couple would bypass all of the techniques described in this chapter and turn to artificial insemination by donor (AID) if they had no moral or theological objection to a third-party contributor.

A second alternative for women who cannot produce eggs is called surrogate embryo transfer (SET). This is considered in the same family of procedures as GIFT, ZIFT, and IVF because of its complexity. It involves transferring an embryo rather than harvesting eggs. Initially it was designed to enable a woman to donate eggs to an infertile couple without enduring the rigors of the hormone therapy and egg retrieval. Most women would not choose to donate eggs since the procedure is so inconvenient for the donor. With embryo transfer, a donor woman would, in effect, donate the egg while it is still inside her body. She would be artificially inseminated with the sperm of the husband of the infertile couple. This might need to be repeated a number of times until she conceives. When that occurs, then the physician flushes the embryo out of her uterus and transfers it to the infertile woman, who will carry the child to term. Though it is certainly less medically complicated to allow the donor woman to give birth to the child as well, it is potentially more complicated legally, since the egg donor has now become a surrogate mother.

Though this procedure makes egg donation much simpler, the outcome has not been good enough to justify most infertility clinics continuing to offer it. Since the process of transferring the embryo is so difficult, the success rate was quite low compared to GIFT, ZIFT, and IVF. The risk to the embryo, that it might be inadvertently destroyed or deformed in the process of transfer, is so great that most clinics do not even present the option to infertile couples as an alternative. Most egg donations today come from women who are having eggs harvested for themselves. Sometimes couples who are having GIFT, ZIFT, or IVF donate their leftover embryos after they have become pregnant. This is

---

5. The complexities involved with surrogate motherhood will be taken up in chapter 7.

often less than optimal for the couple seeking a donation of eggs. They would rather have the egg donated than the embryo because the husband of the recipient couple could use his sperm to fertilize the donor egg, giving the couple at least a partial genetic connection to their child. For many couples, that is very important and justifies the lengths to which they must go to secure such a link. Many couples see no significant difference between receiving a donation of embryos and adoption, since there is no genetic connection with either option. The difference is for the woman in the recipient couple who may want to experience childbirth and the connection to the child that giving birth brings.

For the person who believes that personhood begins at conception, GIFT, ZIFT, and IVF have two potential moral difficulties. It is certainly better for the couple who chooses to use either of these procedures to enter into them aware of the possible problem areas. Many couples do not become aware of the potential problems until after they are deeply involved in the process, and at times, after they are pregnant and thinking that the process is over. This leaves them with some agonizing decisions to make.

The first moral problem is what to do with leftover embryos that are being kept by the clinic in storage. This difficulty is created by the cost of the procedures and their relatively low success rate. Since egg retrieval is so expensive and so inconvenient, the woman attempts to produce as many eggs as possible for the physician to harvest. They are all fertilized at the same time, and only four embryos are actually implanted in the woman's body. The rest are frozen and kept in storage should they be needed if the woman does not become pregnant with the first attempt at implanting embryos. The exception to this is with GIFT, where in most cases four eggs are reinserted with the husband's sperm into the woman's fallopian tubes and fertilization occurs in the body. The rest of the embryos are fertilized in the lab and stored for future use. Should pregnancy not occur in the body, then the couple would revert to trying ZIFT or IVF with the remaining embryos, since this is much less complicated than trying GIFT again.

When the couple has difficulty becoming pregnant through any of these procedures, having the embryos in storage is helpful. The woman avoids repeating the process of egg retrieval, and the couple avoids the substantial additional expense, since egg re-trieval is the most costly part of the process.[6] Most clinics assume that the couple will want to avoid starting over if the first attempt at achieving pregnancy fails. But trying to make the process less medically and financially complicated has made it more ethically complicated for the couple who holds that personhood begins at conception. Of course, for the couple who believes that the un-born acquires personhood at some point after conception, this is not a problem. But for the Christian couple who is trying to be consistent with Scripture in their entire approach to these repro-ductive technologies, what to do with leftover embryos presents a significant problem.

The reason this is a problem is that embryos are persons, de-serving of full human rights. They are not potential persons, a concept that itself is problematic. Either one is a person or one is not a person. To speak of a potential person is philosophically ab-surd, because personhood is not a degreed property.[7] What one normally means by their imprecise use of that term is that the em-bryo (and fetus also) is a person with the potential to become a fully grown adult. It is better to say that the embryo is a "person with potential."

In GIFT, ZIFT, and IVF, leftover embryos are usually dis-carded.[8] In some cases, they are used for experimentation,[9] and if the couple consents, they may be donated to other infertile cou-ples. Donations like this would be seen as the practical equivalent of adoption. The couple would simply put embryos, not newborn babies, up for "adoption." Of course, embryo donation is not

6. Egg retrieval accounts for roughly half to two-thirds of the total cost of GIFT, ZIFT, or IVF.

7. See the discussion of the personhood of the fetus/embryo in chapter four for more details on this concept.

8. In some cases, the couple decides to allow them to die a natural death. They allow them to be in storage past the point at which they could be success-fully thawed and implanted.

9. The debate on embryo experimentation is just beginning in the United States. In late 1994, Congress decided whether to authorize federal funding for embryo research. It has been discouraged since the Reagan and Bush adminis-trations. Embryo research is occurring in parts of Europe at present. See chapter 9 for further discussion of embryo research and experimentation.

anywhere near as complicated as formal adoption, and the infertile couple gets the experience of carrying and delivering a child.

The normal practice of discarding embryos is problematic for couples who hold that personhood begins at conception. Throwing away embryos that a couple does not plan to use is no different morally from abortion at any point during the pregnancy. Only the location of the unborn child and its stage of development are different. Since the embryo has all the capacities to develop into a fully grown adult from the point of conception, needing only the proper environment in which to develop, then the point at which it is destroyed and discarded is irrelevant. A person with a unique genetic endowment and with full potential to become a fully grown adult has been destroyed. Some have further lamented the fact that human embryos are being treated as the equivalent of "industrial waste," a byproduct of the procedure that is thrown out when no longer needed.[10] Experimenting on embryos does not seem to be morally different, since the experiment will usually result in the destruction or deformation of the embryo, and since the embryos that do survive the experiments are usually discarded after they are no longer useful for research.

Not only are there some complicated moral problems raised by leftover embryos, but also there are some legal problems that would have tested the wisdom of Solomon. Two extraordinary cases that attracted worldwide attention illustrate the myriad of legal problems that are possible when couples have embryos left in storage.

In 1981, embryos left in storage were orphaned. Mario and Elsa Rios were a wealthy California couple who had no heirs to their sizeable estate. They traveled to Australia to have IVF performed. In the early days of these procedures, some of the pioneering work was done in England and Australia, which is why they sought out Australian specialists. Mrs. Rios had several eggs of her own fertilized with donor sperm in the lab. A number of embryos were implanted and two were frozen and kept in storage for later use if necessary. The first round of embryos failed to implant. The Rioses returned to California, presumably to return

10. Roger Rosenblatt, *Time*, February 14, 1983, 90.

again and have the remaining two embryos implanted. However, before they could get back to Australia, they were both killed in a plane crash in South America.

Their deaths left the Australian infertility clinic that had the embryos in storage with some difficult problems. The law in Australia had not yet addressed situations like these, so there were no legal guidelines available to the clinic. What were they to do with the Rioses' embryos? No doubt there was a long line of potential surrogate mothers waiting to be implanted with those embryos in order to stake a claim to part or all of the Rioses' estate. A nationally appointed committee looked into the matter and recommended that the embryos be destroyed, thereby solving the problem by eliminating it. The Australian government agreed. But the state of Victoria, in which the clinic was located, saw it differently and mandated that the embryos be implanted in a surrogate mother, then placed for adoption. That created legal nightmares about the distribution of the Rioses' estate. Should the surrogates be entitled to any share of the estate for carrying the embryos? Should the adoptive parents be entitled to child support or a sizeable share of the estate to pay for the children's additional expenses? Or should the estate be divided equally among the children born of these surrogates? It is not hard to imagine these surrogates, once pregnant, being in a strong position to demand whatever they wanted out of the Rioses' estate.

At this point the attorney for the Rioses' estate insisted that the embryos could not be heirs under American law because donor sperm, not Mr. Rios's, was used to fertilize the eggs. But donor sperm is used with the presumption that the man married to the woman who gives birth to the child is the legal father. That is, sperm donors are not presumed to have paternal rights to the child born from their sperm. The clinic attempted to implant the embryos in a surrogate, but when that failed, there was no longer a problem that needed resolution.[11]

11. For more detail on this case see George P. Smith, "Australia's Frozen 'Orphan' Embryos: A Medical, Legal and Ethical Dilemma," *Journal of Family Law* 24, 1 (1985–86): 26–41. See also Donald DeMarco, *Biotechnology and the Assault on Parenthood* (San Francisco: Ignatius, 1991), 104–5.

A second remarkable case involved frozen embryos as the subject of a custody dispute. Unlike the Rios case, this one required court intervention to resolve the dispute. Junior and Mary Sue Davis were a Tennessee couple who underwent IVF six different times, and had seven embryos left in storage at the end of all their attempts. They divorced, leaving the status of the leftover embryos in legal limbo. Mary Sue Davis wanted the embryos implanted in her in order to have a child. Junior Davis wanted them to be left in storage. The first problem that the courts faced was deciding whether the embryos were property, to be divided equally, or children, to be awarded based on what would be in their best interests. The court had to determine whether this was a property or a custody dispute. The trial court decided that they were children and awarded them to Mary Sue Davis. Since she wanted them implanted, born, and reared, the court ruled that that course of action constituted their best interests. In 1990, the appeals court reversed that decision, awarding both parties an equal voice in the embryos' future.[12] This decision was based on the principle of privacy, that no one should be forced to become a parent against one's will, as Junior Davis would have been had the lower court's decision been allowed to stand. In other words, the right to procreate also includes a right not to procreate, according to one's choice. In 1992, the Tennessee Supreme Court essentially upheld the decision of the court of appeals. However, by the time of the Supreme Court decision, Mary Sue Davis had remarried and wished to donate the embryos rather than have them implanted in her. Since there are thousands of embryos in storage around the country, it is likely that other disputes like this one will arise in the future.[13]

What is a couple to do with leftover embryos that they have preserved in storage? The most obvious alternative to discarding the embryos would be for the couple to insist that the clinic freeze

12. *Davis v Davis*, 1990 Tenn App LEXIS 642 (13 September 1990).
13. For further reading on the Davis case, see George J. Annas, "Crazy-Making: Embryos and Gestational Mothers," *Hastings Center Report* 21 (January–February 1991): 35–38, and Alexander Morgan Capron, "Parenthood and Frozen Embryos: More Than Property and Privacy," *Hastings Center Report* 22 (September–October 1992): 32–33.

and store the woman's eggs prior to fertilization in the lab. That way eggs, not embryos, are being stored. The couple has eggs left over to use again in the future, avoiding the entire process of egg retrieval, while at the same time not destroying and discarding embryonic persons. Unfortunately, storing eggs is not a viable alternative medically at this point in the development of these various technologies. When eggs are frozen in order to be stored, there is a serious problem when the clinic attempts to thaw them for fertilization in the lab. They tend to disintegrate upon thawing and though occasionally an egg is thawed successfully, the success rate is so low that virtually no infertility clinic offers it as an alternative to infertile couples. Researchers are moving ahead in this area, however, and some estimate that it will not be long before it will be possible to freeze, store, and thaw a woman's eggs just as effectively as can be done with embryos. If and when that day arrives and the practice becomes widespread, than there will no longer be a problem of leftover embryos, since only the number of embryos to be implanted will be fertilized. Infertile couples will have eggs, not embryos, left in storage for future use should they experience difficulty achieving a pregnancy. However, medical science will undoubtedly still want to experiment on live embryos, so the issue will not entirely disappear. Couples who use these techniques should be prepared for the normal practice of fertilizing all the suitable eggs that are harvested, keeping them in storage for future use, and discarding the ones that will not be used.

A second alternative that some couples have contemplated regarding leftover embryos is to not intentionally discard the embryos but to allow them to die a natural death in the lab. They reason that it is parallel to a miscarriage, only it happens in the lab and not in the body. During a miscarriage, the fetus dies a natural death and is extracted surgically and discarded, or it is expelled naturally from the body if miscarriage occurs at a very early stage of the pregnancy. Many miscarriages occur prior to implantation, when the embryo fails to attach to the women's uterine wall. Roughly half of all conceptions miscarry in this way, and thus many embryonic persons who are successfully conceived die a natural death at a very early phase of pregnancy. Thus, those who suggest this alternative insist that they are allowing something to happen in the lab that happens frequently in the body. They argue that the location in which it occurs, either the body or the lab, should not make a morally significant difference. Thus they would say that allowing embryos to die a natural death is more akin to a miscarriage than to an intentional abortion.

However, there is another morally significant difference between a miscarriage and allowing embryos in storage to die natural deaths. Most miscarriages cannot be prevented. In most cases, no one fully understands why they occur. Many early miscarriages, those that happen prior to implantation, along with other later-term miscarriages, are a mystery to physicians. In many cases, there is not much they can do to prevent future miscarriages. Of course, some miscarriages can be traced to deformities in the fetus or problems in the woman's reproductive system. But a great many miscarriages are random, spontaneous occurrences. However, in the lab, the destruction of embryos in storage is easily prevented. Simply thaw and implant them, either in the woman of the original couple whose genes contributed to the embryo, or in another woman who is seeking an embryo donor. In medicine in general, it is certainly justifiable to allow someone to die a natural death when it cannot be prevented, that is, when further treatment is futile. But to allow someone to die from an easily preventable disease or condition is morally problematic, and people who allow others to die natural deaths in this way are doing the moral equivalent of killing them.

For example, though there may be some technical distinctions,[14] when Christian Science parents refuse treatment for a child suffering from meningitis, easily treated with antibiotics, society is morally outraged, and properly so. Many would say that the parents are, for all practical purposes, killing the child. In the

14. Of course, the legal system would view these differently. More direct killing would surely receive a harsher sentence. Allowing someone to die might carry a manslaughter charge. It is true that most states do not have good Samaritan laws that require people to render aid to someone who is in trouble (physicians are excepted from this and are required to give aid). But most would agree that allowing someone to die when you could have easily prevented his or her death is morally reprehensible.

same way, allowing embryos in storage to die a natural death is the moral equivalent of killing them, since their natural death is easily preventable. There does not seem to be any moral significant difference between discarding embryos when they are no longer needed and allowing them to be discarded when they can no longer be thawed successfully.[15]

A third alternative view that some couples adopt is that personhood begins at implantation, not conception.[16] This has strong appeal because the average person has a difficult time seeing how embryos in a petri dish in the lab can be the moral equivalent of a baby growing in a mother's womb. The embryos in the lab seem so clinical and detached compared to an embryo in a mother in whom they are developing. In addition, they cannot, at least at present, grow or develop outside the womb. Thus the uterine environment is indispensable for the embryo to develop fully. For the abortion debate, this is not a major shift, and it would not likely make any significant difference in the moral acceptability of abortion, since most induced abortions occur after implantation.[17]

The problem with this shift in one's view of when personhood begins is that there is no *essential* difference between the embryo in the lab and one that has been implanted in a woman's womb. The only difference is one of location, and location is unrelated to the essence of what the embryo is. The fact that its capacities cannot yet develop in certain locations is irrelevant to the fact that it still has all the capacities necessary to develop into an adult from the moment of conception onward. By analogy, almost everyone agrees that there is no essential difference between an unborn child one day before birth and a baby one day after birth. The only difference is one of location and dependence, the latter meaning that the baby is dependent upon its mother in a different way than when it was in utero. Location by itself does not make

15. The latest consensus on how long embryos can remain in storage is roughly five years.

16. For further reading on this view, see Francis J. Beckwith, *Politically Correct Death* (Grand Rapids: Baker, 1994). Dr. Beckwith does not hold this view.

17. As Beckwith notes in his discussion, this is the view of a strong pro-life advocate such as Dr. Bernard Nathanson.

a morally significant difference when it comes to the essential nature of the unborn child. Moreover, this view will likely become obsolete when artificial wombs are developed. Already some animals are being brought to term in artificial wombs, a process called ectogenesis. Though its prospect for use with human beings is still in the future, if and when that occurs, advocates of the view that personhood is acquired at implantation will have to admit that developing fetuses are not yet persons. Of course, they might respond that they are in an environment that suits their developmental needs and whether that is a woman's womb is beside the point. But it does suggest that there is nothing mysterious about the location of the female womb that by itself endows the unborn with personhood.

A fourth alternative is to give the embryos away to another infertile couple. Donating the embryos is certainly a possibility that is morally different from discarding them, but most couples are uncomfortable with the idea of donating their embryos to another couple whom they have never met and will never meet or see again. Embryo donation is done anonymously, in many cases, to prevent the donors from attempting to locate the child and intruding on his or her stable family life. The notion of another couple, not to mention one they do not know, rearing a child who is the combination of their genetic materials is very unsettling. As one person who was contemplating embryo donation put it, "I don't want my progeny running around all over the country without my knowledge!" This uncomfortable feeling is often more intense when the couple realizes that they have not one but a number of embryos in storage, all of which would need to be donated to a variety of couples to keep from having to destroy them. Even though donation does not involve discarding the leftover embryos, and is more ethically acceptable, it is a difficult choice to make emotionally for many couples.

The most prudent course for a couple to follow in this circumstance is to avoid having leftover embryos. This can and does happen by chance, that is, if the couple actually uses all the embryos that are produced in the lab through their sperm and eggs. But it can also happen through wise planning. The couple can inform the clinic of their views concerning when personhood begins and state that under no circumstances do they want any leftover embryos. The couple can insist that the clinic is to harvest a sufficient number of eggs for only one round of embryo implants. That is, the number of eggs to be harvested depends on the number of embryos that the couple wants implanted at any one time. This would usually mean that anywhere from four to six eggs would be retrieved. Four embryos are usually implanted, and often some of the eggs do not fertilize in the lab, so it may be prudent to allow for some attrition in the process. But to be perfectly safe, the couple should insist that all the eggs that are harvested be fertilized and implanted. This will mean that fewer eggs will be retrieved and fertilized, and should all the implanted embryos fail to develop, or the eggs retrieved fail to be fertilized, then the couple would be faced with another cycle of egg retrieval and fertilization in the lab. This will likely increase the cost significantly should the couple elect to continue trying to become pregnant with one of these procedures.

Nevertheless, many couples will not be comfortable with these restraints that could drive up the costs of achieving pregnancy, and in an effort to keep the costs down, will harvest and fertilize as many eggs as they can retrieve, and will keep embryos in storage. But for the couple who holds that personhood begins at conception, that is morally problematic. Since the physicians cannot predict how many eggs they will successfully retrieve or how many will fertilize, it may not be technologically feasible to operate within these limits. If it is inevitable that a couple will have leftover embryos, and if they are unwilling to donate those that remain, then this raises serious questions about the moral acceptability of these techniques. The couple should be prepared to work within limits that do not produce leftovers, or be prepared to donate those that remain after they achieve pregnancy.

The difficulties in having leftover embryos are magnified when the couple does not realize the problem until after the embryos are already in storage. They become pregnant, often with more than one child, and they decide that they do not want any more children and thus have no use for the embryos in storage. Then, and only then, do they begin to consider what to do with the leftover embryos and realize that they have a problem. They are left with some uncomfortable alternatives. They can discard them or let them die natural deaths, both choices ethically troubling because there does not seem to be much significant difference between the two. Or they can donate them, an option that is emotionally distressing and theologically somewhat problematic due to Scripture's skepticism of third-party reproductive arrangements. However, donation of embryos can be seen as parallel to adoption, a rescue operation that is the exception to the general rule of parents keeping their children. Scripture clearly allows adoption and does not view it as a violation of the creation model for procreation, but rather as a justifiable exception to it. It may mean that embryo donation can be viewed as a similar emergency rescue operation. The only difference is the time at which the rescue takes place, prior to implantation instead of at birth.

A second and more troubling ethical issue in these techniques results not from the failure of the embryo implants but from their successes. Multiple pregnancies are not uncommon with these technologies. In many cases, couples are so eager to have a child that becoming pregnant is such good news that it matters little how many pregnancies result. But some couples are clearly distressed with multiple pregnancies, because they did not want as many children as the woman is carrying. In rare cases, more embryos will implant than the woman can carry to term without compromising the fetuses' health, or the fetuses' lives.

When either of these situations occurs, clinics will suggest a reduction in the number of pregnancies the woman is carrying. This procedure is also called selective termination. The clinic normally does not perform the reduction but will refer the couple to a practitioner in the area who can decrease the number of pregnancies without risk to the remaining ones. To accomplish this, physicians use a needle that is inserted into the woman's abdominal wall and guided by ultrasound to the embryos in the woman's uterus to be eliminated. A saline solution of potassium chloride is injected into the fetus(es) to be destroyed, and if they have developed to the point at which the heart can be detected by ultrasound, then the injection is made directly into the heart. The injection kills the developing embryo and in the course of time, it dissolves and is absorbed into the mother's body. It is the essential equivalent of saline abortions that are often used for later-term abortions.

For the couple who holds that personhood begins at conception, these reductions are very problematic. There is no morally significant difference between these reductions and abortions of unwanted pregnancies. In fact, these reductions are ethically more troubling than ordinary abortions. With abortion for family-planning reasons, a pregnancy that was not intended is terminated. Though it is true that by virtue of having sex, the couple knew that pregnancy was a possible outcome, it was nevertheless unplanned and accidental. This is particularly so if reasonable birth-control measures were taken and they failed. But with a reduction, the embryos are deliberately implanted in the woman. The couple consented to the implants, knowing from the start that each one might develop in the uterus. There is a degree of intentionality in these techniques that is not a part of abortions of unplanned pregnancies. Embryonic life is deliberately, not accidentally, created in the lab and intentionally implanted in the woman. This makes pregnancy reduction in these cases seem more callous and less respectful of developing personhood than ordinary abortions. To deliberately create human life, implant it in the uterus where it can grow, and then terminate it if the couple does not want that many children is very troubling and disrespectful to the life intentionally created.

Reductions raise complicated questions about the details involved in carrying them out. For example, which embryos are terminated? On what basis is that decision made? And perhaps most importantly, who makes the decision? A close friend recalls going through GIFT and conceiving triplets, after already having one child. This gave the couple four children, clearly more than they had anticipated and originally wanted. Having this many children would significantly stretch their finances. The temptation to undergo a reduction was strong. But they continued the pregnancy, even though it was physically taxing on the woman (she was in a wheelchair for the last three months until delivery, and delivered more than a month early). It was also stressful to have three newborns at the same time, but these parents are glad they made the decision they did. After the triplets were born, one of the man's colleagues at work was in the middle of IVF with his wife. They too had conceived triplets and were seriously contemplating a reduction. The two men talked, and my friend explained that they were offered the same opportunity by their clinic. He admitted that it was difficult to imagine which one of the three children would have been terminated in the reduction or how they would have made that choice. After expressing his view that these were persons growing in his wife's uterus, the colleague later said that they had decided to continue all three pregnancies. These are agonizing decisions even for couples who hold that abortion is justifiable, but they are decisions that can be avoided with proper planning.

In cases in which the woman's life is endangered, it may be justifiable to abort one of the embryos in order to save the mother's life. That is not because the mother's life is any more valuable than that of the unborn children she is carrying, but because if the mother dies, so will all of the children she is carrying. So it is not trading one life for another, but one life for two or perhaps three. If the decision involves a reduction in order to safeguard the mother's ongoing physical health, that is a different question. At the risk of appearing callous toward the woman's health, life takes precedence over physical health, so it would not be justifiable to undertake a reduction unless the mother's life is at stake. This decision can also be avoided.

In some cases a reduction is proposed to safeguard the lives and health of the other fetuses a woman is carrying. For example, if by carrying four fetuses as long as she can, she runs the risk of delivering prematurely, this may seriously compromise the health and even the life of the children who have been delivered early. If such a reduction is medically indicated because the presence of an additional fetus is seriously jeopardizing the others, then it may be appropriate to reduce the number of pregnancies that the woman is carrying. One must be careful not to expand the definition of *medically indicated* to also encompass the emotional and financial health of the family. If there are genuine medical reasons for a reduction, then it is appropriate by extension of the principle that it is justifiable to reduce to save the mother's life. Again, with proper planning at the beginning of the procedure, this kind of difficult decision can be avoided.

The way to avoid the agonizing dilemma created by the prospect of a pregnancy reduction is to limit the number of embryos that are implanted from the start. The couple should insist that the number of embryos being implanted only be as many as they are willing to rear if all of them successfully implant. In addition, they should not implant more embryos than the woman can safely carry to term should all of them successfully implant. This will likely decrease the probability of achieving a pregnancy, but couples who enter into these procedures should be aware of the potential for multiple pregnancies. They are not uncommon, and unless couples are willing to raise twins or triplets, they should be careful about having four embryos implanted just because statistically this number gives a couple the best chance of having one pregnancy.

Micromanipulation and ICSI

One of the most exciting new procedures is an extension of IVF and ZIFT. Instead of putting sperm and eggs together in the lab and hoping that fertilization will occur, three new techniques enable physicians to initiate fertilization more aggressively. These advances give new hope to couples for whom IVF has not worked, particularly for those couples where the man's sperm appears to be incapable of penetrating the egg. These new techniques are all under the general heading of what is called micromanipulation, referring to the microscopic way in which reproductive specialists can maneuver egg and sperm, better enabling the sperm to penetrate the egg and achieve fertilization.

There are three different ways of aggressively initiating artificial fertilization. The more aggressive the attempt to place the sperm in the egg, the more expensive is the procedure and the more risk of damage there is to the egg. The first technique is called partial zona dissection. The physician cuts an opening in the coating around the center of the egg (the zona) and deposits a large number of sperm into the solution surrounding the egg in the lab. In effect, this cuts an opening for sperm to enter the egg. A second way is known as subzonal injection, in which a handful of sperm is injected into the zona, in hopes that one will penetrate the center of the egg and achieve fertilization. These two methods are not ideal because the sperm still needs to penetrate the center of the egg on its own, and in many cases, more than one sperm fertilizes the egg. When that happens, the embryo will be defective and unable to develop. The third and most exciting technique is called intracytoplasmic sperm injection, or single-sperm injection for short. Physicians actually inject a single sperm into the center of the egg. This technique was perfected by researchers in Belgium and is available in only a few centers in the United States. But its popularity is growing, and it is likely that more reproductive centers will offer it in the future. However, it is a difficult process that takes time and skill to master.

Though the techniques look promising, they are expensive and do pose risks. The major ethical question is whether rates of birth defects will actually increase because defective sperm is able to penetrate the egg. Prior to the advent of micromanipulation techniques, natural processes prevented most defective sperm from entering the egg. To date, there are roughly one thousand babies born from this technique, and there is no evidence of an increase in birth defects. But long-term data are not yet available, so it is too early to tell whether the anticipated increase in the incidence of birth defects will come to pass. Since it is not yet possible to look inside the sperm and see if it contains defective genetic material, this will be a risk for couples considering this technique.

A second ethical dilemma will need to be addressed if and when it does become possible to examine the genetic material of a sperm. Then couples will be able to select a sperm based on its genetic content and select for gender and other traits that they consider desirable. This poses significant problems for those concerned with gender equity, since the track record around the world where sex selection through abortion is allowed is not encouraging for the female gender. Many are concerned about enhancement genetic engineering, the science of trying to improve on a process that society still widely views as natural, and in religious circles, the prerogative of God alone. However, this dilemma is potential, not actual, at this point.

Conclusion

GIFT, ZIFT, and IVF can all be used by couples without raising ethical concerns, as long as the procedures are used within certain guidelines informed by the belief that personhood begins at conception. Couples should harvest only the number of eggs that they intend to fertilize and implant, trying as much as possible to leave no leftover embryos in storage. Also they should implant no more embryos than the number of children they are willing to bear and rear,[18] and no more than the woman can safely carry. Though this increases the financial risk to couples in these procedures, it minimizes the moral risk of a callous disregard for unborn personhood.

Although these procedures are generally morally acceptable with the preceding guidelines, couples must recognize that these procedures are very expensive and have a relatively low success rate. The infertility industry is driven by desperate couples willing to go to any lengths to have a child of their own. In fact, the industry has been criticized for being exploitative of infertile couples and being long on hype and hope and short on results.[19] It is not uncommon for couples to assume a great deal of financial risk to undergo these procedures. Couples need to ask themselves hard questions about the lengths they are willing to go to pursue their dream of a child. What does the no-holds-barred pursuit of these technologies say about these couples' courage, persistence, and trust in God's sovereignty? These are questions of virtue and character, and though they must be asked sensitively, they nonetheless need to be asked. Certainly some couples have approached these technologies with a degree of desperation that

18. It might be possible to put one or more of the children born out of these multiple pregnancies up for adoption, but one must question the wisdom of separating siblings in situations like these.

19. For more critical discussion on the infertility industry, see Donald DeMarco, *Biotechnology and the Assault on Parenthood.*

seems inconsistent with the high view of a sovereign, trustworthy God in whom they confess faith. Surely there is little that is unethical with trying new procedures that may help alleviate infertility, but to do so relentlessly, beyond the means to pay for them, raises questions that are perhaps psychological and spiritual, in addition to moral.

7

Surrogate Motherhood

On March 27, 1986, Mary Beth Whitehead gave birth to a little girl whom she named Sara. On that same day, Elizabeth and William Stern named the same baby Melissa. Both were convinced that the child (called Baby M in the press) belonged to them and were prepared to take drastic measures to insure that they took custody. The Sterns had hired Whitehead to bear their child. She was, and is to this day, the most well-publicized person who ever performed the role of a surrogate mother. Their contest over that child was carried on in court for almost two years, and the case illustrates the potential problems and complexities involved with many of the new reproductive technologies.

Surrogate motherhood is the most controversial of the new reproductive technologies. In many cases, the surrogate bears the child for the contracting couple, willingly gives up the child she has borne to the couple, and accepts her role with no difficulty. In those cases, the contracting couple views the surrogate with extreme gratitude for helping their dream of having a child come true. The surrogate also feels a great deal of satisfaction since she has in effect given a gift of life to a previously infertile couple. But in some well-publicized cases, the surrogate wants to keep the child she has borne and fights the natural father for custody. What began as a harmonious relationship between the couple and the surrogate ends with bitter conflicts and many doubts about the wisdom of using this type of reproductive arrangement.

Many supporters of reproductive technologies in general are opposed to surrogacy. Most of the states that have passed laws concerning surrogacy have decided either to prohibit it or to strictly regulate it, and most states have no such restrictions on other reproductive technologies.

A wide variety of surrogacy arrangements are possible today. There is *genetic surrogacy*, in which the surrogate contributes both the egg and the womb, or gestational environment, to the couple who contracts her services.

In some cases, the infertile woman can produce eggs but cannot carry a pregnancy to term. Then a *gestational surrogate* is needed. This is a more complicated and more expensive case, since in vitro fertilization is also required. The infertile woman is hormonally stimulated to produce a number of eggs during one cycle. The eggs are then surgically removed and fertilized with her husband's sperm in the lab. The eggs that fertilize (usually up to four embryos) are implanted in the uterus of the surrogate. Genetic surrogacy is far more common than gestational surrogacy.

When the surrogate is paid a fee for the entire process, that is called *commercial surrogacy*. Most surrogates are paid between ten thousand dollars and fifteen thousand dollars in addition to all medical expenses. Sometimes wages lost due to the pregnancy are reimbursed.

A family member or close friend offers to carry a child for an infertile woman out of kindness. The joy of helping bring a child into the world for a couple who wants to have a child is satisfaction enough for her. This is called *altruistic surrogacy*. The focus of this chapter is on commercial surrogacy, because the vast majority of surrogacy arrangements are done commercially. But there are some problems even with altruistic surrogacy, although that arrangement dodges the main criticism of commercial surrogacy: that it is baby selling.

Surrogacy itself is not new. The Old Testament records two incidents of surrogacy (Gen. 16:1–6; Gen. 30:1–13). It appears that use of a surrogate to circumvent female infertility was an accepted practice in the ancient Near East.[1] Today, surrogacy does

1. Both the Code of Hammurabi (1792–1750 B.C.) and the Nuzi tablets (1520 B.C.) authorize surrogacy, and not only for cases of barrenness. Thus surrogacy was not only widely practiced, but also was the subject of detailed legislation to keep the practice within proper limits.

not normally involve any sophisticated medical technology. Conception normally is accomplished by artificial insemination, though in some cases in vitro fertilization is used to impregnate the surrogate. What makes surrogacy new is the legal context in which reproduction occurs. The presence of lawyers, detailed contracts, and even the idea of legal representation for the unborn child are the new elements in the previously very private area of procreation.

The following three cases illustrate the myriad of complexities that can occur in a surrogate parenting arrangement.

The Baby M Case

In the soap-opera drama of the first well-publicized surrogacy case, the details of which became a television movie, William Stern had a special interest in fathering a child to whom he was genetically related. He was the only living member of his blood line, most of his relatives having been killed during the Holocaust. His wife, Elizabeth, had a mild case of multiple sclerosis and she believed that the health risk of pregnancy was significant.

The Infertility Center of New York matched the Sterns with Mary Beth Whitehead, a woman of moderate means with two children. She agreed to be impregnated and to surrender custody of the child upon birth for a ten-thousand dollar fee and all associated medical expenses. If she miscarried prior to the fifth month, she would receive no fee, but if miscarriage came after the fifth month or if the child was stillborn, she would receive one thousand dollars.

After the child was born, Whitehead sued for custody after regretting her decision to give up the child to the Sterns. The Sterns allowed her to take the child for a week, after which time she fled the area with the child. The child was later recovered by force by the police in Florida and returned to the Sterns.

In a decision handed down in March 1987, the New Jersey Superior Court ruled that the surrogacy contract between the Sterns and Whitehead was valid. Judge Harvey Sorkow ruled that Whitehead was not coerced into signing the contract and therefore it should be enforced. Using the analogy between a sperm donation and a woman "renting her womb," he ruled that a woman had the right to sell her reproductive capacities. Thus Whitehead breached a valid contract when she refused to surrender the child and give up custody.

Even though the contract was upheld, a custody hearing was held since the best interest of the child was the primary concern. Based on the Whiteheads' refusal to obey the court order and their subsequent flight from the state, the judge ruled that custody should be given to the Sterns. They would be able to provide a more stable home for the child, in his view.

Upon appeal to the New Jersey Supreme Court, the decision was reversed, though the final custody outcome remained the same. In February 1988, Judge Robert Wilentz, writing for a unanimous Court, ruled that surrogacy contracts violated the state laws that prohibit the transfer of money for adoptions. Surrogacy was, in effect, baby-selling, and there are some things, namely, human life, that cannot be bought or sold. The Court cited as evidence the way the fee was paid to Whitehead. Significantly less money was to be paid Whitehead if the baby was miscarried or stillborn. Clearly the Sterns were paying for a child and full parental rights, not just for rental of Whitehead's womb.

The Court also cited New Jersey laws that held the fundamental rights of genetic parents to participate in rearing their children. Since Whitehead was not an unfit mother and had not abandoned her child, there was no good reason to deny her her right of association. In addition, the contract violated laws that stipulated a time period for an adoptive mother to change her mind prior to irrevocably giving up her child. Further, the contract violated established New Jersey public policy on custody that gave the natural parents the right to determine who would rear the child. However, precedent dictated that the decision cannot be made prior to the child's birth.

The adoption of the child by Elizabeth Stern (facilitated by Judge Sorkow immediately after his lower court decision) was voided and the Whiteheads were to get visitation rights to be decided by a lower court. They did not receive custody, since the justices held that the child's best interests would be served by custody of the Sterns. Even though Whitehead announced a pregnancy by another man shortly thereafter and separated from her husband, visitation rights were not terminated.

Since both William Stern and Mary Beth Whitehead are considered the legal parents, future complications could ensue. If William Stern dies, even though Elizabeth Stern has been the social mother of the child and has established the stronger bond with her, custody would likely revert to Whitehead. Similarly, should the Sterns divorce, Whitehead would have grounds to mount a custody challenge and would likely win, since the social mother has no legal parental rights. Assuming that Whitehead continued to be a fit mother, there is no compelling reason to deny her custody. In addition, there could be issues of child support in the future. Suppose that as Baby M grows up, she desires to live with Whitehead. Would Stern be liable for child support? Under existing law it would appear that he would. Likewise, should Whitehead become financially able, perhaps through book or film royalties, would she become liable for child support? Again, it would seem that she would.

Johnson v Calvert

In the early 1990s another landmark case was decided. In Orange County, California, Mark and Crispina Calvert hired Anna Johnson to be the surrogate mother for their child. This case was different from Baby M in that the surrogate had no genetic relationship to the child. She literally rented her womb for nine months for ten thousand dollars plus all medical expenses. Toward the beginning of the seventh month, Johnson started having second thoughts about giving up the child she was bearing. A month prior to the child's birth, Johnson sued for custody. When the child was born in mid-September, temporary custody was awarded to the Calverts with daily visitation allowed to Johnson. These visits were later reduced to twice weekly until the final custody hearing.

Orange County Superior Court Judge Richard Parslow ruled that the surrogacy contract was valid and not inherently exploitative. Since Johnson had no genetic stake in the child, she had no parental rights. Thus exclusive custody of the child was given to the Calverts and no visitation was allowed. The judge ruled that the genetic connection took precedence over the fact that Johnson gave birth to the child, and that the best interests of the child would be served by custody of the Calverts in any case. There was testimony that undermined Johnson's fitness as a mother. Her roommate testified to the neglect of her child, and the fact that she was a single mother with minimal financial resources and had difficulty keeping a job contributed to the decision to award custody to the Calverts. In addition, the sincerity of her bond to the child was questioned, since it was never mentioned until the seventh month of the pregnancy, and then in contradiction to numerous earlier statements to the Calverts that she was carrying their child.

In both these cases, an infertile couple hired a surrogate through an intermediary agency to bear a child for them, with what they considered a valid contract governing the procedure. All medical expenses related to the pregnancy were paid by the contracting couple, and the surrogate was to receive a fee of ten thousand dollars for specific performance of the contract. In each case the surrogate changed her mind and sued to retain parental rights to the child she had borne. The judges, in deciding each case, were setting new precedents, since neither had any significant legal precedent upon which they could base their decision. In New Jersey, this was the first surrogacy case to receive broad legal and public attention. But in California, the precedent set in New Jersey was not helpful, since the relation of the surrogate to the child was different. What made this more difficult is that the presumption of the law is that the birth mother is the legal mother, based on the assumption that genetics and gestation go together. However, the result of the two cases was the same, in that the contracting couple was given permanent custody of the child, though the way in which the surrogacy contract was viewed was quite different. The court found in each case that the best interests of the child would be served by living with the contracting couple.

However, there were some significant differences between the two cases, the principal one being the place of genetic relationship between the surrogate and the child. Whitehead was the genetic mother, having supplied the egg, whereas Johnson was the gestational mother, with no genetic link to the child. Thus the view of the surrogacy contract was different. In New Jersey, the judge ruled that the contract was void because it required Whitehead to give up a fundamental right to parent. But in California, the judge ruled that the contract was valid, and since there was no genetic link between the surrogate and the child, there were no parental rights to be considered. That being so, Johnson had no choice but to give the child to the people the judge considered to be the parents. Genetics made all the difference in the custody award in the Calvert case and in voiding the New Jersey contract. Though the view of the contract was quite different, the child ended up with the contracting couple; however, Whitehead was granted liberal visitation rights and Johnson was granted none. In addition, the fitness of the surrogate as a mother was considered differently by the courts. Though Whitehead came in for harsh criticism in the lower court, the New Jersey Supreme Court ruled that she was indeed fit as a mother and that the lower court had been unfairly biased against her. In Orange County, the judge raised significant questions about Johnson's fitness as a mother based on the testimony of her roommate, her status as a single parent, and her employment history.

Moschetta v Moschetta

The most recent well-publicized case, also in Orange County, California, has taken on a strange twist. In this case, a surrogate has sued for custody of a child whom she bore in June 1990. Elvira Jordan gave birth to Marissa, conceived from Robert Moschetta's sperm and Jordan's egg. In November, Robert separated from his wife, Cynthia, and took the child. In filing for legal separation, Cynthia, with whom the child has no genetic link, filed for custody, claiming that bonding had taken place with the child and that her role as social mother should count as significantly as genetics. Jordan also filed a claim to custody, insisting that she did not enter into the surrogate contract to bear a child for a couple who was not going to stay together. So three "parents" all claimed a right to custody. On January 15, 1991, Judge John Woolley awarded temporary custody to the natural father, visitation rights to his estranged wife, and nothing for the natural surrogate mother. In the spring of 1991, the court ruled that Jordan has legitimate parental rights. In September, Judge Nancy Wieben Stock ruled for joint custody, shared between Jordan and the natural father. Jordan would have the child during the work day and Moschetta in the evenings and on weekends.

Arguments in Favor of Surrogate Motherhood

Surrogacy Is Consistent with the Constitutional Tradition of Procreative Liberty

There is a long tradition in the Western world that gives couples the freedom to make their own decisions about childbearing and childrearing. The family has historically been a place in which the right to privacy has reigned, and thus family decisions have for the most part been beyond the scrutiny and the intervention of the government. Laws have been crafted to insure as much freedom as possible for parents to make choices concerning their children.[2]

A number of Supreme Court cases have set this precedent of family privacy in procreative decision-making. For example, in *Meyer v Nebraska*,[3] the Court ruled that one of the protected Constitutional liberties included the freedom for an individual to "marry, establish a home and bring up children."[4] Though at this point the Court could not have anticipated these new reproductive technologies, proponents argue that the freedom to create a

---

2. This freedom assumes, of course, that parents are acting in the best interests of their children and that no harm comes to children in the exercise of freedom on the part of the parents.

3. 262 US 390 (1923). See chapter 3 for further discussion of these cases.

4. Ibid., 399.

family through normal sexual intercourse extends to noncoital means as well.

A second case that opens the door to procreative freedom was *Griswold v Connecticut*,[5] in which the Court decision struck down a Connecticut law that forbade the use of contraceptives. The freedom not to procreate a child was broadened by a later decision, *Eisenstadt v Baird*.[6] In this landmark case, Justice Brennan stated in the majority opinion, "If the right to privacy means anything, it is the right of the individual, married or single, to be free from unwarranted government intrusion in matters so fundamentally affecting a person as the decision whether to bear or beget a child."[7] Though the decision only technically applied to decisions *not* to bear a child, most scholars agree that freedom in decisions to have a child are also protected by the right to privacy.

A final decision broadens this freedom even further. In *Carey v Population Services*,[8] the Court ruled that in the absence of a compelling state interest, the state could not unduly burden someone who wanted to purchase contraceptives. In the most sweeping statement on procreative liberty, the Court affirmed the right to marital privacy in decisions involving bearing a child. The language of the decision goes far beyond the narrow issue of contraception, and in the view of proponents of surrogacy, strongly implies freedom to involve a third party in procreative efforts. The Court stated that "the decision to bear or beget a child is at the very heart of this cluster of Constitutionally protected choices . . . , decisions whether *to accomplish or prevent conception* are among the most private and sensitive . . . , the Constitution protects individual decisions in matters of childbearing from unjustified intrusion by the State."[9]

Thus the right of individuals to make their own decisions about childbearing is well established in American tradition. Whether these decisions apply to surrogacy is not clear, since the

5. 381 US 479 (1965).
6. 405 US 438 (1972).
7. Ibid., 453.
8. 431 US 678 (1977).
9. Ibid., 685, 687.

Court has not specifically ruled on a surrogacy case, and since none of these reproductive technologies were in use at the time of these decisions. But it does appear that the full range of procreative decisions is in view in these Court decisions. The debate is over the degree to which Court decisions that apply to individuals using normal coital means of reproduction extend to individuals using noncoital means.

In response to this argument, the tradition of procreative liberty opens the door only to *altruistic* surrogacy, in which a woman performs the role of surrogate out of a charitable motive, and receives reimbursement only for reasonable expenses incurred during the pregnancy. This is very different from the way in which surrogacy is usually negotiated. Normally, the surrogate is paid at least ten thousand dollars for her services, and another ten thousand to twenty-five thousand dollars is paid to a surrogacy broker for his services in recruiting the surrogate and drawing up the contract that will govern the arrangement. Whether procreative liberty allows for *commercial* surrogacy is another matter, since most states have laws that forbid exchange of money for the transfer of parental rights to a child.[10] Procreative liberty may allow for use of a surrogate, but it does not give the surrogate the right to sell the child produced by the arrangement.

The Fee Paid to the Surrogate Is for Services Rendered, Not the Sale of a Child

Surrogacy proponents are sensitive to the charge that paying a surrogate a large amount of money for bearing a child for another couple is baby-selling. Therefore, proponents argue that the fee pays only for gestational services rendered, and is not the sale of a child. Proponents insist that it is fair for a woman to be compensated for the time, risk, and sacrifice that pregnancy entails. People have a right to be compensated appropriately for services

---

10. This normally applies to adoption. In most states it is against the law to pay birth mothers a fee beyond expenses to give up her child for adoption. The state rightly wants to protect birth mothers from being exploited and children from being objects of barter.

rendered. Just as it is legitimate to pay surrogate *child rearers* in a daycare setting, proponents insist that it should be legitimate to pay surrogate *childbearers.*

This argument fails to take into account that the fee is for much more than childbirth services rendered. The service provided in bearing the child is clearly not the intended end product of the arrangement. What really counts in a surrogacy arrangement is not only the successful birth of the child, but also the transfer of parental rights from the surrogate to the infertile wife. She must adopt the child for the deal to be done. In most surrogacy cases, in which the surrogate supplies both the egg and the womb, she is the legal mother of the child.[11] Should she so desire, she may keep the child and share custody with the natural father. Thus, for any surrogacy arrangement to be completed, she must turn over parental rights to the child. Therefore, the fee also pays for this transfer of parental rights, and that constitutes baby-selling. If the parties in a surrogacy arrangement were actually effecting an adoption, the exchange of money for the transfer of parental rights would be illegal, since this kind of baby-selling is prohibited by most adoption laws.

For example, in the well-known Baby M case (referred to in the beginning of this chapter), only in the event of the surrogate's delivering a healthy baby to the contracting couple and turning over parental rights would she be paid the full ten-thousand dollar fee. If she miscarried prior to the fifth month of pregnancy, she would receive nothing. If she miscarried after the fifth month or gave birth to a stillborn child, she would receive only one thousand dollars. The contract was clearly oriented to the delivery of the end product, not the gestational process. To be consistent, if the fee paid to the surrogate is only for gestational services rendered, the surrogate would be paid the same amount whether or not she turned over the child to the contracting couple. If the fee

11. In cases in which the surrogate does not supply the egg (gestational surrogacy), there is debate over who is actually the mother: the woman who bears the child (the traditional definition), or the genetic contributor. Good arguments can be made for both genetics and gestation being the determinant of motherhood. For further detail on this see Scott B. Rae, *The Ethics of Commercial Surrogate Motherhood* (Westport, Conn.: Praeger, 1994).

pays only for childbirth services, it is hard to see how a couple could take the surrogate to court to get the child, since the surrogate would have fulfilled her part of the contract once the child was born. In addition, if she miscarried at some point in the pregnancy, her fee should be prorated over the number of months that she performed a gestational service. But this would make surrogacy much too risky for the contracting couple, and it is unlikely that they or the brokers could live consistently with a fee-for-gestational-services scheme.

Proponents of surrogacy will respond by saying that the natural father cannot buy back what is already his, and thus surrogacy cannot be baby-selling. But the child is not *all* his. At best, he can only claim the equivalent of joint tenancy in a piece of property, in which he buys out his partner, the surrogate, and thus is still baby-selling.[12]

Surrogacy Is Very Different from Black-Market Adoptions

Some proponents of surrogacy will admit that children are being sold, but that the circumstances are so different from black-market adoptions that there is no harm in exchanging parental rights for money. The laws that prevent payment to birth mothers were designed to prevent black-market adoptions, in which birth mothers were exploited based on their financial need and in which the well-being of the children was not considered the highest priority. Proponents argue that surrogacy is a completely different situation. The natural father is also the adopting father, and surrogacy results from a planned and wanted pregnancy as opposed to an unwanted pregnancy. Thus the child is not going to a stranger but to a genetic relative, and the surrogate is not coerced into making a decision she will later regret.

However, the differences between black-market adoptions and surrogacy are overstated. For example, there is little screening of the contracting couple done in order to insure that they are fit parents and that the best interests of the child are being main-

---

12. This real estate analogy is taken from Alexander M. Capron, "Surrogate Contracts: A Danger Zone," *Los Angeles Times*, April 7, 1987, B5.

tained. In addition, the element of coercion is not entirely absent from a surrogacy arrangement since it is quite possible that the surrogate could end up being coerced by the contract into giving up a child that she wants to keep. Further, given the desperation of the contracting couple to have a child, surrogacy leaves them open to exploitation by the brokers. Thus to say that the environment surrounding surrogacy is free from coercion is not accurate.

Even if the child is treated well and the arrangement involves no coercion, the problem of baby-selling remains. During the Civil War era, there were cases in which slaves were treated well and considered to be family members, but the fact remained that they had been bought and sold and had become objects of barter. The circumstances in which such barter takes place are irrelevant.

Restriction on the Fee Means Restriction on the Practice of Surrogacy

Proponents of commercial surrogacy hold that it is inconsistent to affirm procreative liberty and forbid the fee to the surrogate. If the fee is prohibited, then the number of available surrogates will dramatically decrease and, in all likelihood, curtail the practice. Thus the right to procreate in this way will be an empty right, since the state will have interfered to prevent people from exercising it.

The precedent for this argument is *Carey v Population Services*.[13] In this case the Court struck down a New York law that put burdens on people who wanted to purchase contraceptives, saying that such restrictions infringed on a protected right. This reasoning has been applied to commercial surrogacy by suggesting that a restriction on the fee is tantamount to a restriction on a protected procreative liberty.

However, one should recognize that there is a significant difference between the issue in *Carey* and that in surrogacy. In *Carey*, what is at stake is the sale of *contraceptives*. In surrogacy what is at stake is the sale of *children*. Though one has a fundamental right to procreate, nowhere does one have a right to sell

13. 431 US 678 (1977).

the "product" of procreation. Any restriction on the sale of children is legitimate, and the argument from the *Carey* decision does not apply to surrogacy.

Arguments Against Surrogate Motherhood

Surrogacy Involves the Sale of Children

The most serious objection to commercial surrogacy is that it reduces children to objects of barter by putting a price on them. Most of the arguments in favor of surrogacy are attempts to avoid this problem. Opponents of surrogacy insist that any attempt to deny or minimize the charge of baby-selling fails, and thus surrogacy involves the sale of children. This violates the Thirteenth Amendment that outlawed slavery because it constituted the sale of human beings. It violates commonly and widely held moral principles that safeguard human rights and the dignity of humans, namely, that human beings are made in God's image and are his unique creations. Persons are not fundamentally things that can be purchased and sold for a price. The fact that proponents of surrogacy try so hard to avoid the charge of baby-selling indicates their acceptance of these moral principles. The debate is not whether human beings should be bought and sold. Rather it is over whether commercial surrogacy constitutes such a sale of children. If it does, most would agree that the case against surrogacy is quite strong. As the New Jersey Supreme Court put it in the Baby M case, "There are, in a civilized society, some things that money cannot buy. . . . There are values . . . , that society deems more important than granting to wealth whatever it can buy, be it labor, love or life."[14] The sale of children, which normally results from a surrogacy transaction (the only exception being cases of altruistic surrogacy), is inherently problematic. Irrespective of the other good consequences that the arrangement produces, it is troubling in the same way that slavery is inherently troubling: human beings are not objects for sale.

14. *In re Baby M*, 537 A2d, 1249 (1988).

Surrogacy Involves Potential for Exploitation of the Surrogate

Most people agree on the potential for commercial surrogacy to be exploitative. The combination of desperate infertile couples, low-income surrogates, and surrogacy brokers with varying degrees of moral scruples raises the prospect that the entire commercial enterprise can be exploitative. But statistics on the approximately six hundred surrogacy arrangements to date indicate that this potential for exploitation has not yet materialized. Most surrogates are women of average means (the average income of a surrogate mother is around twenty-five thousand dollars per year),[15] not destitute but also motivated by the money. The fee alone should not be considered exploitation but an inducement to do something that the surrogate would not otherwise do.

However, this does not mean that the potential for exploitation should not be taken seriously. Should surrogacy become more socially acceptable and should states make it legal, it is not difficult to imagine the various ways in which surrogacy brokers would attempt to hold costs down in order to maximize their profit. One of the most attractive ways in which this could be done would be to recruit surrogate mothers from among the poor in this country and particularly from the third world. For example, some experts suggest that those with financial need actually make the best candidates for surrogates since they are the least inclined to keep the child produced by the arrangement.[16] Other people are making plans to actively recruit women from the third world to be brought to the United States to serve as surrogates. The advantage of using these women is that it dramatically reduces the cost of doing surrogacy business. John Stehura, of the

15. The statistics on the annual income of surrogates is a bit misleading since it records the income of women who were selected as surrogates. It does not take into account the women who applied to be surrogates but were not chosen. A 1983 study by psychiatrist Philip Parker found that more than 40 percent of the applicants to provide surrogacy services were receiving some kind of government financial assistance. See "Motivation of Surrogate Mothers: Initial Findings," *American Journal of Psychiatry* 140 (1983): 1.

16. Statement of staff psychologist Howard Adelman of Surrogate Mothering Ltd. in Philadelphia, cited in Gena Corea, *The Mother Machine* (New York: Harper and Row, 1985), 229.

Bionetics Foundation, stated that the surrogates from these countries would receive only the basic necessities and travel expenses for their services. Revealing a strong bias toward exploitation of the surrogates, he stated, "Often they [the potential surrogates] are looking for a survival situation—something to do to pay for the rent and food. They come from underdeveloped countries where food is a serious issue." But he also added that they make good candidates for surrogacy and stated, "they know how to take care of children . . . , it's obviously a perfect match."[17] He further speculates that perhaps one-tenth of the normal fee could be paid these women and that it would not matter if they had other health problems, as long as they had an adequate diet and no problems that would affect the developing child.[18] It is not difficult to see the potential for crass exploitation of poor women in desperate circumstances, a potential that is already being seriously considered by brokers in the industry. It is not clear the degree to which these statements are representative of the entire industry, but with the profit motive being a primary factor it does not take much imagination to see the potential for taking advantage of vulnerable women.

Surrogacy Involves Detachment from the Child in Utero

One of the most serious objections to surrogacy applies to both commercial and altruistic surrogacy. In screening women to select the most ideal surrogates, one looks for the woman's ability to give up the child she is carrying. The less attached the woman is to the child, the easier it is to complete the arrangement. But this is hardly an ideal setting for a pregnancy. Surrogacy sanctions female detachment from the child in the womb, a situation in any other pregnancy that one would never want. This detachment is something that would be strongly discouraged in a traditional pregnancy, but is strongly encouraged in surrogacy. Thus surrogacy actually turns a vice, the ability to detach from the child in utero, into a virtue. Should surrogacy be widely practiced, bio-

17. Cited in ibid., 245.
18. Cited in ibid., 214–15.

ethicist Daniel Callahan of the Hastings Center describes what one of the results would be: "We will be forced to cultivate the services of women with the hardly desirable trait of being willing to gestate and then give up their own children, especially if paid enough to do so . . . . There would still be the need to find women with the capacity to dissociate and distance themselves from their own child. This is not a psychological trait we should want to foster, even in the name of altruism."[19]

Surrogacy Violates the Right of Mothers to Associate with Their Children

Another serious problem with commercial surrogacy might also apply to altruistic surrogacy. In most surrogacy contracts, whether for a fee or not, the surrogate agrees to relinquish any parental rights to the child she is carrying to the couple who contracted her services. In the Baby M case, the police actually had to break into a home to return Baby M to the contracting couple.[20] A surrogacy contract forces a woman to give up the child she has borne to the couple who paid her to do so. Should she have second thoughts and desire to keep the child, under the contract she would be forced to give up her child.

Of course, this assumes the traditional definition of a mother. A mother is defined as the woman who gives birth to the child. Society has never had to carefully define motherhood because medicine had previously not been able to separate the genetic and gestational aspects of motherhood. It is a new phenomenon to have one woman be the genetic contributor and a different woman be the one who carries the child. There is debate over whether genetics or gestation should determine motherhood, but in the great majority of cases of surrogacy, the surrogate provides

19. Daniel Callahan, "Surrogate Motherhood: A Bad Idea," *New York Times*, January 20, 1987, B21.
20. This sounds worse than it may be, since Mary Beth Whitehead had left the area with the child because she wanted so badly to keep her. The police were obeying the dictates of a lower court decision that awarded sole custody of the child to the contracting couple. But in any case, they still took the child by force from the woman who bore her. That behavior struck most people as unfortunate if not barbaric.

both the genetic material and the womb. Thus by any definition, she is the mother of the child. To force her to give up her child under the terms of a surrogacy contract violates her fundamental right to associate with and rear her child.[21] This does not mean that she has exclusive rights to the child. That must be shared with the natural father. But the right of one parent (the natural father) to associate with his child cannot be enforced at the expense of the right of the other (the surrogate).

As a result of this fundamental right, some states that allow a fee to be paid to the surrogate also do not allow the contract to be enforced if the surrogate wants to keep the child. Any contract that requires a woman to agree to give up the child she bears prior to birth is not considered a valid contract. This is similar to the way that most states deal with adoptions. Any agreement prior to birth to give up one's child is not binding and can be revoked if the birth mother changes her mind. Many states that have passed laws on surrogacy have chosen to use the model of adoption law rather than contract law. The problem with allowing the surrogate to keep the child is that it substantially increases the risk to the contracting couple. They might go through the entire process and end with shared custody of a child that they initially thought was to be theirs. To many people, that doesn't seem fair. But to others is it just as unfair to take a child away from his or her mother simply because a contract states that she must. Even in cases where the surrogate does not contribute the egg, gestation determines motherhood.

The notion that gestation should determine motherhood is based principally on the contribution the gestational mother makes during pregnancy and birth. She is anything but a "human incubator," and makes a substantial contribution not only to the physical development of the child, but to its emotional and psychological development as well. The gestational mother has built up what bioethicist Ruth Macklin calls "sweat equity" in the child

21. In *Stanley v Illinois*, the Supreme Court stated that "the rights to conceive and to raise one's children have been deemed essential . . . , basic civil rights of man . . . , far more precious than property rights. It is cardinal with us that the custody, care and nurture of the child reside first in the parents." 405 US 650 (1971), at 651.

she is carrying.[22] The nine-month investment in the child and the labor, literally, involved in giving birth, tilt the equation in favor of the gestational mother. She clearly has made the greater investment in the child in terms of effort and time expended, and thus she should have a greater claim to motherhood. At the end of the process of birth, the woman who gives birth to the child will have contributed much more of herself than the egg donor did in order to bring about the child's birth. For a woman who knows what pregnancy and childbirth involve, the contribution of the egg donor might seem trivial compared to the rigors and demands of pregnancy and birth.

Health law specialist George J. Annas suggests that gestation gives a woman a greater interest in the child she is carrying because of the biological investment being made.[23] Although this investment is difficult to define and more difficult to quantify, it does reflect the substantial difference in involvement between egg donation and pregnancy and birth.[24] It is not accurate to suggest that the "carrier" of the child has no impact on the person into whom the child develops. Although the physical traits and many of the predispositions of the child have their source in the genes, there is a growing body of evidence that points to the gestational environment as a substantial contributor to the child's personality.[25] Similarly, Katharine Bartlett of Duke University Law School argues that the nine-month investment of the gesta-

22. Ruth Macklin, "Artificial Means of Reproduction and Our Understanding of the Family," *Hastings Center Report* 21 (January–February 1991): 9.

23. George J. Annas, "Redefining Parenthood and Protecting Embryos: Why We Need New Laws," *Hastings Center Report* 14 (October 1984): 51. See also George J. Annas and Sherman Elias, "Noncoital Reproduction," *Journal of the American Medical Association* 255 (3 January 1986): 67, and Annas and Elias, "In Vitro Fertilization and Embryo Transfer: Medicolegal Aspects of a New Technique to Create a Family," *Family Law Quarterly* 17 (1983): 216–17.

24. Laurence D. Houlgate, "Whose Child? In re Baby M and the Biological Preference Principle," *Logos (USA)* 9 (1988): 167.

25. See, for example, Thomas Verny, M.D., and John Kelly, *The Secret Life of the Unborn Child* (New York: Delta, 1981), B. R. H. Van den Bergh, "The Influence of Maternal Emotions During Pregnancy on Fetal and Neonatal Behavior," *Pre and Peri-Natal Psychology* 5 (1990): 127, and Peter Hepper, "Foetal Learning: Implications for Psychiatry," *British Journal of Psychiatry* 155 (1989): 289–93.

tional mother, in addition to the pain, risk, and sacrifice involved in carrying and giving birth to a child, greatly outweighs the contribution of the genetic donor.[26]

Similar in importance to the investment and contribution of the gestational mother is the bonding that occurs between her and the child she is carrying. Although significant bonding can take place between any two individuals, the combination of biological investment and the resultant bonding weighs heavily in favor of gestation as the determinant of motherhood.[27] That is, the combination of biology and relationship that is inherent in gestation argues for motherhood being vested in the woman who bears the child. In most pregnancies, this bond is a central part of the pregnant woman's self-concept, and although children do not normally entirely define a woman's life, they are surely integral to what defines her as a person. In most instances, the loss of this bond causes a great deal of grief when a pregnancy is lost. This is even the case in adoption, in which the birth mother realizes that giving up the child is in both the child's and the mother's best interests. One reason that many states have a period in which a birth mother can regain custody of her child prior to the adoption's becoming final is that they recognize the strength of this bond. Similarly, most states do not hold an adoptive mother to a prebirth consent to adoption, since she cannot know the strength of the bond she will feel with her child prior to birth, and thus cannot give genuinely informed consent. In cases in which the surrogate changes her mind and wants to keep the child, it is reasonable to see this bond as similarly important and self-defining.

This sense of bonding makes pregnancy a relationship, not only physiologically, but also emotionally. What makes a woman a mother is the unique relationship developed with the fetus in the nine months of pregnancy and the event of birth. Gestation creates motherhood because of the intense, intimate relationship that is created as a woman carries a developing child. Egg dona-

26. Katharine Bartlett, "Re-expressing Parenthood," *Yale Law Journal* 98 (1988): 329–30.

27. See "Rumplestiltskin Revisited: The Inalienable Rights of Surrogate Mothers," *Harvard Law Review* 99 (June 1986): 1952.

tion and a ten-thousand-dollar fee paid to the surrogate do not compare with the bonding that has been established during pregnancy. Sociologist Barbara Katz Rothman summarizes the argument for gestation in this way: "Any pregnant woman is the mother of the child she bears. Her gestational relationship establishes her motherhood. We will not accept the idea that we can look at a woman, heavy with child, and say the child is not hers. The fetus is part of the woman's body, regardless of the source of the egg and sperm. Biological motherhood is not a service, not a commodity, but a relationship."[28]

Conclusion

With Scripture's skepticism about third-party contributors to procreation, one should be careful about employing even altruistic surrogates. Commercial surrogacy is problematic even for those who do not hold to biblical authority, because it constitutes baby-selling. Baby-selling is morally troubling because it violates the Thirteenth Amendment, which is undergirded by the principle of respect for human dignity, for human beings made in God's image.

28. Barbara Katz Rothman, "Surrogacy Contracts: A Misconception," *Daily Journal Report* 88–6 (1 April 1988): 20.

8

Embryo Cloning

Introduction

On October 13, 1993, at the annual meeting of the American Fertility Society in Montreal, George Washington University infertility researchers Dr. Jerry Hall and Dr. Robert Stillman announced that they had successfully cloned a human embryo for the first time. The scientific community was electric with excitement at what they had accomplished, and Hall and Stillman were thrilled with the prospects of what their achievement held out for infertile couples. Though presented in a low-key fashion at the meeting, news of their discovery spread quickly around the world, bringing the strongest reaction and most intense debate on any issue in medical ethics since in vitro fertilization in the late 1970s. The university's phone and fax lines were overwhelmed with calls and requests from scientists and the press.

Shortly after the release of their research, Hall and Stillman were invited to be guests on "Nightline," "Good Morning America," and "Larry King Live." Particularly on "Larry King Live," as the calls poured in they were caught off guard, astonished at the amount of criticism they received for their work. Interestingly, the disapproval they encountered came from both religious and nonreligious people. Many people who called in that evening had an intuitive reaction that their work was not right, but were unable to pinpoint why. Others had strong reactions based on religious beliefs that cloning was "playing God" with life in the lab, something that was inherently objectionable. Still others were supportive of the progress of science that their work represented and were critical of those who sought to place moral and religious restrictions on scientific research that was clearly well-intentioned. Polls taken around this time showed that roughly three out of four Americans disapproved of the idea of embryo cloning.[1]

The November 8, 1993, issue of *Time* captured the visceral reaction of many people when they heard of this research. It was the cover story that week, and the cover of the magazine was a modified reproduction of Michelangelo's painting of the creation, in which the finger of God touches Adam's finger. Through that touch God extends the breath of life into Adam, who comes alive. *Time* artists altered the painting and instead of God touching one person, he touches five clones of Adam at the same time. The point was clearly that there was "something wrong with this picture," implying that there is similarly something wrong with human beings taking the liberty of copying in the lab what God had already created in the body. It also called into question a fundamental Judeo-Christian assumption about human beings being unique creations of God, since that presumably unique genetic design is now capable of being copied outside of the body.

For many people, human cloning is the stuff of science fiction. From its fictional beginning in Aldous Huxley's *Brave New World* to the mid-seventies novel by Ira Levin, later made into a movie, *The Boys from Brazil*, in which a group of neo-Nazis attempt to clone a whole host of Hitlers, to film's most recent example *Jurassic Park*, cloning has never been viewed as something that society would have to face. It has always been, at best, a remote possibility. In fact, the speculation that has accompanied cloning has been widespread enough to warrant an extended entry on the subject in *The Encyclopedia of Science Fiction*.

1. See, for example, the *Time*/CNN poll in Philip Elmer-Dewitt, "Cloning: Where Do We Draw the Line?" *Time*, November 8, 1993, 65–70.

The Science of Cloning

In light of all the science fiction and the way people's imaginations work when they consider cloning, it is important to recognize exactly what Hall and Stillman accomplished. Perhaps more significantly, it is key to realize what they did not accomplish. To be precise, they cloned a human embryo, that is, they made an exact genetic duplicate of an embryo that had been previously fertilized in vitro in the lab. They reproduced in the lab the same process that occurs in the body when identical twins (or triplets) are produced. Most of the embryos were cloned once. In some cases, they made two duplicates of the same embryo. Two copies of the same embryo appears to be the limit of what their process can accomplish at present. They began the experiment with seventeen different embryos, and produced a total of forty-eight.

However, Hall and Stillman did not clone a person. They only copied the genetic material of a human embryo. Cloning a person involves much more than simply copying his or her genes. It also involves duplicating the developmental environment and experiences that inevitably shape the personality of the person. (That is what the neo-Nazis were trying to do in *The Boys from Brazil*.) Cloning a person is very different and truly belongs in the realm of science fiction. But more importantly, these scientists did not clone adult cells, also the raw material of science fiction. They did not take tissue from a mature adult and copy the DNA code. If this were possible, scientists could conceivably produce an identical twin from adult tissue.

Lest you think that these cloned embryos had started the process of becoming a baby that could grow if implanted in a woman's uterus, that was not quite the case. Since the original embryos were defective, they were incapable of developing for more than a few days. Hall and Stillman were not trying to produce cloned embryos that could be implanted and develop to a full-term pregnancy (a process still two to three years away, they estimate). They only wanted to see if the cloning process could be done. They were not attempting to set up embryo production lines or create any of the more outlandish scenarios that critics of their work fear.

Embryo cloning is neither new nor particularly difficult, though cloning of human embryos does contain some complicated aspects. Researchers have been cloning certain types of animal embryos since the late 1970s. For example, sheep embryos were successfully cloned to produce adult sheep in 1979, and the same result was produced with cattle in 1980. Animal cloning has not become a widespread commercial practice simply because it is too expensive. In fact, the firm that developed and patented the cattle cloning process is now out of business.[2]

The technical process of cloning embryos does not appear to be that complicated, though it does contain a complex procedure. Scientists who work with animal embryos suggest that there is no reason human embryos could not be cloned in the same way it is done with animals. Dr. Arthur Caplan, director of the Center for Bioethics at the University of Pennsylvania, commented that "it doesn't take a Nobel Prize team with a million dollar lab [to accomplish human embryo cloning]. It's fairly simple."[3] Many other scientists were capable of accomplishing Hall's and Stillman's feat, but chose not to do so for fear of the criticism they would receive and the ethical Pandora's box that they would open. Dr. Leeanda Wilton, director of the world-renown Monash In Vitro Fertilization Center in Australia, where much of the pioneering work in IVF was done, suggested that the reason many qualified researchers have not pursued embryo cloning is that they fear opening up ethical issues that society is not equipped to resolve. She stated, "They haven't done so [cloned embryos] because it opens up a can of worms."[4]

To clone the embryos, Hall and Stillman took embryos that had been fertilized in vitro. Fertilization must take place in the lab in order to give researchers the available embryos without risk of their being damaged. All embryo cloning must start with in vitro fertilization. The embryos they used in their experiments had been fertilized by two sperm instead of one, making them ab-

2. That company is Granada Biosciences, who sold the rights to the technology that enables cattle embryos to be cloned, and went out of business in 1992.
3. Quoted in Gina Kolata, "Doctor Clones Human Embryos, Creates Twins," *New York Times,* October 24, 1993, 1.
4. Elmer-Dewitt, "Cloning," 70.

normal embryos and destined to die within a week. This cloning process would be no different if the embryo were properly fertilized and had a normal chance at becoming a baby if implanted. The second step, after fertilization, is to watch the embryo divide in two, as it does in the normal course of development. Once that is done, then the coating that contains enzymes that promote the cell division that is necessary for growth and development (called the zona pellucida) is removed. Then the two cells in the embryo are separated. The coating then must be replaced in order for development of the embryos to continue. Hall and Stillman used an artificial zona pellucida to recoat the now two embryonic cells, enabling development to continue. As the cells grow they form genetically identical embryos, a laboratory equivalent to what occurs naturally in the body when identical twins are conceived. With the group of embryos with which Hall and Stillman worked, growth stopped after six days because they were abnormal embryos.[5]

Ethical Assessment of Human Embryo Cloning

Cloning of human embryos does indeed open up a world of complicated ethical questions. Some countries have elected not to allow human cloning in any form. For example, what Hall and Stillman did would be a federal crime in Germany, Great Britain, and Japan. Germany has strict regulations on cloning and other reproductive technologies for understandable reasons, given its recent experience with the Nazi eugenics program. In Britain, researchers who want to attempt cloning must obtain a government license to do so, and to date, the government refuses to issue them. Other countries, among them United States, have no policy at this time on embryo research and cloning, and anyone who has the inclination and the resources to attempt the research is free to do so. In September 1994, the Clinton administration signaled a willingness to endorse embryo research with federal funding,

5. This description of the technical process of embryo cloning is taken from Elmer-Dewitt, "Cloning," 67.

which when effective would result in removing a long-standing moratorium. The standards that govern the practice of embryo research are voluntary, set by the American Fertility Society. These guidelines for pre-implantation embryo research stipulate that scientists can study embryos not intended for implantation in order to gain information about areas of clinical importance, as long as the study is approved by the institutional review board of the participating facility.[6] Further guidelines were suggested by the embryo research panel of the National Institutes of Health (NIH), which recommended moving ahead with federally funded embryo research in or after 1994.

The ethical dilemmas in cloning human embryos revolve around two areas. The first concerns the question of whether embryo cloning per se is morally allowed. That is, can scientists ethically clone embryos of human beings, irrespective of the uses envisioned for the clones? Is it inherently morally objectionable? There are questions about scientists "playing God" with the basic substance of life in its beginnings. Additionally, there are questions about the unique personal identity of each individual. Does the prospect of cloning, even at the embryonic stage, compromise the right that each individual has to his or her own unique identity?

The second set of ethical dilemmas concerns the potential uses of cloned embryos. Whether cloning is morally allowed depends on how the cloned embryos will be used. In other words, why would someone want to clone human embryos? Are there legitimate reasons for cloning embryos that do not include some of the more extreme scenarios that critics of cloning fear? It may be that some uses of cloned embryos would be ethically acceptable and others would not. Cloning of human embryos would not be objectionable per se, and the morality of cloning would be determined by the uses to which the cloned embryos would be put.

---

6. The institutional review board (IRB) is a committee within a medical facility that approves experiments, particularly those involving human subjects. See Rebecca Kolberg, "Human Embryo Cloning Reported," *Science* 262 (October 29, 1993): 652–53.

Imagine that you and your spouse (if you are married) are patients at a local infertility clinic. You are about to undergo IVF, and the clinic suggests that you think about cloning some of the embryos that you will create when the woman's eggs are fertilized in vitro with her husband's sperm. You have read in *Time* and *Newsweek* about cloning of embryos enhancing a couple's prospects of having a successful pregnancy through infertility treatments. Think about why you might want to have embryos produced from your and your spouse's genetic materials cloned. What could you do with them that might make a difference in your family? What uses would be significant enough to justify the additional expense of cloning embryos.

Embryo Cloning Per Se

First, is cloning of human embryos inherently an ethical problem? Is it an example of scientists taking creative prerogatives that belong only to God? Many people who are uncomfortable with the whole notion of embryo cloning use the idea of playing God as the overarching criticism of the process. But is it a valid charge? If a person holds to the Roman Catholic concept of natural law, which does not allow any interventions in the reproductive process, then this will likely be a problem. It would be similar to fertilization outside the womb in IVF, an unjustified manipulation in a divinely ordained process. It would not be consistent to accept IVF and reject cloning per se, because they are two aspects of the same process. There is little difference between creating embryos in the lab and copying those creations. Both are unnatural in that they do not occur naturally within the body. Both are reproductive interventions that create life. Both processes reproduce in the lab that which the body does naturally. Of course, one can reject both IVF and cloning and be consistent. But is that necessary from the perspective of Christian ethics?

One of the primary reasons noted for rejecting the Catholic natural-law framework for reproduction is based on the concept of general revelation. Science and technologies that generally improve the lot of mankind and specifically help alleviate the effects of the fall of man (of which infertility is one), are part of God's revelation to the human race unveiled outside of Scripture.[7] Of course, most technologies can be put to immoral uses, the result of sinful human beings implementing them. But technology that improves the state of affairs in creation can be seen as a part of the mandate God originally gave mankind at creation, to have dominion over the earth. This task was made more difficult by the entrance of sin into the world, but sin did not and does not today disqualify man from continuing to exercise his dominion over creation. A significant part of that dominion is the human race's gaining an increasing degree of control over itself, namely, over the body. The advances of medicine over the centuries are examples of mankind's increasing dominion over the pinnacle of creation, man and woman themselves. The ability of human beings to discover, synthesize, and apply new information that results in advances in sciences and technology comes from God's common grace, made known by his general revelation. Human beings are continuing to fulfill the creation mandate of Genesis 1–2 by searching out and applying those things that God has revealed in the creation. God's general revelation is not limited to those who know God; it is available generally, to everyone who applies himself or herself. To be sure, not everything that science or technology discovers is an example of general revelation. If such discoveries are proven false later or contradict Scripture, then Scripture is the final authority to resolve the dilemma. It may be that if Scripture and general revelation conflict, our biblical interpretation is incorrect. Or it may be that we must reject what is coming from outside Scripture and conclude that since it contradicts Scripture, it cannot be a legitimate form of general revelation.

Advances in medical technology that alleviate disease, a result of the fall, can surely be seen as a part of God's general revelation. Mankind's increasing mastery over the human body has increased our lifespan, decreased infant mortality, and improved the quality of life for most patients. In some cases, the availability

7. Not everyone views technology as so positive. From a more secular perspective see Neil Postman, *Technopoly* (New York: Vintage, 1992). From a Christian perspective see Jacques Ellul, *The Technological Society* (New York: Knopf, 1964).

of life-sustaining medical technology has resulted in people living with a very low quality of life, but those are the exceptions and not the rule. Medicine has rarely been viewed as playing God with the human body. Since infertility is a result of the fall, reproductive medicine is to infertility what medicine is to disease, a part of God's general revelation and common grace that can be used within limits set by Scripture. If reproductive medicine is not playing God with life in the lab, then it would seem to follow that cloning human embryos per se is not playing God with life in the lab either.

A second objection to cloning per se is that it violates the idea of a person's individual identity. Since cloning produces exact genetic duplicates, that practice calls into question the unique genetic identity that individuals have, and to which, some suggest, they have a right. Daniel Callahan of the Hastings Center, the preeminent bioethics think tank in the United States, questioned the advisability of cloning: "I think we have a right to our own individual genetic identity. I think this [cloning of embryos] could well violate this right."[8] Imagine that a couple underwent IVF, had embryos cloned, implanted some, and kept some in storage for later, anticipating a second child. Then they implanted one of the cloned embryos five years later, so that they had an identical twin born five years after the sibling was born. The older child now has a sibling that is an exact genetic duplicate of him or her. This scenario causes some moral discomfort for many people when they wonder about the effect on the older child of seeing a genetic duplicate for a little brother or sister. When asked if they would have liked being a clone, 86 percent of people surveyed responded negatively, and only 6 percent indicated that they would be comfortable with that.[9]

The objection goes deeper when more than simply harm to the cloned person is considered. It may be that we harm ourselves as well. Theologian and ethicist Richard McCormick put it this way: "It is increasingly easy to shatter our wonder at human diversity and individuality, especially in the era of the Human Ge-

8. Cited in Elmer-Dewitt, "Cloning," 68.
9. Ibid., 65.

nome Project, when we are tempted to collapse the human person into genetic data. It would be ironical were this to happen in an era that prides itself on treasuring of uniqueness and diversity of all kinds."[10] It may be that cloning will cause us to lose our sense of appreciation for the wonder of God's creation and the uniqueness of each individual human being. As McCormick rightly points out, it would be ironic if that happened at the same time that society is emphasizing multiculturalism.

However, there is much more to one's unique personal identity than genetics. A person is born with his or her genetic identity, but the identity of the person develops over time. The personality is formed, dispositions are developed, and the experiences and the environment shape the whole person over time. In fact, the dominant aspects of one's personal identity are the personality and character traits that are learned and developed over time. We should be very careful about reducing a person's uniqueness to his or her genetic makeup alone, especially in view of the Christian doctrine of the soul. What makes individuals unique from a Christian perspective is ultimately their souls. However one views the transmission of the soul, whether it is directly created by God with each new conception or mediated through the parents, it does not appear that the soul presents a problem with embryo cloning. The reason for this is that, again, cloning in the lab duplicates a natural bodily process that occurs when identical twins or triplets are produced. However one would resolve the problem of the soul in those natural cases would be the same in dealing with cloned embryos.[11] In addition, even if a person had a right to a unique genetic identity, particularly if that is seen as the gift of God, then identical twins or trip-

10. Richard A. McCormick, "Blastomere Separation: Some Concerns," *Hastings Center Report* 24 (March–April 1994): 14–16.

11. The technical terms for the ways in which people view the transmission of the soul are traduceanism, whose advocates hold that the soul is mediated through the parents, and creationism, whose advocates hold that each soul is directly created by God. For more on the doctrine of the soul, see J. P. Moreland, "A Defense of a Substance Dualist View of the Soul," in *Christian Perspectives on Being Human: An Interdisciplinary Approach,* ed. J. P. Moreland and David M. Ciocchi (Grand Rapids: Baker, 1993), 55–79.

lets, when produced naturally in the body, would violate that right. But that is logically problematic and calls into question the assumption that people have the right to a unique genetic identity when God himself may violate that right from time to time when identical twins are produced.

From a biblical perspective, our genetic identity is entirely the gift of God and not something to which we have a right. God affirms that we do not have this right each time identical twins or triplets are born. The fact that most people do have a unique genetic identity does not mandate that it is our right. Thus, embryo cloning does not appear to be playing God in the lab nor does it violate our notion of individual personal identity. However, we may run the risk of losing the proper valuation of human diversity and individuality. That concern is worth taking seriously, but by itself is not sufficient to warrant prohibiting embryo cloning.

Possible Uses of Cloned Embryos

Infertility Enhancement

Cloning was developed by infertility specialists to help couples increase their chances of having a baby. The most commonly mentioned and least controversial uses for cloned embryos are for enhancing IVF or ZIFT and keeping the costs down. Imagine that you and your spouse are patients in the infertility clinic. To your disappointment, after an entire cycle of expensive hormone treatments, only four eggs can be retrieved, far fewer than normal. When it comes time to have embryos implanted, you are told that only two of the eggs have been fertilized. You know that the best chances for achieving one pregnancy come from having four embryos implanted. So instead of risking the entire expensive procedure on only two embryos, the clinic offers to clone two more, giving you statistically the best odds at becoming pregnant.

A second scenario is perhaps more likely to occur. Since couples routinely fail to achieve pregnancy in any given round of IVF, frequently they face the decision whether to try again. This means another cycle of hormone treatments, egg retrieval, laboratory fertilization and reimplantation, all procedures involving considerable expense, must be borne again. It is not uncommon for some couples to go through the cycle repeatedly, spending tens of thousands of dollars. Couples who wish to avoid the expense and physical demands on the woman that superovulation involves could have one cycle that produces a number of embryos, some of which are implanted; of the balance to be kept in storage, one could be cloned. Whenever all the noncloned embryos were implanted, the cloned embryo would still be available for implantation should the treatment fail to produce a pregnancy. This would enable the couple to attempt implantation again without egg retrieval. A variant of this scenario is that if the couple decides to try for another child at a later date, there would be cloned embryos available for subsequent children if there are no noncloned embryos left after the cycle that achieves the first pregnancy. Thus, cloned embryos could be used to help infertile couples avoid a second egg retrieval procedure should the first implants fail or should they want another child in the future.

For example, suppose that during the initial cycle of egg retrieval, the couple produced five embryos suitable for implantation. Four are implanted, and the one that is left is cloned to produce three more embryos. Should the original implants fail to produce a pregnancy, three more embryos are waiting to be used when the couple wants to try again. If they become pregnant during the first implants and want another child three years later, then embryos are waiting to be implanted at that time.

The problem with these scenarios is no different than with IVF or ZIFT. With both of these procedures, as many eggs are harvested as possible and fertilized to keep in storage, in order to keep the costs down. If they are not needed should the couple become pregnant, they are routinely discarded. In some cases they are donated. The same would be true of cloned embryos used for infertility enhancement. Any clones that are not needed would be discarded. That raises the same problems that IVF and ZIFT raised. Intentionally ending the lives of embryonic persons is the moral equivalent of abortion. The proper way to use cloned embryos is the same way that embryos are used in IVF and ZIFT. A couple should authorize only the number of embryos cloned (instead of created with IVF and ZIFT) that they intend to implant and are prepared to rear. A couple should not put themselves in the position of having leftover embryos in storage, whether cloned or produced by IVF. In addition, a couple should avoid the prospect of selective termination should more embryos, cloned or not, implant than they are prepared to carry or rear. In other words, use of cloned embryos for infertility enhancement should be subject to the same guidelines as IVF and ZIFT.

One objection to using cloned embryos for infertility does not apply to IVF and ZIFT. Should a couple use them and more than one pregnancy occurs, they have deliberately created identical twins. In this case, there does not seem to be any significant moral difference than what takes place naturally when identical twins are conceived. It would not seem to be any different than a scenario in which twins or triplets are conceived by GIFT, IVF or ZIFT. When more than one pregnancy develops, technology has duplicated what takes place in the body naturally. The only difference is that the twins created are identical, not fraternal as are created by GIFT, IVF, or ZIFT.

There is a bit more discomfort when the twin is born later, the result of a second round of implants. But there is a problem only if one reduces personal identity to genetics. The second child's personality, character, environment, and experiences will be different from his earlier born twin. Since that is the dominant part of one's identity as a whole person, it is difficult to see how having a genetic duplicate can be problematic, since the younger twin will become a much different person, though sharing some of the same physical traits and predispositions.

Life and Health Insurance[12]

In Orange County, California, the Ayala family made the national headlines in 1990 when their teenage daughter contracted leukemia and needed a bone-marrow transplant.[13] A donor whose bone marrow was compatible with hers could not

12. This helpful term for this use of the cloned embryos is taken from John A. Robertson, "The Question of Human Cloning," *Hastings Center Report* 24 (March–April 1994): 6–14.
13. For more on this story, see *Orange County Register,* August 31, 1990, B1.

be found, so the family decided to conceive a child in the hope that he or she would be a match and could contribute the bone marrow necessary to save their daughter's life. They were able to discover in utero whether the baby was a match for the daughter. The family maintained that they would not abort the pregnancy should the unborn child not be a tissue match, and they would love the child and welcome it into their family. This story had a happy ending, since the child turned out to be a match and in 1993 donated the bone marrow that enabled her sister to make great progress in her fight against leukemia.

Had the Ayalas had a clone of their older daughter's embryo in storage, they would have been assured of a tissue match. They would have thawed the embryo and implanted it and waited for the child to reach the age at which she could be a bone-marrow donor. Or, if their older daughter had died of leukemia, her cloned embryo could be implanted and "replace" her. That is, in the first case, the embryo provided health insurance for the family, and in the second, it provided a form of life insurance.

One can imagine the pressures that such a donor might face. One has been conceived primarily to be a bone-marrow donor, though the parents valued the child and welcomed her into the family. The parents made it clear that had she not been a tissue match for her older sister, the parents would not have aborted her. However, it would have been very difficult to say no to a request for tissue. Donating bone marrow can be a painful experience, one that most people would not undergo for a stranger. But family relationships often create pressures to do things that people ordinarily would not do. Situations like these raise the question of informed consent. That is, all medical treatment, particularly organ and tissue donation, must proceed with the consent of the patient or donor. It must be informed consent, consent that is based on adequate information. In other words, the donor must know exactly what he or she is getting into and cannot be coerced or manipulated into granting consent. Most minors are presumed incapable of giving consent because of their age. The bone marrow donor in the Ayala case would surely be asked to donate while still a child, likely at an age where he or she is incapable of understanding all that is necessary to give informed consent. Parents are usually authorized to give consent for treatment for their children, but parents authorizing organ and tissue donations from one of their children is something quite different. Society does not ask children to be organ or tissue donors, unless they have died tragically. Then parents, as next of kin, can authorize organ donation. But informed consent is such an important value in medicine that society has been hesitant to morally obligate children to donate, even for family members. To clone and save embryos for the purpose of tissue compatibility, or health insurance, raises serious questions about the consent of the donor. This is even more so the case when the donor has been conceived, born, and reared for the primary purpose of donating tissue.

A second problem with this kind of health insurance is society's intrinsic view of a person. It is axiomatic among civilized people that a human being is not to be treated as a means to an end, but as an end with intrinsic value. They are treasured because, as persons, they are inherently valuable, irrespective of what they accomplish. With a scenario such as the bone-marrow donation, it is hard to escape the conclusion that these donors are considered as having instrumental as opposed to inherent value. That is, they are valued primarily for their tissue compatibility.

Whether these two problems, informed consent and viewing the person as a means to an end, are enough to outweigh the obligations to do good and prevent harm when it is in one's power to do so is a difficult question. One way to view it is to weigh the potential benefits to the recipient with the risks to the donor. The greater the risk to the donor and the less the potential benefit to the recipient, the less the obligation to provide the donation. The problem with this kind of weighing is that it assumes that the person making the decision about donation can make a rational, objective decision. But when you are that person, and you know that you were cloned and implanted for the primary purpose of making this donation, being able to make an objective decision in the midst of family pressures seems unrealistic.

A second and perhaps unlikely scenario is that couples would use cloned embryos as a form of life insurance; that is, to "replace" a child who has died a tragic and premature death. Though the thought of replacing children with genetic twins is an interesting thought, especially for couples grieving the loss of a child, this use of cloned embryos is improbable. The only way this could be done is by the couple setting aside some embryos in in vitro fertilization for cloning and storage. Though it is possible that couples could undergo IVF for the purpose of providing such a backup, that would be rare because of the cost involved. However, it may be the couples already undergoing IVF would welcome the chance to store embryos in case the unthinkable happens. In addition, couples using IVF usually want to maximize the number of embryos available for implantation, and it is improbable that they would set some aside for such life insurance. Furthermore, it is hard to imagine couples planning in advance to replace a child who might, by some chance, die tragically. In fact, having a genetic twin as a replacement for a deceased child would probably increase the sadness and sense of loss for the child who had died. Every day of that twin's life would be a reminder to the parents that another child who looks like him or her had died in his or her youth. It would likely make it more difficult for the parents and other siblings to appropriately grieve their loss and get on with their lives.

Genetic Screening and Research

Embryo cloning could enhance the efficiency of both genetic screening and embryonic research. Imagine a couple with a family history of genetic disease, Down's syndrome, for example. Instead of trying to conceive naturally, they may decide to conceive through IVF and have the embryos screened for the gene for Down's syndrome. Those embryos carrying the gene for the disease would be discarded and only those in which the gene was absent would be considered for implantation. This seems like a great benefit to the couple who genuinely wants a healthy child and desires to avoid the prospect of giving birth to a handicapped baby. This type of screening could also be used for sex and trait selection. Only embryos with the desired gender or traits would be candidates for implantation.

Some clinics can already do this type of genetic screening of embryos with IVF.[14] But in some cases, embryos are damaged or

14. This will be discussed in more detail in chapter 9.

even destroyed by the screening process. Cloning helps increase the chances that a couple will have embryos without the genetic disease they fear, because it is not a significant setback if some embryos are damaged in the process when other cloned duplicates are available.

As significant a benefit as this use of cloned embryos appears, there are problems involved. First, if one takes the position that personhood begins at conception, then any process that damages, destroys, or results in embryos being discarded is problematic. This happens both in the process of screening and as a result of information gained from the screening. In the latter case, there does not seem to be any morally significant difference between discarding the defective embryos and aborting a defective fetus when the defect is discovered during pregnancy. Second, most acknowledge that any kind of sex selection is morally troubling because of the gender bias toward boys and against girls. For example, in China, which has had restrictive population-control policies, it is common for families to abort female fetuses and keep male ones. In addition, trait selection is viewed as playing God and moving society toward eugenics, the term used to describe the use of technology to produce a specific type of human being. This preferential breeding is often considered a flight into science fiction, but there are already sperm banks of Nobel Prize winners and other similarly gifted people from which couples can select a sperm donor for their child.[15]

Using cloned embryos for research and experimentation has the potential for producing great scientific advances in our knowledge of embryonic life. But such research usually damages or destroys the embryos involved and, as such, is problematic for the person who holds that personhood begins at conception. In research of this sort, wholesale discarding of embryos damaged in the experiments is highly likely, and this presents a moral problem. Nevertheless, embryo research is moving ahead with the endorsement of the current administration. Even if one does not hold that personhood begins at conception, at the least one must

15. The most notable one of these is Robert Graham's clinic called the Repository for Germinal Choice, in Escondido, California.

acknowledge that embryos should be given high value because of their potential to become fully functioning human beings. In the right setting in the womb, embryos become babies, and given their potential to do so, they are entitled to respect beyond their use as morally neutral objects for research and experimentation.

For Profit and Sale

Imagine the possibilities if there were a market for embryos. People could shop for the right combination of genetic traits to produce a "designer child." Embryos banks would spring up where prospective parents could select a child with all their desired traits. Bioethicist and law professor George Annas remarked in the aftermath of Hall's and Stillman's announcement, "Without regulation, it will only be a matter of time before some entrepreneur tries to market embryos derived from Michael Jordan or Cindy Crawford."[16] The appeal of embryos with the genetic material of superstar athletes or supermodels is not hard to imagine, nor is the potential for profit in such a market. A commercial market in human embryos is the nightmare that most experts in this field fear.

However, upon further thought, such a market may be unlikely to develop. First, it is highly probable that any governing body that oversees embryo research will prohibit purchase and sale of human embryos. Such a body does not exist now, but with embryo research scheduled to move forward, it will not likely move forward without a board of scientists and ethicists to set guidelines for the research. All indications from the debate at the National Institutes of Health in Washington, D.C., are that the government will prohibit a commercial market in embryos. Of course, the degree to which that can be enforced is another question. For example, most state laws make purchasing a child for adoption illegal, that is, prospective adoptive parents cannot pay a birth mother a fee beyond reasonable expenses for her child. But there is a thriving black market for adoptable children in which children are undoubtedly bought and sold. It is clearly difficult to enforce adoption laws that prohibit such a market. It may

16. Cited in Elmer-Dewitt, "Cloning," 69.

be that enforcing a prohibition against the sale of embryos will be similarly difficult. Just because there are black-market adoptions does not justify prohibiting legal adoptions. Some argue that it is not overkill to prohibit cloning entirely because of the prospect of a commercial market in human embryos.

A second reason that fears of a commercial market may be overstated is that the demand for cloned embryos may not be as great as people suspect. It may appeal to some to have a child with the genetic endowment of a superstar athlete or model, but most prospective parents desire a child with their genetic material, not someone else's. Most couples who could afford to purchase cloned embryos and who could have their own children would probably choose to have a child of their own, that is, with their genetic materials. It is true that they may want to have some control over the process by genetic screening or even by embryo screening. Though there may be many potential sellers of embryos in the market, it is debatable how many potential buyers there would be. Surely couples or single people might view a child from a cloned embryo of a gifted athlete or model as a ticket to fame or wealth. But with the technology needed to clone embryos being so costly and the time required for such a child to mature to fulfill its intended purpose so lengthy, such motives are unrealistic.

Society should avoid a market for embryos for the same reason it should avoid a market for human beings and for body parts.[17] Persons are not inherently objects of barter. They are not commodities that can be bought and sold on the open market. The inherent dignity of the individual person made in God's image should prevent people from being viewed as market commodities.

---

17. There is some debate, however, on both a market for babies in adoption and a market for body parts. For the merits of an open adoption market see Elisabeth M. Landes and Richard A. Posner, "The Economics of the Baby Shortage," *Journal of Legal Studies* 7 (1978): 323–48. For the discussion of a market for body parts, a California Court of Appeals (upheld by the state Supreme Court) ruled that human beings have a property interest in their own body parts. The court did not rule on the right to financial compensation. See *Moore v Regents of the University of California*, 249 Cal Rptr 494 (1988).

Conclusion

Cloning of human embryos is a cutting-edge technology with promise to help infertile couples undergoing IVF. Since the process essentially duplicates in the lab what the body does naturally when it produces identical twins, as a technology it poses no problems. The moral problems come when the clones are used in certain ways. These are the same issues related to the disposition of leftover embryos as in IVF. There are problems of informed consent when clones are contemplated for health insurance, and it is unlikely that they would be used for life insurance. There are problems with using the clones for genetic screening and research, since they are often damaged or destroyed in the process. And there are serious problems with a commercial market for cloned embryos, for the same reason that there are problems with the sale of babies and body parts. Should a couple follow the guidelines set out for IVF, GIFT, and ZIFT in chapter 6, there is no reason cloned embryos cannot be used to enhance infertility treatments.

9

Prenatal Genetic Testing

Introduction

Tim and Barbara are about to have their first experience with genetic testing and counseling. They married in their mid-thirties
and, because of their ages, tried to start a family shortly after their
honeymoon. As is more common with older couples attempting
conception, it took some time before a pregnancy resulted. Barbara is now thirty-eight and three months pregnant with their first
child. They are thrilled that she is expecting, but understandably
concerned about what they have heard are the higher risks of their
child being born with certain genetic abnormalities such as
Down's syndrome. Their obstetrician routinely suggests prenatal
testing for all patients, usually by a simple procedure such as ultrasound. For patients over thirty-five, their physician suggests
that more detailed testing might be in order, since the risks of
Down's syndrome seem to be greater the older the woman is at
the time of pregnancy. This involves a bit riskier test known as
amniocentesis, which enables the physician to examine cells from
the baby itself. Since one of Barbara's sisters has a mild case of
Down's syndrome, Barbara has an additional risk factor and
agrees to have the testing done. She is somewhat anxious about
the results.

Though her sister has lived a relatively normal life with
Down's syndrome, Barbara has seen others, both children and

adults, with more severe cases, and she is afraid that her child might also suffer from Down's. She has some reservations about bringing a severely deformed child into the world, both out of concern for the child and concern for her and her husband. She has told her husband that she would consider ending the pregnancy if the tests reveal genetic abnormalities in their child. If you were her friend and she came to you for your counsel, what would you advise her about the wisdom of using this genetic testing and her options based on the results of the tests?

Or consider Dave and Diane. Dave's family medical history includes some individuals who have suffered from Huntington's disease. Huntington's disease is a terrible degenerative neurological disease that internally destroys a person, but the symptoms usually do not begin to appear until the person with the disease reaches roughly age thirty. It is called a late-onset genetic disease. Dave is a carrier of the disease. Since Dave carries the gene, there is a chance that any children that he and Diane have will inherit the gene and end up with the disease. They are concerned about the welfare of any children that they might have. Dave knows about the ravages of the disease from his own research into its symptoms, and both he and Diane are fairly sure that they do not want to subject a child to the horrors of Huntington's disease. But they want children very badly, and so far they are not comfortable with either adoption or a sperm donor that would enable them to bypass Dave's genes and still have children. They consider prenatal genetic testing to be non-negotiable, and they will have whatever tests are necessary to determine if their child will suffer from Huntington's disease. Though they admit that ending a pregnancy would be difficult, both of them would do so if they discovered through testing that their baby would be destined to endure Huntington's disease. What would you tell this couple about the wisdom of genetic testing and what they would do with the information from the tests?

Or take Dave and Diane's predicament one step further. In order to insure the best probability of a child without the gene for Huntington's disease, they have decided to do a much more sophisticated form of prenatal genetic testing. They are going to test for the gene before Diane even becomes pregnant. The way they can do this is by using in vitro fertilization instead of natural conception. Even though they do not have an infertility problem, they think that it would make sense to have conception occur outside the womb. They will go through the normal procedure of having Diane's eggs harvested and fertilized in the lab with Dave's sperm. Then they will test the embryos to see which ones do not have the gene. They will implant the one that does not have the defective gene and discard the ones that do have it. This way they insure that the child will not be afflicted with Huntington's disease. It will help to have a number of embryos from which to choose, since some will likely have the gene and others will likely be damaged or destroyed in the process of testing them for the gene. Another way to accomplish the same result would be to clone some of the embryos. That way if a particular embryo is damaged during the testing and found to be without the gene, other exact duplicates would still be available for implantation. If you were friends of this couple, how would you advise them about this kind of prenatal genetic testing?

Or finally, take the case of Jim and Lori. They have three boys. They very much want a girl. In fact, the only reason that they are trying to have a fourth child is that they might have a girl. They don't want a larger family but think that the additional expense and effort would be worthwhile to have a girl. They are interested in prenatal genetic testing to determine if the child Lori is carrying is a girl. If it is not, then they admit that they would be faced with a difficult decision. They acknowledge that they might consider ending the pregnancy if they found out that the child was a boy. They are interested in genetic testing for the purpose of sex selection. How would you advise them about the testing for this purpose? Why?

Testing for sex/gender selection is normally opposed by most bioethics scholars, but in clinics across the country it occurs more frequently than one might suppose. Of course, it is rarely admitted that a couple is ending a pregnancy for that reason. But it does happen in the United States and other parts of the West. It occurs with alarming regularity in other countries where women's rights are not as valued as they are in the West. For example, in India, where male children are valued much more highly than female children, physicians and genetic counselors are in a difficult bind, wanting to offer the testing but fully aware that some couples will routinely end the pregnancy if testing reveals that the child is a girl. In China, where access to such testing is available, the government's restrictive population policies pressure couples to end pregnancies when the fetus is female. Many developing areas do not have access to this kind of medical technology, and thus instead of aborting female fetuses, infanticide of female newborns is sometimes practiced. But where the testing is available, and where one gender is valued more than the other, scenarios like Jim's and Lori's occur regularly.

Different Types of Prenatal Testing

In the last twenty-five years, screening for genetic and other types of fetal defects has become a routine part of a pregnant woman's maternity care. It is done is a wide variety of ways. Almost every pregnant woman with adequate prenatal care receives an ultrasound image of her uterus and the fetus growing inside it. This is usually the first picture the couple has of the developing child. Ultrasounds are normally done around the end of the first trimester of pregnancy. As the pregnancy progresses, the image of the fetus becomes clearer, until late in the pregnancy when the fetus is too large to be viewed well. The gender of the child is usually apparent to the trained eye, and some anomalies can be detected through ultrasound.

A second and routine test that has been developed recently is a simple blood test that indicates a variety of fetal abnormalities. It is called the alphafetoprotein (AFP) test. If there is a high level of AFP in the mother's blood this can be an indication that this key protein is leaking from the fetus into the mother's blood. This condition can suggest that the fetus has a neural tube defect such as anencephaly. It can also indicate that the fetus has not developed any cerebral cortex in the brain, or that the fetus has spina bifida, an opening in the sac that surrounds the spinal cord. (The closer to the brain the opening, the more nerve damage will result.) In addition, a low level of AFP can indicate Down's syndrome in a fetus. Since the test was initially developed, it has been refined to correct the high number of false positives and negatives. It is a much more reliable test today than it was five to ten years ago, and it is considered routine for pregnant women today. Some states, such as California, require doctors to offer the AFP test to all their maternity patients.

A third type of prenatal test is usually reserved for women who are considered at high risk for fetal abnormalities. These are often women who are older or who have a family history that would indicate a higher likelihood of a defect being passed along to the child. This test is known as amniocentesis and is normally done between the sixteenth and twentieth weeks of pregnancy. In this test, the physician inserts a needle, guided by ultrasound to help insure that the fetus is not damaged, into the woman's abdomen and draws out some of the amniotic fluid in which the fetus is swimming. The fetus normally sloughs off cells during development that can be obtained through the mother's amniotic fluid. The physician draws out some of the fetus's cells through the fluid and analyzes them. The physician can determine if the developing fetus has any genetic anomalies. Amniocentesis is invasive for the mother and can be risky for both mother and fetus. Occasionally, amniocentesis causes a miscarriage, in approximately 1/2–1 percent of cases.

A fourth and a bit riskier prenatal test is called chorionic villus sampling (CVS). This test too captures some of the fetus's cells but gets them from a different place in the woman's body. The chorionic villi make up the edges of the placenta, and they look like a cluster of small hairs that surround the sides of the placenta. The physician will obtain the chorionic villi either through the woman's abdomen or through the cervix with a catheter. The advantage of this test is that it can be performed earlier in the pregnancy, around the tenth to twelfth weeks, during the first trimester of pregnancy. Should the couple find that their child has abnormalities and they decide not to continue the pregnancy, it is emotionally easier on some couples to terminate the pregnancy in the first rather than in the second trimester. But this is riskier for the mother and fetus and results in miscarriages in roughly 1–2 percent of cases. Some studies have suggested that a variety of birth defects can result from CVS testing.[1]

A final type of testing can be done prior to a pregnancy.[2] Embryos obtained through IVF can be screened for abnormalities prior to implantation so that only embryos without genetic defects are candidates for implantation. In the future, it may be that the woman's eggs can be tested, so that prior to fertilization a couple can know vital genetic information and enhance their chances at having a child without any genetic anomalies.

Backdrop of the Human Genome Project

One of the primary reasons prenatal genetic testing is becoming more widespread is that the amount of genetic information available to couples has increased exponentially in the past few years. This is because of a project called the Human Genome Project, an enormous worldwide effort designed to map the entire human genetic code.[3] Work is proceeding at numerous laboratories and universities, and participants believe that the entire project will be complete by the year 2005. It is funded in this country by the National Institutes of Health and the Energy Department, for approximately $160 million annually for fifteen years, a total of around $2.5 billion dollars. The goal is to identify which genes are responsible for which traits in the human genetic code. Researchers are discovering heretofore unknown (but suspected) genetic links with numerous diseases, or at least predispositions to certain diseases. For example, genetic links to

1. Elizabeth Kristol, "Picture Perfect: The Politics of Prenatal Testing," *First Things* (April 1993): 17–24, 18.

2. There are some more experimental types of testing such as cordocentesis, a test that analyzes the blood of the fetus that has been drawn from the umbilical cord, fetal skin sampling, and fetoscopy.

3. For further information on the project at a more popular level, see Robert Shapiro, *The Human Blueprint* (New York: St. Martin's Press, 1991) and Lois Wingerson, *Mapping Our Genes* (New York: Plume, 1990). For a more academic view see George J. Annas and Sherman Elias, *Gene Mapping* (New York: Oxford University Press, 1992).

both colon and breast cancer were discovered in the past three years. Once the link is pinpointed to a specific gene, then a diagnostic test can usually be developed without much difficulty to enable a couple to have prenatal testing done. The project promises to produce an abundance of genetic information that can be used by couples who wish to know what genetic predispositions their child has inherited. Of course, a number of diseases have well-known genetic links, such as Down's syndrome and Huntington's disease, but the number of conditions for which a fetus can be tested will increase dramatically in the next decade.

Though the project raises the prospect of genetic engineering for genetic enhancement, the more immediate promise of the project is the information it will provide. Some conditions can be treated in utero through the exciting field of fetal therapy. But in many cases, the information available to the couple will help them prepare for their child. In some cases, what a couple finds out about their child will likely result in their terminating the pregnancy.

Couples undergoing prenatal testing are not the only ones interested in this information. Employers and insurance carriers are sure to demand access to a person's genetic information. It is understandable that an employer would be reluctant to hire someone if that employer knew the person would develop a crippling disease that would end his or her career, as is the case in Huntington's disease. Or, if the person were hired, the employer might argue that there is a right to know factors that materially affect a person's ability to perform a job. Insurance carriers, particularly in life and health insurance, argue that knowledge of a client's genetic background is essential if they are to accurately assess the risks of insuring this person. From their perspective, this information is critical to anticipating the costs of doing business, something that every company must do to stay in business.

It is not difficult, however, to envision a new class of people who are victims of genetic discrimination. Surely such discrimination parallels discrimination on the basis of race and gender, since a person inherits his or her genetic code in the same way he or she inherits race and gender. They could certainly argue that their right to privacy makes information about their genetic makeup their own, to disclose at their discretion.

Some interest groups also have a great deal of interest in the project. For example, gay and lesbian advocacy groups are eager for the project to discover a genetic link to homosexuality. If such a link is found, it would add strength to their claim that homosexuals deserve minority status and the protection from discrimination that such a status brings.

But back to the happy, excited, expecting couple, for whom a whole new world of information is opening up. The genome project may make genetic testing routine because the number of conditions that are detectable in the womb are increasing annually. (In the past, genetic testing was primarily for those couples whose family history indicated some possibility of a genetic disease.) There seems to be little doubt about the potential demand for testing. Of all the questions that prospective parents ask when they find out they are pregnant—Is it a boy or girl? What will it look like? Who will it favor? What will its temperament be? Will it be an easy baby?—the most anxiety-producing question is no doubt, Will it be healthy? This desire for reassurance about the baby's health gnaws at most parents-to-be and drives them to genetic testing and genetic counselors if they have concerns about the baby's health.

The Ethics of Prenatal Genetic Testing

In the biblical and theological framework for reproductive technologies that was laid out in the opening chapters, one of the conclusions drawn was that the medical technology that generally improves the lot of the human race and helps alleviate effects of the entrance of sin into the world is an aspect of God's general revelation. The ability of human beings to look into the womb and examine the genetic structure of tiny babies and even smaller embryos ultimately comes from God. His wisdom revealed outside of Scripture has enabled human beings to develop the technology that identifies the results of sin in general in the world in the form of genetic diseases.[4] Thus, prenatal genetic testing per se does not appear to be wrong. That does not suggest that couples are morally obligated to use the available testing technology. But it is important that couples acknowledge that the womb is still "the secret place" over which God alone ultimately has control (Ps. 139:15). Further, they should realize that these tests are not infallible (all have some margin of error, greater for some than for others) and some do involve a degree of risk both to the mother and the fetus. If the benefit of obtaining the information is greater than or proportionate to the risk incurred in the test, then utilizing genetic testing technology is morally appropriate.

However, what couples do with the information gleaned from prenatal genetic testing is quite another matter. Most genetic counselors will say that they operate with the presumption of objectivity. Their role is to give information and maximize reproductive choice for the couple.[5] Yet when public health officials talk about the benefits of prenatal screening in reducing the incidence of genetic diseases, that discussion assumes that couples will end their pregnancy if they receive bad news from their testing.[6] In some of the medical literature, the term *amniocentesis* is used to refer not only to the process of testing but also to the abor-

---

4. That is not to say that any specific genetic disease is the result of a specific sin committed by one of the parents of the child in question. Far from it. Genetic diseases are the result of the general presence of sin in the world.

5. Even the scholarly literature on the subject makes this presumption. For example, Kathleen Nolan, M.D., an associate of the Hastings Center, states that "out of respect for reproductive decisionmaking and genetic privacy, and to prevent abuses such as attempts at eugenic control, virtually all genetic counselors espouse the ideals of value-neutral counseling and autonomous decisionmaking." "First Fruits: Genetic Screening," in "Genetic Grammar: Health, Illness and the Human Genome Project," *Hastings Center Report* 22, Special Supplement (July–August 1992): S2–4.

6. Though also lamenting the loss of choice for parents who desire to rear a handicapped child, sociologist Barbara Katz Rothman nevertheless makes this assumption when she states that "although some people have discussed the value of being forewarned of genetic or other diseases even in a pregnancy the woman intends to carry to term, abortion is an integral part of this new technology [of prenatal testing]." "The Products of Conception: The Social Context of Reproductive Choices," *Journal of Medical Ethics* 11 (1985): 188–92, at 189.

tion that the authors assume a couple will authorize if their fetus is discovered to have some genetic defect.[7]

Public health authorities sometimes suggest that prenatal testing is a great help in eliminating the incidence of genetic diseases. But the only way it can be helpful in that way is if couples end their pregnancies and thus eliminate the genetic disease. Genetic disease is thus being eliminated, but preemptively, and at the expense of the child who has the disease. It is one thing to decrease the incidence of these genetic diseases, but quite another to do so by eliminating the person who has the disease. The incidence of every disease would decrease dramatically if medical practitioners had the liberty to do away with afflicted patients. There is a difference between finding a solution to a problem and eliminating the problem. In many genetic counseling offices, there is an assumption that if tests indicate genetic defects, the couple will end the pregnancy. Couples who utilize prenatal genetic testing should be aware of this assumption prior to the start of the testing.

This assumption is understandable. Couples who discover that their child has a genetic abnormality are often pulled by the desire to end their pregnancy. After the anticipation of conception and the excitement of pregnancy, to find out that the child you are carrying has genetic defects can be a crushing disappointment that many couples wish to put behind them by ending the pregnancy. In addition, couples want to avoid the difficulties—physical, emotional, and financial—of rearing a handicapped child.

However, the difficulty of undergoing an abortion of a genetically deformed fetus should not be underestimated. Most genetic anomalies are detected by amniocentesis or other tests that are not performed, and the results not available, until the second trimester of pregnancy. By this time the fetus is beginning to resemble a baby and its features are becoming more pronounced and visible by ultrasound. This is not to say that the appearance of humanness is a valid criterion for the right to life, but rather, that the more the fetus resembles a baby, the more emotionally difficult it is for the parents to authorize the abortion. Many couples expe-

7. Kristol, "Picture Perfect," 18, 20.

rience profound grief, loss, and guilt when abortion for deformity is performed.

What counts the most is not the emotional element involved in the decision to terminate a pregnancy when the fetus is genetically defective. What matters is what reason and Scripture have to say about the personhood of the unborn. If it's true that the fetus is a substance and the result of a continuous process of development that begins at conception, in which there is no metaphysically relevant decisive moment, then the fetus, irrespective of its stage of development, is a fully human person deserving all the rights to life. The problematic element in prenatal genetic testing is the decision to end a pregnancy because of the information that the testing reveals.

The presence of a genetically deformed child in the womb is often used to justify abortion. There is no doubt that finding out that one's child in utero is not healthy is a difficult situation. But let's analyze the decision to end a pregnancy because of genetic anomalies and how it is justified. It is most frequently justified by a quality-of-life argument. That is, the child born with such abnormalities is deemed incapable of having a life worth living. The child may never have what is considered to be normal mental capacity, and in some cases will not even have normal bodily functions. In many cases the child may have a life filled with suffering. For example, children with severe Down's syndrome or spina bifida may be incapable of meaningful interaction and function. In extreme and severe cases such as anencephaly (a condition in which the child is born with the majority of its brain missing; only the brain stem, which controls the involuntary functions, is present), the argument is made that the child is so deformed that it cannot properly be called a person, and thus has no rights to life.

Even if a couple receives testing results that indicate a genetic anomaly in their child, that does not justify ending the pregnancy. First, the couple must realize that these tests are not infallible and should not be taken by the couple as error-free. The AFP test is notorious for both false positives and negatives, often requiring involved follow-up testing and substantial anxiety to the couple who is awaiting the results. Even amniocentesis is not 100 percent reliable, and couples should be very careful about terminating a pregnancy based on tests that can be in error.

Second, assuming that the tests are entirely accurate, the degree of deformity that the child will experience is difficult to predict. For example, there are varying degrees of abnormality with Down's syndrome. Some cases are severe and others are mild. Those with mild cases often lead relatively normal lives and are virtually indistinguishable to the casual observer. For example, a recent network television series, "Life Goes On," was about a high school student with mild Down's syndrome. He attended school with his friends and did most things that his peers did. Other genetic diseases such as Huntington's disease do not onset until later in life. Until the symptoms develop, usually sometime between the ages of thirty and forty, the person lives a normal life.

Third, assuming that the degree of deformity experienced can be predicted with certainty, it is presumptuous to suggest that the lives of genetically or otherwise disabled persons are not worth living. That is a value judgment, not a medical fact, and no one should have the right to impose that kind of value judgment upon another person, especially when doing so results in his or her death. Not even parents should have the right to set the standard of a life worth living for their child. In many cases in which abortion is contemplated, the parents may confuse the burden of life for the child with the burden of the parents caring for the child. Though society should not underestimate the challenge of a lifetime of caring for these children, the notion of a life not worth living for the child should not be used to disguise what is often the real reason the child is being aborted: the burden on the parents. The hardship on the parents does not justify ending the pregnancy, any more than the financial hardship of a poor woman justifies her ending her pregnancy.

It is presumptuous to suggest that the life of the genetically handicapped fetus is not worth living, because there is no inherent connection between disability and unhappiness. Nor is there any intrinsic link between disability and personal fulfillment. It would be interesting to take an informal and anecdotal survey of handicapped individuals and ask them if, on account of their disability, they viewed their life as not worth living and would have preferred never to have been born. You would surely find that un-happiness does not necessarily follow from possession of a hand-icap. Some of the most fulfilled and happy people around are those who have succeeded in overcoming their handicaps, and they would likely be offended at the suggestion that their lives are unhappy, not to mention not worth living.

A fourth and the most important reason that handicap does not justify ending a pregnancy is that the entity in the womb, however genetically deformed, is still a person. Those who de-fend the moral right of parents to abort genetically defective chil-dren assume that the fetus is less than a person. They have to hold this assumption in order for this justification of abortion to make any sense. Unless one assumes that the handicapped unborn is not a person, there is no morally significant difference between abortion for reasons of genetic deformity and executing adults who are genetically handicapped. Yet very few people consider executing handicapped adults simply on the basis of their handi-cap, for the reason that society acknowledges that they are per-sons with the right to life. In fact, the handicapped are deemed more worthy of protection from discrimination, not less, because of their vulnerability. The decision to end a pregnancy on the basis of genetic deformity alone is no different from eliminating adults because they are handicapped. If the fetus, irrespective of genetic defect, is a person, then the decision to abort based on such defect cannot be justified. Surely it is better to suffer the tragedy of accepting a child with genetic abnormalities than to in-flict tragedy on another person by abortion.[8]

However, some anomalies are so severe that they may seem in-consistent with the child being a person. For example, a child with anencephaly, perhaps the most severe abnormality with which a child can be born, will have no ability to do anything ex-cept maintain essential bodily functions. The child is born with only a brain stem and has no cerebral part of the brain. Thus the child will have no sense of self-consciousness, no awareness of his

8. Francis J. Beckwith, *Politically Correct Death: Answering the Arguments for Abortion Rights* (Grand Rapids: Baker, 1992). For more detail on this and other justifications for abortion, his work is extremely helpful.

or her environment, and no ability to interact or form any kind of human relationships. For many people, the decision to abort an anencephalic child is an easy one, and many medical professionals have concluded that anencephalics are not persons because they are so deformed.[9] But because the child does not have the capacity to perform certain functions, it does not follow that the child is not a person. Functional definitions of personhood are both metaphysically inconsistent and socially potentially dangerous.[10] Personhood is a matter of essence, not function.

However, admitting that the anencephalic child is a person does not by itself mean that all treatment to save its life, once born, is appropriate. An anencephalic child is born with a terminal illness. Most anencephalics die within the first month of life, though some live for as long as a year. There is no obligation to treat a terminally ill patient when the treatment is futile, that is, when it would not improve the patient's condition and restore health. Since the anencephalic child is imminently dying from birth, there is no obligation to offer aggressive medical treatment. Of course, for all dying patients, there is the obligation to provide comfort and dignity, that is, care that maintains comfort and dignity while allowing the disease to take its natural course. Thus, one does not have to deny personhood to the anencephalic child in order to justify not providing aggressive treatment.

One can ask, "If it is legitimate to provide only comfort and dignity care for anencephalics and let their condition take its natural course, why is it not acceptable to end the pregnancy?" This is a troublesome and emotionally arduous situation, and one can understand the difficulty in continuing a pregnancy in which the child a woman is carrying is anencephalic. But I am hesitant to

9. Some time ago I overheard a nurse discussing the care of an anencephalic child. The parents were trying to decide how much treatment to authorize, and the nurse suggested that "this decision is easy. Take the child home and let it die. It's not a person."

10. For further discussion of this aspect of personhood see the material in chapter 4. See also Scott B. Rae, "Views of Human Nature at the Edges of Life: Personhood and Medical Ethics," in *Christian Perspectives on Being Human: A Multidisciplinary Approach to Integration,* ed. J. P. Moreland and David M. Ciocchi (Grand Rapids: Baker, 1993): 235–56.

endorse ending such a pregnancy for two reasons. First, there are often questions about the diagnosis and the severity of the deformity that cannot be confirmed until after birth. Thus, it seems best to wait until after birth to make decisions about the care of the child instead of ending the pregnancy. Second, there is a significant moral difference between actively taking someone's life and passively allowing a natural death to occur. In the latter the cause of death is the disease or condition afflicting the child, but in the former, the cause of death is the action of the physician performing the abortion.[11]

If couples do not accept the abortion assumption behind a good deal of prenatal genetic testing, then it would seem to be an appropriate bit of technology that they can utilize. But if a couple is committed to continuing the pregnancy regardless of the results of the tests, then one might ask, "What is the purpose for having the testing done?" It would seem pointless and perhaps even foolish to submit to the risks of some of these tests when the results will not affect the decision about continuing the pregnancy. In some cases that is true, and it would be unwise to undergo the riskier tests without a compelling reason to do so. However, it is legitimate to use prenatal genetic testing to prepare for the arrival of a child who will have a genetic defect. There does not seem to be any good reason not to have the tests that carry little risk and are not invasive, such as ultrasound imaging and the AFP blood test.[12] In fact, seeing their child on the ultrasound monitor for the first time is one of the most thrilling experiences most couples can have. The ultrasound image can usually identify the gender of the child if the parents desire to know that prior to birth. If there are good reasons, such as a family history of genetic disease or advanced age of the mother, to indicate further genetic testing, then these too are legitimate if the tests are used either to reassure the parents that their child is healthy or to pre-

11. For more detail on this voluminous debate see, J. P. Moreland, "James Rachels and the Active Euthanasia Debate," *Journal of the Evangelical Theological Society* 31 (March 1988): 81–94, and idem, "Review of *The End of Life*," *The Thomist* 53 (October 1989): 714–22.

12. There is still some debate over the long-term risk of ultrasound imaging. See Kristol, "Picture Perfect," 17–18.

pare them emotionally and perhaps financially for the rigors of raising a handicapped child. Even couples who have a strong preference for one gender over another would be well served by ultrasound and disclosure of the child's gender. This may be the case with a couple who has a number of children of the same gender and who want the next child to be a different sex. If the child is not of the desired gender, then the parents have time to work through the disappointment prior to the delivery date. By the time of the child's birth, they are emotionally prepared to bond properly with that newborn child, a process that is crucial to the child's development.

In addition, some genetic anomalies can be treated if care is initiated shortly after birth. For example, with spina bifida, physicians can close the sac surrounding the spinal column after birth. But to do this, the child must go immediately from the delivery room to the operating room, minimizing the exposure to the spinal column. It is very helpful to everyone concerned if this condition is known prior to birth.[13] Furthermore, the field of fetal therapy is developing some exciting technologies that enable physicians to treat some conditions and even perform limited surgery on developing fetuses in the womb. As this field continues to grow, more conditions will likely be treatable in utero, contributing to further legitimate demand for prenatal testing.

Use of prenatal genetic testing is morally legitimate when it is used to get information about the child in utero in order to prepare the parents for care of this child and, if necessary, prepare physicians for appropriate treatment of the child. That is the

---

13. One of the tragedies associated with spina bifida happens when the parents do not authorize the surgery at birth, choosing not to give aggressive treatment. The parents then take the child home, and it usually dies at home within the first two years. But during that time, the parents have become attached to the child and come later to regret their decision to refuse the surgery. Discovering that the child has spina bifida through prenatal testing can enable the parents to work through this decision while they have time to do so. Spina bifida is less severe than anencephaly and the surgery does help in most cases. The child with spina bifida is not born with a terminal illness, though the deformities can be severe. Thus authorizing the treatment would be obligatory with spina bifida, since the treatment would not be futile. Refusing to authorize the surgery for spina bifida would be the moral equivalent of abortion based on the child's anomaly.

proper use of the information gleaned from the testing. To use the results to authorize and justify ending the pregnancy is not legitimate, since the parents would be condemning the handicapped unborn to death on the basis of its genetic anomaly. The only way this can be justified is to assume that the fetus with inherited abnormalities is less than a fully human person, an assumption that cannot be maintained. But if the handicapped unborn is indeed a person, then ending a pregnancy on the basis of the handicap is the most vicious form of discrimination.

Genetic Testing of Preimplantation Embryos

Technology has recently taken prenatal genetic testing back a step, to testing embryos prior to implantation. Genetic structure of the embryo can now be analyzed for genetic abnormalities. This technology has developed quickly and quietly. Until late 1993, with the cloning of embryos, there had not been much media attention paid to testing of embryos. Many clinics across the country are prepared to engage in embryo testing, and in late 1994, embryo research received the approval of a panel of experts appointed by the National Institutes of Health.

Embryo testing can be done only when IVF is used as an infertility treatment. Thus for the foreseeable future, testing of embryos will not likely become widespread or routine for couples who do not need technological assistance in conception. But since couples who use IVF or other sophisticated reproductive technologies often have amniocentesis or CVS testing done, it would seem to make sense to encourage embryo testing as a routine part of IVF. The defective embryos could be discarded instead of implanted, and the couple would have greater assurance that their fetus would not carry any deleterious genes. Some researchers see embryo testing as a means to move toward eliminating certain types of genetic diseases, while others see it as a first step in actually correcting such defects through genetic engineering. In the same way that physicians can treat some defects in utero through fetal therapy, it may be possible in the future to treat some conditions through embryo therapy.

The development of embryo testing has brought increasing pressure for government to give its sanction and begin funding research using human embryos. During the Reagan and Bush administrations, there had been a moratorium on any federal funding for embryo research, severely limiting the amount of research that could be done. In 1993, President Clinton ended the moratorium and appointed a panel from the National Institutes of Health to issue ethical guidelines for such research. In September 1994, the panel recommended that research on embryos be allowed, and federal funding was encouraged to help close a significant gap in our knowledge of embryology. The panel proposed to limit research to the first fourteen days of development and to allow embryos to be created specifically for compelling research projects. It also proposed that no market for embryos should be created and that sex selection of embryos is not appropriate.[14]

The most controversial part of the panel's recommendation clearly was its acceptance of creating embryos for research purposes. President Clinton rejected that aspect of the proposal and denied federal funding for institutions that create embryos solely for the purpose of research. That leaves as the only source of embryos for study those that are leftover embryos created by couples undergoing IVF. Many commentators objected to the panel's recommendation, suggesting that the deliberate creation of embryos in order to conduct research on them and then discard them smacked of Huxley's *Brave New World*. Ironically, the panel acknowledged that the embryo deserves special respect because of its potential to become a full human being. As one writer put it, "The NIH panel acknowledges that, should its recommendation be followed, scientists will be creating, manipulating and then destroying 'developing human life' that deserves 'serious moral consideration.'"[15]

Embryo research in general and embryo testing for individual couples face the same moral problem. If personhood begins at

14. National Institutes of Health, *Report of the Human Embryo Research Panel* (Washington, D.C.: United States Government Printing Office, September 27, 1994).

15. George Weigel, "A Brave New World Is Hatched," *Los Angeles Times*, November 27, 1994, B6.

conception, then there is no moral difference between aborting a fetus and discarding an embryo. If the results of genetic testing indicate that certain embryos are defective, then there is no moral difference between discarding them and aborting defective fetuses (and executing handicapped adults).[16] In addition, in the process of testing, the embryos are sometimes unintentionally damaged and then are discarded, and this is problematic for the same reason that research that damages the embryo is a problem. In general, research on a human being that is not for its benefit, is done without its consent, and could likely lead to its destruction should not be allowed in society. Similarly, embryo testing that damages embryos or leads to their being discarded is morally problematic.

However, embryo testing for couples at risk for transmitting genetic diseases seems to be a responsible way of procreating children. Rather than taking their chances, using embryo testing gives them a measure of control and assures them of not passing on harmful genes to their child or children. To deny the legitimacy of embryo testing would seem to take away the only responsible way of procreating a genetically related child for couples who have a history of genetic disease. However, the underlying reasoning that justifies embryo testing in this case is a crude form of utilitarianism, in which the ends justify the means, and in which results are subservient to moral principles. It is problematic for the results of any technology to be the moral trump card that is the overriding consideration in determining the proper use of such a technology. Though one cannot help but have a good deal of empathy for couples with a history of genetic disease, sac-

---

16. Even though the NIH panel for embryo research recognized that special moral status should be granted to the embryo, the panel and many others do not see embryos on the same moral level with fetuses. For example, Professor Andrea Bonnicksen states that "arguably it is morally more acceptable to discard embryos than to abort fetuses." She further adds that "deliberately discarding faulty embryos is arguably no worse than the constant threat in IVF of embryo loss due to biological fluke." In the first statement, she apparently assumes that implantation makes a morally significant difference in determining personhood, but that is a difference only in location, not in essence. In the second statement, she ignores the obvious difference between accidental death of embryos and intentional discarding of defective embryos. "Genetic Diagnosis of Human Embryos," *Hastings Center Report* 22, Special Supplement (July–August 1992): S5–11, at 5–6.

rificing embryonic persons for the sake of a couple having a healthy child is too high a cost for the Christian couple who holds that personhood begins at conception. Of course, for the couple who denies the personhood of the unborn or holds that its personhood begins at some later point in pregnancy, this presents no moral dilemma and can be considered a responsible way to avert some of the risks of procreation.

Social Concerns about Prenatal Testing

Beyond the clinical issues about when prenatal genetic testing is legitimate to use, there are other concerns about prenatal genetic testing in general. What kind of cultural ethos is being created by the growing prevalence of this kind of testing and routine abortion when the results are not what the couple desires? How is the growing availability of prenatal testing affecting the way society thinks about reproduction? Two potential effects of this growth in genetic testing are worth further thought.

The first relates to how society views the disabled adult population. Disability advocacy groups are understandably concerned about the abortion assumption inherent in a good deal of genetic testing. They fear that the loss of respect for the disabled unborn will translate into less respect for the adult disabled population. There is a curious double standard at work here. Virtually everyone writing on medical ethics condemns abortion for the purpose of sex selection, on the grounds that it makes a powerful statement about the relative value of the female gender. Since most people who contemplate sex selection favor boys, a preference that is overwhelmingly the case in much of the third world and in places where there are restrictive population policies, feminist groups are rightly concerned about what that says about the value of their gender in society. But when it comes to the disabled, no such concern is apparent, since society has already sanctioned abortion for virtually any disability that the testing uncovers.[17] We are content to draw our moral lines at gender but

17. Kristol, "Picture Perfect," 23.

not at disability. The landmark President's Commission on Bioethics in the 1980s illustrates this double standard. The commission gives approval for genetic testing, but also condemns use of such testing for sex selection: "[sex selection] is incompatible with the attitude of virtually unconditional acceptance that developmental psychologists have found to be essential to successful parenting. For the good of all children, society's efforts should go into promoting the acceptance of each individual—with his or her particular strengths and weaknesses—rather than reinforcing the negative attitudes that lead to rejection."[18] What holds for gender should also hold for disability. One can argue that the disabled, because of their greater degree of vulnerability, are owed this acceptance even more so than healthy children, irrespective of gender.

The unconditional love and acceptance that are at the heart of all responsible parenthood may also be affected by the cultural ethos produced by widespread genetic screening. Testing can involve a conflict between unconditional love for a child and a parental desire to have the best for children. Sociologist Barbara Katz Rothman asks pointedly, "What does it do to motherhood, to women, and to men as fathers too, when we make parental acceptance conditional, pending further testing. We ask the mother and her family to say in essence, 'These are my standards. If you meet these standards of acceptability, then you are mine and I will love you and accept you totally. After you pass this [genetic] test.'"[19] The extreme form of this occurs in the futuristic scenarios in which parents use testing and genetic engineering to customize their children by selecting the most desirable traits and gender. Though trait selection for children is still in the future, the mentality that underlies it may already be present. Though it is legitimate for parents to want every advantage for their children, seeking such advantage must not come at the expense of the unconditional acceptance that is what ultimately gives children their greatest advantage. To the degree that prenatal testing encourages a way of thinking that undercuts parental love and ac-

18. Cited in ibid., 23.
19. Rothman, "The Products of Conception," 190.

ceptance toward children, society should be careful about endorsing its widespread use. This is one further reason why, for the Christian, the morally acceptable use of testing should be for preparation, not abortion. Children and the disabled are marginalized enough in Western culture. Society in general and individual couples in particular should be cautious about endorsing prenatal genetic testing if indeed it undermines one of the essentials of responsible parenthood.

10

Maternal-Fetal Conflicts

Introduction

The new reproductive technologies are not only designed for new
ways to conceive a child. Some of the most remarkable new technologies provide great help in managing a pregnancy. For example, new discoveries in fetal therapy enable physicians to treat
fetal conditions in the womb. In addition, new social issues such
as AIDS and drug addiction affect the way a woman might man-
age her pregnancy. The combination of new fetal medicine and
new social issues have set up conflicts between the freedom of the
pregnant woman and the rights of the unborn child. Many of
these conflicts are not new. The issue of compelled Cesarean sections for women with endangered fetuses has been debated for
some time, though with new intensity recently because of the impact of the women's movement. But new techniques and new
trends in society have raised other situations in which the rights
of women to do with their own bodies what they deem best conflict with the best interests of the children they are carrying. The
following scenarios illustrate the variety of maternal-fetal conflicts that can arise during a pregnancy.

Scenario 1—Trusting God for Successful Delivery

In December 1993, a Chicago woman refused to consent to a
Cesarean section (C-section) that her physicians deemed neces-

sary to protect the life of her unborn child. The woman, a Christian in the Pentecostal tradition, believed strongly that God was in control of her pregnancy. She was trusting him to bring her through it and give her the gift that she claimed he had promised to her, a healthy baby. Yet she suffered from complications in pregnancy, and her doctors were quite certain that unless she delivered by C-section, the child would be significantly harmed and would not likely survive a normal vaginal delivery.

The more the physicians tried to convince this woman to have the C-section, the more adamant she became in her refusal. The way in which she cited her religious convictions as the basis for her refusal made it more difficult for the physicians to convince her to have the surgery, since they are often sensitive to a patient's religious freedom. But the physicians acknowledged that this case was different because it involved another person, the unborn child. The hospital believed that the physicians were acting in the best interests of the child about to be born, and that the mother was making decisions that were not in her child's best interests. As a result, the hospital requested a court order that would give the right to perform the C-section without the mother's consent.[1]

Interestingly, the American Civil Liberties Union (ACLU) provided the legal counsel for the woman. The ACLU defended her rights to make decisions about what happens to her body as a fundamental civil right guaranteed her by the right to privacy. It struck most people as somewhat odd that the group would defend her, since the ACLU is not well known for advocacy on behalf of conservative Christian causes or individuals. However, they maintained that this was a civil rights issue with an underlying concern for the religious liberty of the pregnant woman. The woman won her case in court and the Court of Appeals refused to hear the case. Thus, the hospital and her physicians were not able to insist on a C-section, leaving them to hope that the child would not be harmed by vaginal delivery. Two days later the

1. The physicians and the hospital could not proceed with the C-section without a court order since that would have constituted battery, for which they could be arrested. Court orders normally can be obtained in a short time.

mother went into labor, and after a difficult delivery, gave birth to a healthy baby.

Scenario 2—Fetal Surgery and Therapy

Jane is six months pregnant with her third child. She has two healthy children already and is not anticipating any complications with this pregnancy. During one of her monthly office visits, her doctor suggests an ultrasound, to insure that the baby is developing normally. During the procedure, the doctor notices a condition in the baby that she had not seen prior to this time. She tells Jane that it is a moderate to serious condition for the baby, but that the technology of fetal therapy is progressing rapidly and can likely be effective in treating her child's condition. In fact, some medical centers can even perform fetal surgery. Although it is still a young discipline, physicians who specialize in it are very competent. Nevertheless, it is quite an invasive procedure for the mother, since physicians must go through her abdomen to perform it.

Jane remembers her physician telling her things about her two earlier pregnancies: how there were some things that the doctor had noticed about her two children, but she was not to worry. If the condition worsened, the child would be delivered by C-section and have the necessary surgery, or they could wait, preferably until the full gestation period was complete, deliver the child, and then perform any necessary procedures. At the time of those earlier pregnancies, fetal therapy was still an experimental procedure, not yet approved for widespread clinical use, so Jane's options were more limited then than they are today. For this current pregnancy, Jane is concerned about the risks and the invasiveness of the fetal surgery being proposed, and she is not sure that she wants to authorize it. The condition can be corrected after birth, but it would be better to attempt to correct it now. Yet she looks at her two healthy children and is not sure that there is that much cause for concern. The physician feels that the in utero surgery would be very helpful, but she is concerned about Jane's reluctance to consent to it. Though this not a matter of life and death for the child, the physician feels that the surgery should be done, and the sooner the better.

Scenario 3—AIDS Testing and AZT Treatment

Physicians working in public hospitals and clinics see their share of pregnant women who are infected with the AIDS virus. HIV-infected pregnant women frequently pass the virus on to the child in the womb. In a recent study in the *New England Journal of Medicine*, researchers in the United States and France discovered that AZT treatment dramatically reduced the rate at which pregnant women transmitted the virus to their unborn children.[2] The infection rate was reduced by two-thirds compared to the control group, suggesting that AZT treatment is highly effective in preventing the spread of HIV to children in utero.

These new findings raise ethical questions about compelling pregnant women, especially those at risk for HIV, to be tested and to get the AZT treatment for their unborn child. At present, society is hesitant about requiring mandatory AIDS testing, and in some states not even rapists can be forced to submit to HIV testing. Yet AZT offers great promise not only in treating the symptoms in the mother but also in preventing the spread of this deadly disease to the children that they carry. Furthermore, it is much less expensive for public hospitals to treat a pregnant woman with AZT than it is to treat a child born with the HIV virus. Physicians now have a significant weapon in their arsenal to help prevent the spread of AIDS. Should pregnant women in public facilities be required to submit to AIDS testing, and if they test positive, be required to take AZT for the sake of their unborn child, and for public health? At present the law does not allow physicians to do this. Not only would it deter women from seeking treatment, but one of the chief dictates of medical ethics, enforced by the law, is that people cannot be forced into either testing or treatment without their informed consent. But would these women not have a moral obligation to be tested and take the

2. "A Gain Against AIDS That Carries Ethical Questions," *Los Angeles Times*, November 14, 1994, B12.

treatment so that their unborn child could come into the world with a chance to live AIDS-free? Would not the physicians have the obligation to urge testing and treatment on these women, irrespective of the social stigma that may result from having the HIV virus?

Scenario 4—Get Drug Treatment or Go to Jail

In an effort to protect the welfare of children born to mothers addicted to drugs, a South Carolina hospital initiated a new policy that would force drug-addicted pregnant women being treated at this medical center to go into treatment or face arrest for endangering an unborn child. It was a controversial policy, and whether the policy will stand up to Constitutional scrutiny is still in question. Lawyers for one pregnant woman sued the hospital, claiming that it violated the mother's right to privacy. No one, they insisted, could be coerced into drug treatment, and there were no sufficient grounds to have the woman put into jail for her drug use. The hospital argued that pregnant women have a responsibility to avoid endangering their unborn children. Even though they have the right to end the pregnancy, once they decide to keep the child, pregnant women have a responsibility not to place the fetus in danger by compromising its health and its chances for a good start in life. The hospital had seen so many drug-addicted pregnant women that it felt that its hard-line stand was justified to protect the interests of children not yet born. Yet this seriously compromises the freedom of pregnant women to make decisions about their lives in privacy, apart from bureaucratic interference. Yet to stand by while addicted pregnant women continue to take drugs seriously compromises the future health of the unborn child. To many in the community, the hospital's stand seemed fair and reasonable, and they felt that it was about time that someone stood up for the interests of the unborn child.

Scenario 5—The Pregnant Woman Who Drinks and Smokes

Your next-door neighbor has just informed you of the exciting news of her pregnancy. She and her husband are having their first child, and though they are both young, they are thrilled to be having a child and seem to be as well prepared as possible for the demanding task of parenthood. But one thing about this pregnancy disturbs you. Both the prospective mother and father smoke habitually. You don't know exactly how much they smoke, but it seems that almost every time you see them, one or both of them have a cigarette in their hands, and every time you are in their house, it is evident that someone has been smoking recently. You also know that they both drink, and it seems to you that it is more than simply social drinking. In fact, when you take your trash out each week you notice that there are always a lot of liquor bottles that have been emptied during the week, as well as a good number of beer bottles. The parents' drinking and smoking habits are troubling to you, but you don't know whether to mind your own business or to say something about it to them. You decide to give them the benefit of the doubt for now, hoping that for the sake of their unborn child, they will stop smoking and the woman will limit her drinking.

However, after the first couple of months of the pregnancy, you notice that there have not been any changes. Both parents still smoke, and the amount of empty liquor bottles in the trash every week appears to be the same. You are understandably concerned for the health of their unborn child, yet you are hesitant to step into someone else's private life. You finally decide to say something to them, hoping that they are not aware of the dangers to the child of their smoking and drinking. They shrug and tell you that their doctor told them the same thing, but they don't believe that it's any big deal. They tell you that many of their friends smoked and drank through their pregnancies, and they have perfectly healthy children. In fact, both of their parents smoked and drank their way through all their pregnancies, not knowing any better, and nothing happened to any of their children. So they politely tell you thanks for the concern, but they're confident that everything will be OK. You realize there's nothing more you can do, but you wish there was a way to compel them to stop doing things that endanger the health of their child. You also want to respect their privacy, and you are uncomfortable about how restrictions on their endangering habits would be enforced.

Scenario 6—Workplace Harm to Pregnant Women

Marie has been working at a chemical plant for the past few years. She enjoys her high-paying job and has been promoted several times since she has been there. Her boss has assured her that her job is secure despite recent downsizing and that, in fact, she has a bright future with the company should she decide to stay. However, she has recently discovered that she is pregnant. She and her husband planned this pregnancy, and she anticipates taking the company-provided maternity leave and returning to work within a year. In her first pregnancy exam, her doctor asked her about her employment. When she replied that she works in a chemical plant, her doctor expressed great concern about her exposure to chemicals that could cause birth defects in her child. She recommended that Marie do whatever was necessary to eliminate or substantially minimize her exposure to dangerous chemicals. This was a major concern for Marie, since she knew it would limit her professionally.

After her employer found out she was pregnant, Marie was informed about the company's policy that encouraged reassignment of pregnant women to areas of the company that would not involve exposure to dangerous chemicals. This meant a job that was much less stimulating than her present one, and she felt that the company was discriminating against her since the same policies did not and could not apply to men. She knew that policies like this one had been challenged in court, but she was hesitant to say anything because she was anticipating resuming work there after her maternity leave. She felt strongly that the decisions about her pregnancy and her employment should be hers to make, yet she felt uncomfortable about exposing her child to potentially harmful chemicals. She also had to think about her future with the company and her family's financial needs, part of which were and would continue to be met by her income.

All the preceding scenarios involve a conflict between the rights of the pregnant woman and the best interests of her unborn child. To put it in the language of bioethics, it is a conflict between the autonomy of the mother, that is, the right of the mother to make her own decisions about her life and pregnancy apart from state interference, and the responsibility of benefi-cence toward the unborn child, that is, the obligation to do what is in the child's best interests. At the least, the mother has the ob-ligation of what is called nonmalifescence, which means that she has the obligation to do no harm to the child in her womb. The rights of the woman are grounded in the right to privacy, well es-tablished in the interpretative tradition of the Supreme Court since the early part of this century. The cultural milieu that places great emphasis on individual rights and the women's movement of the past three decades have contributed to the em-phasis on the woman's freedom in pregnancy. In addition, since the *Roe v Wade* (1973) decision that legalized abortion on de-mand, the interests of the fetus have been downplayed.[3] As a re-sult, the interests of the mother are normally given priority over the interests of the fetus.

Thus, Cesarean sections are not normally forced on women whose unborn children would be endangered by vaginal birth. Fetal therapy and surgery require consent of the mother, and physicians hesitate to pressure women to have this done. AIDS testing for pregnant women and forced treatment of AZT is not likely in the near future due to the social stigmatization that comes from AIDS. Giving pregnant women the choice between drug treatment or arrest is considered by many in society as a dra-conian solution to drug addiction during pregnancy. It would be virtually unthinkable that the state would intervene against preg-nant women who smoke and drink during pregnancy, and the courts have upheld pregnant women's claims of gender discrim-ination against companies that have policies restricting a preg-nant woman's employment. In the law and in society, the trend is toward protecting women's rights at the expense of the inter-ests of the fetus.

3. *Roe v Wade*, 410 US 113 (1973). With the *Doe v Bolton* decision, handed down that same day, *Roe* made abortion on demand legal for the entire nine months of pregnancy. The Court ruled in *Doe* that the freedom to end a preg-nancy in the last trimester based on the threat to the woman's life included her health and well-being, emotionally, physically, and financially. *Doe v Bolton*, 410 US 179 (1973).

However, it is unsettling to think that a pregnant woman would refuse a C-section or fetal therapy, knowing that the health of her unborn child could be improved or its life saved. It is equally disturbing to realize that babies are born with drug addiction and the HIV virus or with other birth defects that can be traced to smoking, drinking, or workplace hazards. We normally consider that society has the greatest moral and legal obligation to protect its most vulnerable members. Society has placed a high priority on a woman's privacy, especially during pregnancy. But the exercise of that freedom, when it harms the fetus in the womb, leaves one wondering about the appropriate limits on a pregnant woman's freedom to live her life as she chooses.

For the majority of pregnant women, there is no maternal-fetal conflict. In most cases, pregnant women willingly relinquish their freedom to do whatever is in the best interests of their unborn child. This is likely because the loss of freedom is considered a nominal sacrifice when compared with the anticipated benefit to the fetus. In addition, as pregnancy progresses a bonding normally occurs between the unborn child and its mother, bringing out the woman's maternal instincts to care for the child that is developing inside her womb. Most women, though they do not want the invasiveness of C-section or fetal therapy, consent to these if they are convinced that the procedures are necessary for their child. Many women stop drinking and smoking when they find out that they are pregnant. They respond to noncoercive persuasion to do what is in the child's best interests. But when it comes to using the compulsion of the state to force women to act in their child's best interests, that is a somewhat different matter. There are cases that garner a good bit of publicity when the pregnant woman refuses to yield her freedom to order her life according to her choice, even if it means additional risk for her unborn child.

For the Christian couple, this may not be an issue of great debate, since the position most consistent with Scripture is that the fetus is a person from conception forward.[4] Since the fetus is a person, it has the rights to protection from harm. Further, since Scripture indicates a stronger obligation to protect the most vul-

4. For development of this position, see chapter 4.

nerable (for example, the poor and the disabled), the unborn surely fit in that category. Since the fetus is a person with rights to life, the mother's freedom should be limited when the interests of the fetus conflict with the liberty of the mother. Normally, when life conflicts with liberty, life takes precedence, and if both parties are persons with full rights, then maternal-fetal conflicts are no different. As is the case with so many bioethics issues, the foundational question is the personhood of the fetus. However, even if a person denies the fundamental personhood of the fetus and accepts the right of a woman to an abortion, a good case can still be made that the fetus's best interests should normally take priority over the mother's freedom.

The Legal Status of the Fetus

Fetuses occupy a position of legal limbo when it comes to their rights and the corresponding duties of society to protect them. Ever since *Roe v Wade*, which forms the broad umbrella under which fetal rights are viewed, society has exhibited a peculiar ambivalence about the legal standing of the fetus. Clearly the *Roe* decision seriously undermined any claims to fetal personhood and the attendant rights to life. But that is not to say that the fetus does not have any rights or protections under the law. For example, fetuses have inheritance rights in many states. Further, fetuses are protected from prenatal injury in that, after birth, they may sue the parents for injuries inflicted during pregnancy. The assumption underlying this notion is that children have the right to begin life with a sound mind and body, giving them the right to a pregnancy free from harm.[5] Traditionally, criminal law did not view the death of a fetus as murder unless it was born alive and then killed. But recently some states have statutes in which the death of a wanted fetus can bring a manslaughter charge,[6] and in some states, if the fetus is killed in an automobile accident, the

5. For the judicial precedent for this, see *Smith v Brennan*, 157 A2d 497 (New Jersey 1960). See also Margery W. Shaw, "Conditional Prospective Rights of the Fetus," *Journal of Legal Medicine* 5 (1984): 63–116.
6. *Commonwealth v Kass*, 467 NE 2d 1324 (Mass. 1984).

charge can be vehicular homicide.[7] In California, it is first-degree murder to kill a fetus with premeditated malice.[8] The California Supreme Court will hear its first fetal murder case in which a man injured a pregnant woman during a convenience-store robbery and her viable fetus died. If the Court rules that the man is guilty of murder, then that decision will significantly advance the rights of fetuses to be protected from prenatal injury.

In the law and in much of the literature, the only fetuses that have rights and protections are apparently those that are wanted. This conclusion seems inescapable given the rights granted to women by the *Roe* and *Doe* Supreme Court decisions for abortion on demand throughout the entire pregnancy. Even though *Roe* suggests a gradually increasing value and thus protections as pregnancy progresses, the combination of the *Roe* and *Doe* rulings effectively gave women the freedom to end a pregnancy at any point. It is difficult to see how the fetus could have any meaningful rights if it is denied the most basic right, the right to life. However, because the fetus does have some rights, it does not necessarily follow that it has full human rights according to the law. But there is a sense of ambivalence in the law about the status and corresponding rights of the fetus. The exact legal status of the unborn is characterized by ambiguity and difficulty in interpretation. The law presupposes that fetuses are not full persons but have increasing value as gestation progresses, and they are entitled to some protections consistent with their development. Yet under *Roe v Wade* and *Doe v Bolton,* they can be aborted at virtually any time during pregnancy.

The Fetus as a Patient

Maternal-fetal conflicts presuppose the notion that the fetus is a patient. The discussion of maternal-fetal conflicts presumes that

7. *State v Willis,* 457 So2d 959 (Miss. 1984).
8. *People v Smith,* 59 Cal App 3d 75d1 (Cal App 1976). The citations in notes 6–8 are taken from Lawrence J. Nelson and Nancy Milliken, "Compelled Medical Treatment of Pregnant Women," in *Ethical Issues in the New Reproductive Technology,* ed. Richard T. Hull (Belmont, Calif.: Wadsworth, 1990), 224–40.

the fetus is wanted, and that its wantedness gives the pregnant woman a greater obligation toward the child in utero.[9] One of the indications of this obligation is the increasing number of publicly and privately funded educational and prenatal care programs aimed at pregnant women. Society puts a great deal of emphasis on proper care for pregnant women out of an obligation to give children the best possible start in life. It may seem inconsistent to emphasize prenatal care and allow for abortion on demand at the same time, but if one makes the distinction between fetuses not yet born and fetuses who will not be born (and also children already born), then one can see how different levels of obligation to the unborn can arise.[10] Of course, whether a child is wanted is irrelevant to its essence as a person, and the idea that wantedness can bestow rights and corresponding obligations on individuals and society is highly arbitrary. As is true in the debate over abortion, whether a child is wanted is not a commentary on the essence of its personhood. Rather, it is a commentary on the parents who either do or do not want a particular child.[11]

Because the fetus is a patient under obstetric care during the pregnancy and at times needing therapy or surgery, it does not follow that it is a full person. The ability of medical technology to increasingly treat a fetus and thus to view it as a patient is irrelevant to the discussion of the fetus's personhood. The progress of medicine in fetal therapy is a commentary on the progress of medicine, not on the essence of the fetus. However, the increasing accessibility of the fetus to medical treatment in utero has generated a particularly troubling situation. At present, the law

9. One justification for this is that the wanted fetus is at least a "future child" to whom the mother has certain obligations. See the rest of the chapter for further discussion of this notion.

10. For example, see Thomas H. Murray, "Moral Obligations to the Not Yet Born: The Fetus as Patient," in Hull, *Ethical Issues in the New Reproductive Technology*, 211–12.

11. One of the most common arguments in favor of abortion rights is that legalized abortion keeps women from bringing unwanted children into the world. They might be unwanted because of interruption to the mother's career, financial difficulties, physical or mental deformity, or a variety of other reasons. The response of the pro-life movement to this argument is that whether a child is wanted is more reflective of the parents than the essence of the child.

allows a woman to abort a fetus at the same gestational age at which medicine can perform heroic life-saving procedures on the same fetus. Ethicist Daniel Callahan of the Hastings Center says that "this disparity of treatment calls attention to the arbitrary and contingent value of the fetus: an abortable product of conception from one value perspective, and a cherished baby and patient from another, but the same organism in either case."[12] However, the ability to perform procedures on the fetus does not by itself impart personhood to the fetus. But the growing technology of fetal therapy helps illustrate the ambiguity and ambivalence in society about the personhood of the fetus. The greater the degree to which the fetus can be treated medically like a newborn child, the closer the parallel to that newborn will appear and the greater the inconsistency with the fact that medicine can heroically save lives that the law gives women the right to abort on demand.

What makes maternal fetal conflicts such a difficult discussion is that the fetus is not the only patient in view. That is why laws aimed at protecting children from abuse and abandonment do not apply precisely here. Compelling treatment of children involves only a court order for parental consent. But compelling treatment of a fetus in utero is more complicated, because to treat the fetus, the physician must go through the pregnant women. She needs to give her consent, not only because she is the child's mother, but also because the treatment will infringe on her body.

The Moral Obligation to Act in the Fetus's Best Interests

A pregnant woman has a moral obligation to the fetus she is carrying to act in its best interest and to avoid acting in ways that bring harm to it.[13] This discussion presumes that the woman desires to keep the fetus and rear it as her child. She has the legal

12. Daniel Callahan and Sidney Callahan, *Abortion: Understanding Differences* (New York: Plenum, 1984): 34.
13. I am indebted to my colleague Dr. Paul M. Cox for his insights in this section.

right to end the pregnancy, though, as has been argued in chapter 4, she does not have the moral right to do so since the fetus is a person from conception. However, the question of abortion has complicated the obligation of the mother to act in the fetus's best interests. For example, ethicist John Fletcher is rightly concerned about "the inconsistency of encouraging fetal therapy and respecting parental choice about abortion. . . ."[14] Philosopher Marc Lappe suggests that "whatever social, medical or legal sanctions existed for protecting the fetus against potential abuse during pregnancy in the past may now have been seriously compromised by the Supreme Court's abortion decision."[15] It is confusing at the least to pregnant women to urge them to consent to invasive procedures that are in the fetus's best interests while at the same time allowing them to abort the same fetus at virtually any time during pregnancy. This confusion further illustrates the ambivalence and ambiguity with which society views the moral status of the unborn.

However, should a woman decide to keep the child, she incurs a responsibility to care properly for it. This is because the woman, by rejecting the option of abortion and deciding to carry the child to term, has decided to procreate, and thus she becomes responsible for the child she is procreating.[16] This is not to say that the wantedness of the fetus contributes anything to the essential nature of the fetus, only to say that irrespective of how one views abortion, wantedness brings at least a further responsibility to act in the fetus's welfare. To be entirely consistent, since the fetus is indeed a person from conception, pregnant women have the moral responsibility to do what will give the unborn child the best chance at a healthy start in life, including refusing to consider abortion an option. But even for the woman who sees abortion as a live option, if she decides to keep the child, she has entered into a relationship of responsibility for the child she is carrying.

14. John Fletcher, "The Fetus as Patient: Ethical Issues," *Journal of the American Medical Association* 246 (August 14, 1981): 772–73.

15. Marc Lappe, "The Moral Claims of the Wanted Fetus," *Hastings Center Report* 5 (1975): 11–13.

16. John A. Robertson, *Children of Choice: Freedom and the New Reproductive Technologies* (Princeton, N. J.: Princeton University Press, 1994), 178.

This obligation to act in the fetus's best interests is particularly clear if the woman holds that the fetus is indeed a person. In that case, any maternal-fetal conflict would pit the woman's freedom to order her life as she sees fit and to be free from invasive medicine that she does not want against the fetus's best interests. Her moral responsibility toward the fetus is greater than her responsibility toward any other person because of the degree of dependence which the fetus has upon her and the fetus's general vulnerability. Her moral obligation would parallel her obligation to her other children if she has them. However, it is not an exact parallel because to treat the fetus the physician must go through the mother, both figuratively for consent, and literally for the actual treatment. In general, when life conflicts with liberty, life takes precedence. When the life or significant health of the child in the womb conflicts with the liberty of the mother to avoid invasive procedures or make sacrifices in her lifestyle, the life of the child in utero normally takes preference. Thus a pregnant woman would have a moral obligation to avoid actions that would bring harm to her fetus and to authorize necessary treatment for her fetus, even if it is invasive for her. Whether this moral obligation should also be a legal obligation is a different question that will be addressed later.

Even those who believe in the legitimacy of abortion have an obligation to the unborn. Although the right to abortion is legally established, once the mother decides to keep the child, she incurs a responsibility to act in the child's best interests. Though she does have the right to end the pregnancy, she becomes responsible for the fetus once she decides to have the child. It does not necessarily follow that the fetus then becomes a person to whom the mother has a responsibility, for wantedness does not change the essential nature of the fetus. That is, it does not follow that if the woman has the right to an abortion, she also has freedom to behave any way she desires during the pregnancy. On what basis does she incur a moral obligation to act in the fetus's best interests?

If the woman does not hold that the fetus is a person, she would technically not have an obligation to the fetus she is carrying. Rather, she has an obligation to the child who will emerge from her womb at birth. Of course, a substance view of the fetus would dictate that there is no essential difference between the fetus and the child. They are not two different beings. The difference is only one of development along the continuum in which there are no morally significant breaks. And this is not to say that the moral status of the fetus is in any way determined by the subjective belief of the pregnant woman. The fetus's standing is a matter of objective fact, not subjective belief. It does not matter whether a particular pregnant woman believes that the entity she is carrying is a person. However, even the woman who holds that her fetus is not a person has an obligation to act in its best interests based on her obligation to her future child. Her obligation is to insure that her child, when born, will have the best chance she can give him or her of a healthy start in life. Virtually everyone agrees that a newborn child is a person with full protection under the law, and if the pregnant woman decides to bring her child to term, the child is a person at the time of birth. Her moral obligation is technically not to the fetus, but to the future child. Since her actions while pregnant affect the child while developing in the womb, she has a responsibility to act in his or her best interests. Law professor Margery Shaw, using legal terms, argues that the pregnant woman who decides to carry her fetus to term incurs a "conditional prospective liability for negligent acts toward her fetus if it should be born alive." That is, the fetus has the right to have a healthy start and the mother has the responsibility to provide it such that the fetus could be a potential plaintiff if abuse in the womb produces clear and significant harm.[17] There is legal precedent for this view in a New Jersey case in which the court ruled that

> justice requires the principle that a child has a legal right to begin life with a sound mind and body. If wrongful conduct of another interferes with that right, and it can be established by competent proof that there is a causal connection between the wrongful interference and the harm suffered by the child, damages for such harm should be recoverable by the child.[18]

17. Margery Shaw, "The Potential Plaintiff: Preconception and Prenatal Torts," in Aubrey Milunsky and George J. Annas, eds., *Genetics and the Law II* (New York: Plenum, 1980), 228.
18. *Smith v Brennan*, 157 A2d 497, NJ (1960).

Once the language of the law has been introduced into this discussion, the focus shifts from the moral to the legal obligation of the pregnant woman, and the degree to which the law should coerce pregnant women to act in the best interests of their future children. Consistent with the fundamental Constitutional notions of individual liberty and the right of individual autonomy and self-determination, there is a long tradition of noninterference with parental authority over children that has been extended in recent years to include pregnant women with their fetuses. With the emphasis on women's rights in the last two decades, courts have been even more hesitant to compel fetal therapy because it is invasive for the mother. Historically the law has been properly hesitant to involve itself in matters between parents and children, unless, of course, there is clear evidence of parental abuse, neglect, or unfitness. One example, however, in which the state has consistently interfered with parental decisions about medical care for children is when Christian Scientist parents refuse treatment for their seriously ill children. Periodically, one reads of a child in a Christian Science family who has contracted meningitis, whose parents deny access to the antibiotics necessary to cure the infection and prevent serious brain damage and death. According to Christian Science tradition, they treat the child with prayer and other nonmedical treatments. Medical centers often seek court orders against such parents and are normally granted them. But court-compelled medical treatment is the exception rather than the rule, and there is usually broad latitude given to parents to act in the best interests of their children.

The state clearly has a legitimate interest in protecting its most vulnerable citizens, children, from harm, even from harm at the hands of their parents. But when should the state intervene and override parental authority in medical matters? Clearly these state interventions should be kept to a minimum. Few people want the government to coerce medical care any more than necessary.

The scenario of the government as the "pregnancy police" is not appealing, and the difficulty in enforcement of the behavior of pregnant women is virtually impossible and would involve intolerable invasions of privacy to do so. But under what circumstances would it be necessary? The criteria for deciding when the state should compel treatment of fetuses (and children) might be this:[19]

1. There is a high probability of harm to the fetus/child occurring without the necessary treatment.
2. There is a high probability of a high magnitude of harm; that is, the child will die or suffer grave bodily harm without the necessary treatment.
3. With the necessary treatment, the harm can be avoided and the child can live a relatively normal life; that is, the treatment must be proven to be reliable and must be capable of restoring the normal health of the fetus or child.
4. The harm avoided must be proportional to harm inflicted by the treatment.

These criteria would keep state interference at a minimum and prevent the state from overreaching its bounds, but also would protect children who are at risk from treatable illness. Thus, the state should interfere only when the harm to the future child is sure and great and when the treatment can restore normal life without inflicting a worse burden.

Forced Cesarean Sections

The most difficult maternal-fetal conflict to resolve occurs when a pregnant woman refuses to deliver her baby by C-section when her physicians deem it necessary to safeguard the life or health of the child. In most cases, women who need them do not refuse C-sections. But having a C-section is considered major surgery, and no one should underestimate the rigors of maintaining a newborn child while recovering from a C-section. The medical profession has received a good deal of criticism for overuse of C-sections,

19. Joseph Goldstein, "Medical Care for the Child at Risk: On State Supervision of Parental Autonomy," in *Who Speaks for the Child?: The Problems of Proxy Consent,* eds. Willard Gaylin and Ruth Macklin (New York: Plenum, 1982), 162. See also Michael Wald, "State Intervention on Behalf of Neglected Children, A Search for Realistic Standards," *Stanford Law Review* 27 (1984–85): 985.

performing them when they were not necessary, either for reasons of convenience or, more likely, as protection from liability.

A survey in 1987 was done of 76 heads of maternal-fetal medicine programs and 14 directors of divisions of maternal-fetal medicine, all at major university medical centers.[20] Eighty-three percent responded, and this group represented forty-five states. Forty-six percent of the heads of these programs thought a woman who refused medical treatment that endangered her fetus's life should be detained, and 47 percent supported obtaining court orders for intrauterine transfusions and emergency C-sections. The conclusion that emerges is that there is sharp division in the obstetric community on the issue of whether physicians should seek court orders to perform C-sections on pregnant women who refuse them.

Most obstetric practice is properly moving toward what is called a two-patient model for obstetric care.[21] In the past, the pregnant woman and her fetus were treated as essentially one patient, since the actions of the woman were for the most part all that could be monitored. One of the main reasons for this shift to a two-patient model is the improvement in diagnostic tools for observing the fetus. Such observation no longer needs to be done using the mother as the source of the data for the fetus's condition. The technological improvement has enabled and encouraged physicians to regard the fetus as a patient in its own right.

This two-patient model is supported by an increasing body of research that recognizes that a significant degree of bonding occurs in utero and that the contribution of the pregnant women's gestational environment can affect the child's character and personality. An entire discipline known as prenatal psychology has

20. Veronika E. B. Kolder, Janet Gallagher, and Michael T. Parsons, "Court Ordered Obstetrical Interventions," *New England Journal of Medicine* 316 (May 7, 1987): 1192–96.

21. The exception to this is in the case of abortion, in which the one-patient model is still widely used. For example, notice that the principal argument for the legitimacy of abortion is that the fetus is *part of the woman's body* and thus to regulate abortion is to violate her right to bodily integrity. For further discussion on the one- and two-patient models for obstetric care, see Susan S. Mattingly, "The Maternal-Fetal Dyad: Exploring the Two-Patient Obstetric Model," *Hastings Center Report* 22 (January–February 1992): 13–18.

arisen in order to maximize the development of the child in utero. This science views the fetus not only as a patient but also as a developing person.[22]

Under the one-patient model, the fetus and the mother are seen as an organic whole, in which the burdens and benefits are balanced with both in view. The benefits to the fetus are balanced against the burdens to the mother. In the two-patient model, the distribution of benefits and burdens is irrelevant. In this model, one cannot justify imposing risk on one patient to benefit another. Common examples of this are organ donation, bone-marrow transplants, and blood donation; these cannot be forced upon a person, irrespective of the benefit to another, and even if the one who would benefit is a close relative or family member.[23] Most states do not have what are called good Samaritan laws that give a legal duty to render aid to someone whose life is at risk. Not even parents can be forced to donate organs or undergo significant risks for their children. When treatment is indicated for the fetus and contraindicated for the mother, under this model the pregnant woman's refusal of C-section must be observed. Thus, what appears at first glance to be a move toward greater protection of the fetus turns out to be less protection.

The problem with the implications of the two-patient model is that the maternal-fetal relationship is entirely unique and qualitatively different from any other relationship, even one with one's own children after birth. The in utero relationship is unparalleled in the dependence that the fetus has on the mother, and thus it may be that the argument that one need not undergo risks for which another benefits does not apply here. It is not like a relationship to a stranger, but one of total dependence. It would seem that in cases in which the mother has decided to carry the child to

22. See, for example, Thomas Verny, *The Secret Life of the Unborn Child* (New York: Delta, 1981), in addition to the journal *Pre- and Perinatal Psychology*.

23. For example, a 1990 well-publicized Orange County, California, case in which a couple conceived a child in the hope that it would be a bone-marrow match for their teenage daughter with leukemia. Great ethical concerns were raised about the consent of the donor to the donation. The ethical analysis of this case worked from the two-patient model, and reflects a commonly held sentiment, that another cannot be asked to assume risk for the benefit of another.

term, there has been a decision either to become a parent or to give up the child for adoption. In either case, the decision to go to term creates an obligation to act in the interests of the child a woman is carrying. Future children have a prima facie claim to be protected from injury inflicted during pregnancy. Should the mother choose not to act in the best interests of the fetus, it has no one left to be its advocate.[24] In our society, we have consistently maintained advocacy of the most vulnerable, namely, children and the developmentally disabled.[25] One should be cautious with forcing medical interventions upon pregnant women, but the way in which the welfare of the fetus is dismissed after moving to a two-patient model is disturbing.

Another way to look at this is to weigh the comparative risk to the fetus and to the mother. When the exercise of a liberty costs someone his or her life, life generally overrides liberty. Cases of forced C-sections can be seen as the conflict between grave risk to the fetus and moderate risk to the mother. Even the Supreme Court in *Roe v Wade* admits that in the third trimester, in which these cases occur, the life of the fetus admits significant protection and infringes on the liberty of abortion. In addition, the mother will most likely recover from the C-section; if it is not performed, the fetus most likely will not. Thus it may be that the degree of risk involved to the fetus and the unique relationship of mother to child in utero gives one cause for caution in applying to this relationship the principle that one cannot force a person to assume risk for another's benefit. Thus it would seem that there is a prima facie case for forced C-sections when the life of the fetus is in jeopardy.

However, there are some significant problems with giving greater weight to the life of the fetus over the health risk of the

---

24. Susan Mattingly illustrates how vulnerable the fetus is in the two-patient model when she states, "A woman's failure to volunteer for fetal therapy may seriously violate her fiduciary responsibilities to the fetus, thus disqualifying her as a proxy, but the physician's duties to her as patient remain intact." "The Maternal-Fetal Dyad: Exploring the Two-Patient Obstetric Model," *Hastings Center Report* 22 (1992): 16.

25. Of course, abortion is the exception to this, but *Roe v Wade* recognizes that the state has an interest in protecting fetal life in the third trimester, clearly after viability. This part of the ruling recognized the principle that protection must be most afforded to the most vulnerable.

mother. First, fetal diagnosis is still an uncertain practice, and in many cases of apparent fetal distress the fetus was delivered vaginally without any compromise to its health. Second, forced C-sections can foster an adversarial relationship between a woman and her primary physician, and may deter some women from delivering in hospitals. Third, it may be the beginning of a slippery slope in which women will be forced to submit to fetal surgery and prohibitions on smoking and drinking during pregnancy. Part of this slippery slope is that it generally weakens the liberty of pregnant women, who also have interests that need to be protected.

Since the law does not require people to be good Samaritans by putting themselves at risk for others, it would seem that the obligation toward an unborn child should not exceed a parent's obligation to already born children. But the mother-child relationship in utero is unique, and the degree of dependence that exists between mother and child in the womb suggests that pregnant women have greater obligations toward their unborn children than parents have toward children in general. If there is no alternative to a forced C-section, then it may be justifiable in order to save the life of the unborn child. But given the problems with forced C-sections, one should be very careful about turning a woman's moral obligation into a legal obligation as well. Education and moral persuasion are better tools than the law for getting pregnant women to act in the best interests of their future children.

A Pastoral Word to Infertile Couples

When we met John and Mary in the introduction to this book, we met a couple who was in a great deal of pain about their inability to have a child. Most of this book has dealt with the ethical dimension of infertility and the various new technologies to overcome infertility. But that is hardly the only important aspect in dealing with infertility. Long before a couple considers the technologies that have been the focus of this book, they sometimes talk to close friends, family members, or a professional such as their pastor or a counselor. More often than not, the person they share their struggles with is not particularly equipped to help them work through the things that are troubling them. That person can offer a listening ear and a compassionate shoulder on which to cry, both of which are valuable. But well-meaning individuals can increase the pain by the advice they give. Suggestions such as "relax, you're trying too hard," or "it's not the right time," often do more harm than good because they inadvertently communicate to the couple that their struggle is not significant. What may be worse are the spiritualized words of "encouragement" that tell a couple to trust in God or suggest that a couple may be childless because God has some other purpose for them. Both comments may be true, but when they are offered as advice, these comments seem callous and unfeeling, and a denial of the pain that the couple feels.

My wife and I dealt with infertility for about three years before our first child was born. We have three children today, and some people think that disqualifies us from having anything credible to say to struggling infertile couples. But we remember the pain we experienced, and we believe that we can offer genuine empathy and sound advice to an infertile couple. My wife, Sally, is also a marriage and family counselor who has led infertility support groups for some time. If you and your spouse are struggling with infertility, or you know a couple going through this struggle and want to be helpful to them, this next section is especially for you. It summarizes our thoughts about dealing with the trauma of infertility.

Advice for the Infertile Couple

Admit that infertility produces real and deep pain. For couples who strongly desire a child, the inability to have one produces a strange mixture of emotions. The primary ones are anger, frustration, and disappointment that may reach the point of despair after a prolonged struggle with infertility. Being around families, especially those with babies or young children, may make these feelings more acute, and it is understandable that you may want to avoid family functions and family related holidays. My wife and I stopped going to church on Mother's Day and Father's Day. The Christmas season was particularly difficult because so many of our friends were celebrating the holidays with their families. Each time we were reminded of our empty nest.

One of the main reasons that infertility causes so much pain is because the ability to produce a child is at the heart of many people's gender identity. Many men feel deeply inadequate if they cannot father a child. Many women feel incomplete as a woman if they are unable to have a child. This can produce anger and resentment at the partner who is the "problem." Be careful not to let anyone minimize the pain you feel. Resist those who would subtly encourage denial of the anguish you feel. Spend your time with those people who can empathize with you and who can encourage you without use of pious platitudes that will probably make you more angry and will not alleviate your pain.

Share your feelings about your struggle with infertility openly with your partner. During this time, both of you will be bubbling cauldrons of emotion. It is not helpful to keep these emotions inside. Men frequently have a difficult time talking about infertility and sharing how they feel about it. The more you can encourage this kind of discussion, allowing for breaks from it from time to time, the better. It is appropriate and helpful to talk with another person of the same gender, and to get together with other couples who are in the same position as you. There are many support networks available for infertile couples, either through your church (you may even encourage your pastor to start one if your church does not have one already) or through a counselor or a therapist in your community. RESOLVE is a national support network for infertile couples, and Christian groups like Stepping Stones and Focus on the Family can provide additional resources.[1]

It is particularly helpful to be honest with God with your feelings about infertility. Many couples are angry at God and doubt his sovereignty over them and loving care for them. The psalmists in the Old Testament were extremely honest with God with their feelings, and there is never any indication that God thought less of them for being so honest. To question God and to express anger at him is not unusual for infertile couples who believe that God has a family in his plan for them. Many couples feel let down, that God has not kept his promises to them. Most infertile couples would make wonderful parents, and it is not clear sometimes what God is doing in the lives of these couples.

Resist the urge to focus on the question "why?" Whenever a couple or an individual experiences a trauma or a difficult time in life, the natural and obvious question is "Why is this happening to me?" For a Christian, there is a bit of a twist to the question when he or she asks, "What is God trying to teach me through this time?"

---

1. Stepping Stones publishes a regular newsletter and may be reached at the following address: Central Christian Church, 2900 N. Rock Rd., Wichita, KS, 67226–1198. RESOLVE Inc. can be reached at 1310 Broadway, Dept. DA, Somerville, MA, 02144-1731.

For the infertile couple, as for anyone enduring hard times, this question is not only unfruitful, but may be unanswerable this side of eternity. Though it is true that sometimes a look in the mirror answers the question, those cases are clear and usually involve unmistakable sin that is apparent to everyone. Infertility, however, does not fit into that category, even if the root cause of a couple's infertility can be medically pinpointed. The medical cause does not normally answer the deeper question of "why?" Though it is true that infertility is the result of the entrance of sin into the world, it is not normally the case that infertility is the result of some specific sin of a particular couple.[2] Ecclesiastes 3:11 helps put the question into perspective. Solomon writes, "He has made everything beautiful in its time. He has also set eternity in the hearts of men; yet they cannot fathom what God has done from beginning to end." Similarly, in Ecclesiastes 11:6, with a figure of speech particularly appropriate for infertility, he writes, "As you do not know the path of the wind, or how the body is formed in a mother's womb, so you cannot understand the work of God, the Maker of all things." These verses indicate that there are significant limits to what human beings this side of eternity can know about the plan of God for their lives, especially how things fit together into a coherent whole. It is much like viewing an Oriental rug, but from the underside. When someone looks at the rug in that way, he or she will see many knots and loose ends and can only faintly make out the pattern. But when the same person sees the rug from the top, he or she can see the intricate design in all its fullness and beauty. Until Christ comes back, we see life, and especially infertility, from the underside of the Oriental rug of God's plan. That view, and our ability to answer the question "why," will not change until we meet Christ face to face. Thus it is not a fruitful way to expend emotional energy, and it can be presumptuous to suggest such an answer to a struggling infertile couple. The more fruitful questions are "How can we cope with this?" and "Where can we get support in this?" rather

2. The exception to this may be in cases where one or more of the partners has had a history of sexually transmitted disease. This can be a cause of infertility, though clearly not in every case.

than spending a good deal of emotional energy trying to unscrew the inscrutable and answer the unanswerable question of "Why."

Be careful that desperation does not cloud your judgment. There is little doubt that by the time many couples seriously consider some of the more expensive reproductive options, they have become desperate to have a child. Becoming pregnant can become practically an obsession for them. To be sure, this springs out of a natural inclination to procreate, and the sense of desperation is understandable because of the way that infertility strikes at a person's sense of gender identity. But it is also true that this desperation can lead couples to do things that they would not otherwise do. For example, it is not uncommon for couples to go into deep debt in order to pursue the latest round of reproductive technology. It is also not uncommon for couples to be totally engrossed in this process, occasionally to the point of not being able to take care of other important aspects of life. Though I would want to be careful in talking to an infertile couple about this sense of desperation, it is an appropriate concern.

The desperation to conceive a child needs to be evaluated in light of some important biblical virtues. Trust in God's care for and sovereignty over a couple is an important aspect of developing Christlike maturity. Patience, longsuffering, courage, and endurance are other significant Christian virtues that are sometimes compromised in the process of infertility. This sense of desperation for a child, and the feeling that a couple is not complete without one, should not be taken as a given, but rather be brought to the light of Scripture. This is not to further add to the guilt and frustration that many infertile couples feel, and anyone who counsels an infertile couple and mentions their desperation should have earned the right to say things like these through their commitment to the couple and their consistent support of them in the process. These are not questions to be brought up prior to the couple's understanding your commitment to them and unconditional love for them. But support and love for a couple sometimes involves pointing out things about which they may not be aware. The virtue of the couple in the process of infertility does matter, and these questions should be faced, though never used as a club to bludgeon the couple into further guilt.

Set a limit on how much reproductive technology you will pursue. In light of the fact that couples normally become more desperate the further into the process they go, it is helpful to decide at the outset how far you will go. Moral parameters will help you set these boundaries, as well as financial and emotional considerations. To be sure, you should not make any final decisions until all the medical facts are in. Because of your strong desire for a child, you are in a vulnerable position when it comes to making decisions about how far to take the process. Many couples can be persuaded to try once more, when the chances may not be any better than on the previous tries. The "one more try" may produce a child, but statistically, the chances of assisted conception after repeated failures are not high. But the frustration level and the total expense increase with every try that does not result in a pregnancy. At the beginning of the process, when you are more objective, set some limits on how far you will pursue different reproductive options. One of the hardest decisions you may make in your life is the decision to stop employing assisted reproductive technology, thus accepting childlessness or pursuing adoption as alternatives. But the decision may also be one of the wisest.

Infertility is one of the most painful things a person and a couple can experience. Those who have not experienced it have a difficult time identifying with those who cannot conceive the child of their dreams. If you are currently infertile, our heart goes out to you. We hope the encouragement of this chapter and the general guidelines of this book have been helpful to you. If you are in the position of walking with friends through infertility, we hope this book has helped direct you into ways that can be both helpful and encouraging to your friends. Please appreciate how intense their struggle is and how deep their pain is. Allow them to share their feelings with you without being judgmental of them, and especially without offering pious platitudes that will likely alienate you from them. Pray consistently for them, for ultimately it is God who opens the womb. In spite of all our sophisticated technology that enables us to look into the womb, it is still the "secret place" over which God alone has ultimate control.

Index

Scott B. Rae is associate professor of biblical studies and Christian ethics at Talbot School of Theology and the author of *Moral Choices: An Introduction to Ethics* and *The Ethics of Surrogate Motherhood*. His Th.M. degree is from Dallas Theological Seminary; his Ph.D. in social ethics is from the University of Southern California.